BATTLE *of* BRITAIN 85

As I type this, it is nearly 85 years since the start of the Battle of Britain. Of all the young men who fought with Fighter Command in the skies over Britain in the summer and autumn of 1940, the last of them, Group Captain John Allman Hemingway, DFC, AE, originally of Dublin, Ireland, passed away aged 105 in March, 2025.

Even after such a span of time, the legacy of the Battle of Britain remains. What would the map of Europe look like today if the RAF had been vanquished? Thousands of books have been written on the subject, many recording the deeds of the young men involved. This one aims to provide an overview of the campaign, the aircraft flown by both sides and those that remain from the thousands built.

The cover artwork comes from Roy Grinnell. When I first saw Achtung Spitfire! I knew it was what I wanted for this Battle of Britain special. Further research revealed the breadth of artist Roy's passion for aviation – and other subjects. For those who want to see more, I strongly urge them to visit: www.roygrinnellart.com

David Willis
April 2025

BELOW:
The Shuttleworth Collection's Gloster Gladiator in the colours worn by 247 Squadron during 1940. Key-Duncan Cubitt **Shuttleworth's Gloster Gladiat**

ISBN: 978 1 83632 090 6
Editor: David Willis
Senior editor, specials: Roger Mortimer
Email: roger.mortimer@keypublishing.com
Cover Design: Steve Donovan
Design: SJmagic DESIGN SERVICES, India
Advertising Sales Manager: Sam Clark
Email: sam.clark@keypublishing.com
Tel: 01780 755131
Advertising Production: Becky Antoniades
Email: Rebecca.antoniades@keypublishing.com

SUBSCRIPTION/MAIL ORDER
Key Publishing Ltd, PO Box 300, Stamford, Lincs, PE9 1NA

Tel: 01780 480404
Subscriptions email:
subs@keypublishing.com
Mail Order email: orders@keypublishing.com
Website: www.keypublishing.com/shop

PUBLISHING
Group CEO and Publisher: Adrian Cox

Published by
Key Publishing Ltd, PO Box 100, Stamford, Lincs, PE9 1XQ
Tel: 01780 755131
Website: www.keypublishing.com

PRINTING
Precision Colour Printing Ltd, Haldane, Halesfield 1, Telford, Shropshire. TF7 4QQ

DISTRIBUTION
Seymour Distribution Ltd, 2 Poultry Avenue, London, EC1A 9PU
Enquiries Line: 02074 294000.

We are unable to guarantee the bona fides of any of our advertisers. Readers are strongly recommended to take their own precautions before parting with any information or item of value, including, but not limited to money, manuscripts, photographs, or personal

CONTENTS

Hawker Hurricane cockpit.
National Museum of the US Air Force

Messerschmitt Bf 109 cockpit.
Eric Long/Smithsonian Institute

SECTION THREE: THE LUFTWAFFE

SECTION FOUR: A LASTING LEGACY

RIGHT: Two types of fighter and three different bombers – such as these Dornier Do 17Zs of Kampfgeschwader ('bomber wing') 76 – bore the brunt of the Luftwaffe's offensive against Britain during the second half of 1940.
Malcom V Lowe Collection

BOTTOM: For the British public, the 'star' of the Battle of Britain was the Spitfire. This Mk Ia of 19 Squadron lifts off from Fowlmere, on the borders of Cambridgeshire and Hertfordshire, in the summer of 1940.
Aeroplane Collection

BELOW: The legacy of the Battle of Britain runs deep in the collective British psyche. This stamp, issued in 2008, depicts an RAF Plotter of the WAAF (Women's Auxiliary Air Force) in 1940.

Eighty-five years ago in the skies over southern England, one of the most important conflicts of the 20th century was fought. What was called the 'Battle of Britain' by the British Prime Minister Winston Churchill, during a speech he gave in the House of Commons on June 18, 1940, was the first time opposing air forces alone determined the fate of a country. The Royal Air Force (RAF) faced the might of the German Luftwaffe in a battle that would have great repercussions for the rest of the war.

WEST THEN EAST

Swift victories across the continent gave the German armed forces a mystique of invincibility. By mid-1940 all that was left to do to secure the west was to force the stubborn British government to the peace table. Then, with no threat on his western border, the German leader (Führer) Adolph Hitler could pursue his plans of expanding the Reich into the seemingly endless plains of the Soviet Union to the east.

Unlike most of the previous campaigns undertaken in the first nine months of the war, where the German army could 'simply' advance across the border, the English Channel meant that a seaborne invasion, supported by airborne troops, would have to be organised. Recent experience during the Norwegian campaign, during which German shipping suffered several losses from air attacks, made the Kriegsmarine (navy) wary of what many within the German leadership viewed as a mere 'river crossing'. Before any invasion could be mounted, air supremacy had to gained over the British Isles. This meant the elimination of Fighter Command, a role that could only be accomplished by the Luftwaffe.

PLACE IN TIME

Defining the Battle of Britain is problematic. For a start it was a campaign, rather than a single battle, composed of several distinct phases as the Luftwaffe changed tactics to achieve its aims. There was no definitive start or end; Luftwaffe aircraft operated over Britain before and continued to do so afterwards.

In 1942, when the Air Ministry decided to compile a record of those who had lost their lives in the fighting, the Battle of Britain was deemed to have taken place between August 7 and October 31, 1940. In November 1960, the start date was brought forward to July 10, 1940, which remains the generally accepted dates within the United Kingdom today. This excludes much of the night time Blitz on the cities and towns, during which thousands of civilians lost their lives. To German historians, the Battle of Britain is part of the ongoing campaign against the British Isles, known as die Luftschlacht um England ('the Air Battle for England'), which started soon after the fall of France in June 1940 and continued into 1941.

YOUNG MEN

That the names of the vast majority of those who fought with Fighter Command during the summer and autumn of 1940 are known today is down to the dedication and hard work of many individuals. Most Luftwaffe records were destroyed by the end of the war, making the task more difficult, although again over the years researchers have managed to put together at least part of the picture. The common factor of those involved in the Battle of Britain was that they were all young men, in the prime of their lives – and many never got to grow old.

Churchill's speech on June 18 concluded: "Let us therefore brace ourselves to our duties, and so bear ourselves, that if the British Empire and its Commonwealth last for a thousand years, men will say, 'This was their finest hour.'" While the nations of the former Empire are now independent countries, the legacy of the Battle of Britain remains strong in the British psyche and many born after the generation that lived through the summer of 1940 still agree with Churchill's sentiment.

The FINEST HOUR

"What General Weygand has called the Battle of France is over... the Battle of Britain is about to begin." Prime Minister Winston Churchill – June 18, 1940.

NINE MONTHS *of War*

The Battle of Britain followed a series of German victories that saw all opposing forces swept aside. From September 1939 to June 1940, the Luftwaffe had supported the German army as it rolled across Europe.

Preparations for the German invasion of Poland started on April 3, 1939, when the Führer Adolf Hitler issued plans for Fall Weiss (Case White). Crucial to the plan was the application of Blitzkrieg (Lightning War), tactics for which had been refined during army exercises and by the Luftwaffe's experience in the Spanish Civil War.

Core to the concept of Blitzkrieg was mobility and manoeuvre, advancing against the enemy using overwhelming force to crush resistance and bypassing positions when that was not possible. Concentrations of tanks and armoured vehicles would break through defences with enough momentum so that the enemy did not have time to retreat and re-group. Air power played a major role in such operations, undertaking reconnaissance ahead of the army and attacking enemy positions just prior to the arrival of German troops, as well as striking targets around the battlefield. Co-ordination between the army and the air force was vital for such operations. Blitzkrieg offered Germany the opportunity to achieve its military

aims quickly, avoiding the costly attrition of the static trench warfare of World War One.

CASE WHITE

At 0445hrs on September 1, the ground forces of the Wehrmacht ('defence force') advanced east across the Polish border. They were preceded 19 minutes earlier by three Junkers Ju 87B-1 Stuka dive bombers of 3. Staffel, Stukageschwader ('dive bomber wing') 1, which attacked Polish sappers before they could blow up the vital Tczew (Dirschau) bridge over the Vistula. Poland's capital Warsaw was attacked on the first morning of the war.

The roles of the Luftwaffe were to first neutralise the Polish Air Force and then to provide close air support to the army. To achieve them it deployed approximately 1,580 frontline aircraft of Luftflotten ('air fleets') 1 and 4 based in the north and south of Germany. A considerable reserve was held in Germany in case France or Great Britain intervened.

Poland fielded 433 frontline aircraft in 15 fighter squadrons, equipped with

around 150 PZL P7s and P11s, and 12 reconnaissance bomber units with PZL P23s and P37s, plus army co-operation squadrons. While Polish crews were well trained, their aircraft were no match for those of the Germans.

By the end of the first day, the Luftwaffe had flown 1,250 sorties, crippling much of the Polish Air Force. Around 300 Stukas hit airfields, bridges, railways and troop concentrations, operating with little opposition. Nine Kampfgeschwader ('bomber wings') equipped with Dornier Do 17s and nine Gruppen ('groups') of Heinkel He 111s hit both tactical and strategic targets. Messerschmitt Bf 109 fighters operated at the extremes of their range, while the Bf 110 achieved considerable success, using dive-and-climb attacks on the Polish fighters.

From September 3, the day France and Great Britain declared war on Germany, the Luftwaffe was being used to eliminate Polish formation bypassed by the advancing army. As the Polish presence in the air diminished, Luftwaffe fighters turned to strafing attacks. »

ABOVE: Junkers Ju 87 Stukas over Poland in September 1939.
Key Collection

The Wehrmacht's advance was halted briefly on September 9 crossing the Bzura River, around 50 miles (80km) west of Warsaw, until reinforcements were brought up to the front. On the same day, the first assault was launched on the capital by the 4th Panzer Division, meeting stiff resistance. Luftwaffe bombers launched a heavy raid on the city on September 24, during which 1,150 sorties were flown. The capital surrendered five days later.

The fate of Poland had been sealed by a secret protocol of the Molotov-Ribbentrop Pact, a non-aggression agreement signed on August 23, 1939, by the foreign ministers of Germany and the Soviet Union. It divided the country into 'spheres of influence'. Soviet forces invaded Poland from the east on September 17, advancing quickly, as most Polish units were deployed against the Germans.

Fighting in Poland effectively stopped on October 6. However, many Polish pilots and soldiers escaped to Romania and Hungary, eventually making their way to England. There they continued the fight, the airmen serving in the Polish squadrons of the RAF making a vital contribution to the defeat of the Luftwaffe during the Battle of Britain.

SITZKRIEG

From September 1939 to early May 1940, the lack of activity on the ground in the west gave rise to the name 'Phoney War' for the period, also known as 'Sitzkrieg' to the east of the frontline. Upon declaring war on Germany, Britain bolstered the air and land forces it had deployed to France, known as the British Expeditionary Force (BEF). The army in France was supported by two RAF formations. The RAF Component of the BEF ('Air Component') comprised six army co-operations squadrons with Westland Lysanders, three fighter squadrons of Hawker Hurricanes and one of Gladiators (later re-equipped with Hurricanes), and two bomber-reconnaissance units of Bristol Blenheim IVs.

The Advanced Air Striking Force (AASF), formed on August 24, 1939, was independent of the BEF. It had ten squadrons of Fairey Battles from 1 Group of RAF Bomber Command. The bombers were deployed to French bases from September 2 and began photo-reconnaissance sorties eight days later. From December 1939, the Battles of 15 and 40 Squadrons were withdrawn and replaced by 114 and 139 Squadrons, equipped with Blenheim IVs. British Air Forces in France (BAFF), established on January 15, 1940, controlled the activities of the AASF and Air Component.

The Armée de l'Air (French Air Force) had close to 1,500 aircraft, half of which were fighters, although many were approaching obsolescence. Eleven fighter groups were equipped with the Morane-Saulnier MS406, which proved under-powered and slow compared with the Bf 109E, as was the Curtiss 75A Hawk. The best French fighter was the Dewotine D520, equal to the Luftwaffe single-seat Bf 109, but only in service with two units. Facing the Allies were more than 1,000 aircraft of Luftflotten 2 and 3, the number growing to over 3,000 as Germany prepared for operations in the west.

DENMARK AND NORWAY

The strategic importance of Norway was not lost on both sides during early 1940. By the time Germany launched Operation Weserübung ('Weser exercise') on April 9, the Royal Navy was already heading for the north of the country. Weserübung was a combined sea and air assault.

Securing Norway guaranteed German access to the iron ore in Sweden, which had been interrupted by British mining operations. Getting to Norway meant occupying Denmark, with its vital airfields at Aalborg in Jutland. Denmark succumbed within a day of the German forces crossing its border. Aalborg became a major staging post for operations against Norway.

The Kriegsmarine was heavily involved in Weserübung, as was the Luftwaffe, operating at the extremes of its aircraft's range. Around 290 bombers, He 111s and Ju 88s were deployed, along with 70 Bf 110Cs and 40 Ju 87R long-range versions of the Stuka. Both Denmark and Norway had little in the way of modern fighters. The Danish fighter force comprised around 35 Gloster Gauntlet and Hawker Nimrod biplanes and Fokker D.XXI monoplanes, and Norway 12 Gloster Gladiators. Against these the Luftwaffe committed only some 30 Bf 109Es.

"The Danish fighter force comprised around 35 Gloster Gauntlet and Hawker Nimrod biplanes and Fokker D.XXI monoplanes"

(KG, 'bomber wing') 2, Johannes Fink, on July 2, when he was appointed Kanalkampfführer ('Channel war leader'). The first major attack targeted the Portland naval base in Dorset two days later, and was undertaken by Junkers Ju 87 Stukas of III. Gruppe of Sturzkampfgeschwader 51 (III./StG 51). The Stuka's ability to accurately drop bombs on floating targets was extensively demonstrated during the Kanalkampf phase of the Battle of Britain, the large formations attracting RAF fighters to engage in combat. The Luftwaffe's medium bombers were also involved, attacking maritime targets directly as well as sowing mines.

Although RAF Coastal Command was initially responsible for protecting convoys, it was not equipped with aircraft that could meet the Luftwaffe on an equal footing, so at the start of the war the task was transferred to Fighter

Command. Operating over water on the fringes of its air defence system, the command struggled to counter the Luftwaffe raids. Both sides gained experience during Kanalkampf. It also gave the Luftwaffe's commanders time to agree on exactly how they would go about eliminating the RAF.

The Luftwaffe announced on July 29 that major air attacks could begin in early August and on August 1 Führer Directive No. 17 instructed intensified air and sea operations to "establish the necessary conditions for the final conquest of England". Concerted attacks on RAF airfields and infrastructure were to start on August 13.

EAGLE ATTACK

The second phase of the Battle of Britain focused on destroying Fighter Command on the ground and in the air. Large bomber formations operating in daylight would attack the airfields the defenders flew from, forcing the RAF aircraft to be scrambled and shot down by the Luftwaffe's fighters. The

plan was codenamed Adlerangriff – 'Eagle Attack'.

German intelligence was aware of the importance of the Chain Home radar stations to the British defence system and efforts were made to destroy some of the sites to prevent Fighter Command receiving early warning of Luftwaffe raids. On August 12, the test and development group Erprobungsgruppe (EprGr) 210 struck four stations with its Messerschmitt Bf 110 and Bf 109 fighter-bombers. But the tall masts at the sites remained standing and, as rapid repairs were undertaken that made them operational again by the end of the day, the Germans thought the raids had failed to damage the sites. On the same day, the radar station at Ventnor on the Isle of Wight was hit by Ju 88s of KG 51, knocking it out of action for several weeks. The gap in coverage was partially filled by a mobile station and the Germans picked up the emitted radar signals. Believing Ventnor remained operational, the site was again targeted by Stukas four days later.

It seemed to the Germans that destroying Chain Home stations was a difficult proposal. Instead of persevering against the targets – vital to the defenders – only sporadic attacks were attempted thereafter. August 12 also saw the initial daylight raids on RAF airfields, when EprGr 210 and KG 2 struck Manston and Hawkinge, both in the frontline county of Kent.

The main assault against airfields was due to be launched the next day, August 13, which had been designated Adlertag ('Eagle Day'), the opening sorties of Adlerangriff. It was a fiasco. Plans for the attack had been distributed to Luftwaffe units, but it was decided to postpone the operation at the last minute because of bad weather. Not every unit received the cancellation order, resulting in bombers launching without their fighter escort, or Messerschmitts flying unproductive sweeps without the Dorniers, Heinkels or Junkers they were expected to protect.

The bombers of KG 2 struck Eastchurch in Kent, a Coastal Command airfield, while KG 54 was sent against Odiham and Farnborough, both in Hampshire, but did not reach them due to a combination of RAF fighters and dense cloud cover. The Ju 88s of Lehrgeschwader 1 (LG 1, a tactic development unit) hit Andover airfield (but were after Middle Wallop) and badly damaged the docks at Southampton, all in Hampshire. Middle Wallop also escaped an attack by Stukas, which also failed to find Warmwell, Dorset, although significant damage was inflicted on Detling in Kent, which did not belong to Fighter Command. Adlertag cost the Luftwaffe 39 aircraft; the RAF lost 15.

Luftflotte 5 based in Scandinavia entered the Battle of Britain on August 15. Large formations of RAF »

ABOVE: Hawker Hurricane Is of 242 Squadron based at Coltishall in Norfolk during the Battle of Britain.

LEFT: Contrails hanging above a barrage balloon, a familiar sight over southern England during the summer of 1940.

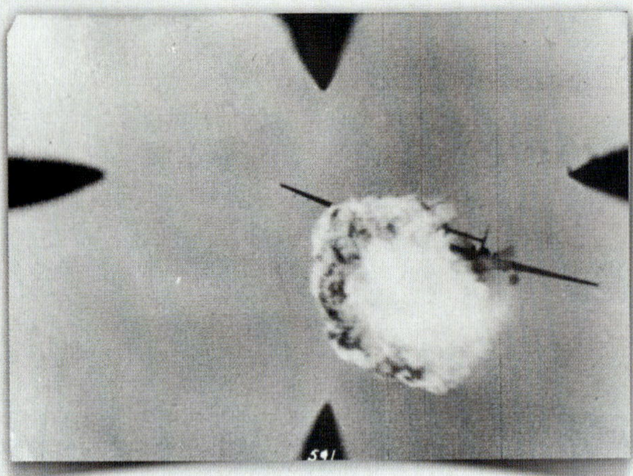

ABOVE: Gun camera image showing the demise of a Messerschmitt Bf 110. All Key Collection unless stated

fighters encountered by the Luftwaffe in southern England led German intelligence to believe that the north of the country was virtually undefended.

More than 60 He 111s of KG 26 departed their base at Stavanger in Norway on August 15, heading for targets around Newcastle in Tyne and Wear, escorted by Bf 110s of I./ZG 76. KG 26 was intercepted by fighters from several RAF fighter squadrons, which shot down eight He 111s and seven Bf 110 escorts. Other He 111s jettisoned their bombs into the sea. Junkers Ju 88s of KG 30, operating from Aalborg in Denmark, bombed the airfield at Driffield in Yorkshire, destroyed several Armstrong Whitworth Whitley bombers.

The Luftwaffe lost 76 aircraft on August 15; the RAF 35.

MOUNTING PRESSURE

By mid-August, with losses increasing among the Kampfgeschwader crews, the Jadgflieger ('fighter pilots') were ordered to devote more fighters to providing close escort for the bombers. During the second half of the month bomber losses declined, but it limited the opportunities for the Bf 109E pilots to hunt down the RAF fighters, their primary mission.

Other new tactics were also tried. Instead of the fighters and bombers forming up before crossing the Channel,

RIGHT: Fighter Command had reserves of aircraft during the Battle of Britain, but lacked sufficient numbers of pilots to fly them. Jim Winchester Collection

BELOW: Messerschmitt Bf 109E-4 'Black 7' of 5./JG 54 was brought down near Lydd in Kent on October 25, 1940. Crown

the bomber formations were massed over the Pas de Calais on the French coast, flying in circles for up to an hour. The armadas would set off across the Channel as soon as the fighter escort took off, rather than the two formating beforehand. It was hoped the RAF would launch its fighters once the radar stations picked up the bombers, and would have to return to their airfields to refuel by the time the formation was heading west. It seldom worked. Instead it left the Messerschmitts struggling to gain altitude while crossing the Channel. In order to keep the RAF guessing where the bombers were heading, several raids were mounted simultaneously while other formations were launched on feint attacks, returning to base before engaging the enemy.

The assault upon Fighter Command's airfields caused great damage to their buildings and facilities, but not enough to permanently put them out of action. Airfields are difficult targets to render unopperative. Fighters – especially the Hurricane, with its wide landing gear track – could operate from grass, while craters could be filled in. The main Fighter Command airfields had been provided with satellite fields, to which aircraft could be dispersed.

The greatest impact of the attacks was on the pilots of the command, many of whom were exhausted after scrambling several times a day to meet the Luftwaffe, often returning to an airfield with fresh holes in it. Early mornings, the lack of sleep, the loss of comrades in the squadron and wondering when your time would come – with no clear end in sight to the fighting – all played on the nerves. This was succinctly encapsulated by the 'fighter pilot's breakfast': two cigarettes and a 'puke'.

Fighter Command rotated its squadrons between its different Groups, which were responsible for regions within the British Isles. Squadrons with heavy attrition were released by 10 and 11 (Fighter) Groups based in the south of England, to be replaced by 'fresh' units, usually drawn from 13 (Fighter) Group, which controlled Fighter Command assets in northern England and Scotland. While the squadrons sent north remained operational and frequently scrambled to intercept German intruders, the general level of activity was much lower than in the south, allowing the unit to make good its losses. Stocks of Spitfires and Hurricanes were available to replace losses, but the number of trained fighter pilots was severely limited.

> *"The RAF claimed 185 enemy aircraft destroyed"*

By September 1940, the Luftwaffe was close to destroying Fighter Command. German attacks began to escalate on August 24, with major attacks on RAF airfields two days later, and the pressure on Fighter Command built up as the days passed. On August 31, RAF losses peaked at 41 aircraft; 39 Luftwaffe aircraft were destroyed. More than 460 RAF aircraft were destroyed or badly damaged between August 23 and September 6, while many fighter airfields were reduced to a state of shambles. More than 100 pilots had been killed and a further 130 injured, a quarter of Fighter Command's total. Even with new pilots rushed through their training, many squadrons only had an average of ten out of the usual establishment of 26.

German intelligence had no way of determining the effect its attacks were having on the human assets of Fighter Command. It only knew that Luftwaffe fighter and bomber crews continued to report that the RAF was still vigorously defending its airspace. As German dissatisfaction with the progress being made towards eliminating the RAF grew, another change of tactics was sought.

LONDON

Bomber Command raided Berlin in response to the scattered bombing of the outskirts of London on August 23. From August 29, the Luftwaffe struck Liverpool, Birmingham, Manchester and other targets by night and, on September 3, in response to the RAF attack on the German capital, it was decided to concentrate the forthcoming bomber campaign on London. The German high command believed that such raids would destroy the morale of the British population and force the government to sue for peace.

The first raid occurred on September 7. A total of 348 bombers from five Kampfgeschwader, escorted by 617 fighters, most of which were Bf 109s, headed for London. RAF Fighter Command was taken by surprise. It expected the formations to break up and head for the airfields, so the defending fighter squadrons were ordered to cover their bases and other strategically important sites. Thus the armada reached its targets nearly unopposed, causing heavy damage to areas in the east of the capital, including the docks, the fires guiding further bombers to the target during the night.

By 1630hrs, Fighter Command had 21 squadrons in the air and large dogfights ensued. The RAF claimed 41 Luftwaffe aircraft for 28 of its own.

London was the target of further raids over the following days. While heavy cloud cover over the capital

made it difficult for the Luftwaffe to hit individual targets in the metropolis, it also hampered the defenders trying to intercept the bombers. London's agony gave Fighter Command the respite needed to repair its airfields.

BATTLE OF BRITAIN DAY

By September, Luftwaffe intelligence estimated that the RAF was down to its last 50 Spitfires. It was hoped that a single large dogfight would be able to cripple Fighter Command once and for all. Two raids were planned for September 15, with the aim of engaging the 'few' remaining RAF fighters.

The first involved 25 Dornier Do 17s and 20 Bf 109 fighter-bombers sent against a railway junction outside Battersea in London, escorted by a further 120 Bf 109 fighters. The RAF responded to the bait, targeting and badly mauling the bombers.

Elements of four Kampfgeschwader were involved in the second attack, which targeted three docks in London. A total of 361 Messerschmitts escorted the bombers and 31 RAF squadrons intercepted the raiders, resulting in furious dogfights over Kent and Sussex. At the end of the day, the RAF claimed 185 enemy aircraft destroyed, for the loss of 26 fighters and 13 pilots killed. The true figures were 61 Luftwaffe and 31 RAF aircraft shot down, but the tally still clearly favoured the RAF. German losses proved that Fighter Command was far from being a spent force.

A week later, German tactics changed again, with smaller bomber formations sent against London while attacks on British aircraft factories increased. Bristol's facility at Filton,

Gloucestershire, was targeted on September 25 and Vickers Supermarine's works in Southampton was badly damaged the next day, effectively halting Spitfire production. Attacks on London continued, with 300 German bombers setting out on September 27, the Luftwaffe losing 57 aircraft during all operations over Britain on that date. By the end of the month, most Kampfgeschwader had switched to nocturnal operations, leaving the fighter-bombers to continue daylight raids. The last mass daylight attack occurred on October 31, the official end of the Battle of Britain.

By then the threat of invasion had receded, the Luftwaffe having failed to gain the necessary air supremacy before the onset of the winter months. Luftwaffe operations continued at night, with many British cities suffering during the Blitz, which continued into May 1941, by which time most of the Kampfgeschwader had been withdrawn in preparation for the assault on the Soviet Union.

Fighting for SURVIVAL

German forces faced more than just Fighter Command during the Battle of Britain.

At the end of what Prime Minister Winston Churchill called the 'Battle of France', Great Britain stood alone, with the prospect of a German invasion launched from the recently occupied European mainland a very real threat. It was clear to the leadership of both sides that before German forces could be landed in England, the Luftwaffe would need to gain control of the skies and neutralise the Royal Navy. The role of the RAF was to stop this happening.

The primary defence against the Luftwaffe in the summer and autumn of 1940 was RAF Fighter Command, its frontline squadrons the most visible part of a defence system that included the early warning network of coastal radar stations, an overland aircraft tracking system (provided by the Observer Corps) and a dispersed command and control infrastructure. The system was developed under the leadership of the head of Fighter Command, Air Chief Marshal Hugh C T Dowding, who embraced new technology to increase the effectiveness of his force.

Fighter Command was not the only British military service facing the Luftwaffe during the Battle of Britain. The army was responsible for manning the anti-aircraft guns and searchlights ranged around strategically important sites across the country. By July 1940, its Anti-Aircraft Command had 1,280 medium and 517 light anti-aircraft guns, plus more than 4,000 searchlights.

A further layer of defence was provided by the barrage balloons of RAF Balloon Command. The balloons were tethered at sites likely to be attacked, a further hazard to German bomber crews concentrating on their run up to the target. The command had 1,466 balloons by July 1940 and they proved dangerous to aircraft of friend and foe alike.

COASTAL COMMAND

While the Battle of Britain will forever be associated with Fighter Command, other RAF organisations also played a role in the campaign – disrupting German preparations for an invasion, interdicting supplies for the Luftwaffe in occupied Europe and attacking the airfields from which it operated, or protecting the vessels off the British coast.

Three Blenheim squadrons of Coastal Command (Nos 235, 236 and 248) were officially credited as taking part in the Battle of Britain. They protected convoys and patrolled the French coast, covering all the ports where barges were being gathered for the planned invasion, as well as escorting aircraft heading for targets along the European coast. They occasionally shot down German fighters and bombers with, for example, 235 Squadron intercepting 40 Heinkel He 111s off the Danish coast in August 15, 1940, shooting down two. No. 236 Squadron strafed Cherbourg airfield in France on August 1, losing two crews during the attack. Reconnaissance missions were flown by 248 Squadron until September, when it concentrated on anti-shipping strikes.

Coastal Command's other squadrons also played a role on the sidelines of the campaign, especially during the early phases when the Luftwaffe focused on British shipping. Squadrons equipped with Avro Anson and Lockheed Hudson general (maritime) reconnaissance aircraft flew countless sorties over coastal convoys, while Bristol Beauforts were used to sow mines. The command also became responsible for photo-reconnaissance from June 16, 1940, with 212 Squadron flying specially modified Spitfire Is to acquire images of invasion preparations in ports and harbours.

BOMBERS

The contribution of Bomber Command to the Battle of Britain is often overlooked. Its commander-in-chief, Air Marshal Charles Portal was directed by the Air Ministry on June 20, 1940, to hit targets that would reduce the scale of German attacks on Britain, such as equipment depots and communications (railways and canals) to stop supplies reaching Luftwaffe units in the occupied countries. Armstrong Whitleys, Handley Page Hampdens and Vickers Wellingtons were to attack German aircraft factories by night, while Blenheim light bombers of 2 Group would raid airfields in occupied territory by day. Losses of Blenheims resulted in a switch to night operations on August 12. During that month, Bomber Command mounted 714 sorties against airfields in Europe, nearly twice as many as in July.

The priority of targets changed frequently. From late August it was shipping assembled for a possible invasion in northern German ports and along the French Channel coast. Bomber Command aircraft also sowed mines in the coastal waters around Europe.

On the night of August 25-26, Bomber Command hit Berlin, in retaliation for the inadvertent bombing of London. The demand for retribution from the German leadership resulted in the Luftwaffe being directed on September 6 to attack the British capital.

Growing the RAF

Key to providing Fighter Command with the aircraft it required during the Battle of Britain were the successive expansion schemes designed to increase the size of the RAF during the five years leading up to the war. They formed the foundation for the successful defence of the country during the summer and autumn of 1940.

MAIN PICTURE: Supermarine Spitfire Is of 19 Squadron, the first Fighter Command unit to re-equip with the eight-gun design.

After World War One, it was assumed that there would not be a major war in Europe for at least ten years. As a result, the budget for the armed forces was severely limited and they were reduced to a shadow of their former sizes. By 1923, the RAF had a frontline strength of only 371 aircraft. Although the number increased slowly during the later half of the 1920s, to maintain parity with the French Air Force, it was not until March 1932 that the assumption of 'ten years of peace' was finally abandoned by the British government.

The catalyst for the change in policy was the growing realisation that Germany was rearming at a fast rate following the rise of Adolph Hitler and the National Socialist Party in that country. In 1934, the RAF had around 800 aircraft in 42 frontline squadrons based in the British Isles. Between then and 1939 this increased to 3,700 in 157 squadrons. The expansion of frontline strength was mirrored in the training infrastructure required to turn out new pilots and ground crew, while investment in the British aviation industry permitted rates of production to be further increased in case of war.

EXPANSION PLANS

On July 18, 1934, RAF Expansion Scheme A was approved as part of a wider effort to bolster the country's armed services. Earlier that year, the government had announced its decision to establish parity with Germany in the air. Scheme A would increase RAF strength by March 1939 to 111 frontline squadrons with 1,252 aircraft, plus 213 within 16 units of the Fleet Air Arm. Scheme A was concerned with increasing the quantity, rather than the quality, of the aircraft in service, by placing orders for existing types. It was the start of a build up that continued well after World War Two had started, although initial progress was slow because of the reluctance to allocate adequate finance to the programme and the hope that the various well-meaning, but ultimately unsuccessful, disarmament initiatives of the period would take root.

On March 10, 1935, Hermann Göring revealed the existence of the Luftwaffe during an interview with a representative of the *London Daily Mail*, adding further impetus to the expansion efforts. In response, the Air Ministry outlined a new plan that would also introduce more technologically advanced aircraft as well as increase the overall size of the force; the improvement in both quality and quantity required by the RAF. Known as Expansion Scheme F, it was sanctioned by the government in February 1936. It called for the delivery of 8,000 aircraft by 1939, including new monoplane types such as the Armstrong Whitworth Whitley, Bristol Blenheim, Fairey Battle, Handley Page Hampden, and Vickers Wellesley and Wellington bombers, plus Hawker Hurricane and Supermarine Spitfire fighters. Development and production of these aircraft proceeded slowly and by the time Scheme F was superseded in the spring of 1938, only the Blenheim, Hurricane and Whitley had entered service with the RAF.

The main obstacle to the programme continued to be financial. This changed when Hitler annexed Austria in March 1938, when the plan was again revised to cover 12,000 aircraft to be delivered within two years, a figure arrived at because it was deemed to be the maximum the British industry could possibly deliver within the time allocated.

Authorisation for the new plan, known as Scheme L, was granted by the government on April 27, 1938. All at once, funding was no longer a problem; the new limiting factors becoming a shortage of labour

and some raw materials. During March 1938, the industry produced 210 aircraft and, despite efforts to increase that figure in the months that followed, it remained constantly around the 200-mark until the fourth quarter of the year, when output began to rise steeply.

The Munich Agreement of September 30, 1938, which ceded the Sudetenland from Czechoslovakia to Germany, demonstrated Hitler's willingness to threaten military action to achieve his demands. That he got his way was in a large part because the British and French governments did not have confidence that their militaries were capable of meeting the German armed forces on an equal footing.

QUANTITY AND QUALITY

The Munich Crisis underlined the weakness of Britain's military preparations. Prime Minister Neville Chamberlain's announcement of "peace in our time" upon returning from his meeting with Hitler was greeted with scepticism within the armed forces and resulted in a redoubling of efforts to improve Britain's defences.

Of the 30 operational squadrons within Fighter Command at the time, only six were re-equipping with new monoplane fighters (five with Hurricanes, one flying Spitfires). The development of infrastructure was also falling behind schedule with, for example, only 16 of a planned 63 satellite airfields ready. Scheme L had to deliver quicker if the RAF was to reach parity with the Luftwaffe.

Production of 12,000 aircraft by the spring of 1940, with the potential of building 2,000 a month if war started, remained the central focus during the early months of 1939. At the start of that year, the industry delivered more than 450 aircraft, which increased to approximately 700 by the middle of the year.

As the likelihood of war increased, the Air Ministry continued to review and refine the expansion programme. In the three months before the German invasion of Poland in September 1939, a number of 'follow-on' orders were placed with the aviation industry for a further 5,500 aircraft to be delivered after April 1, 1940. They included new types such as the four-engine Handley Page Halifax and Shorts Stirling heavy bombers. This raised the total of aircraft planned to 17,500.

By the start of the war, the supply of arms to the British services had improved greatly since October 1938. »

ABOVE: The Gloster Gauntlet served at home in the front line between May 1935 and November 1939. It was typical of the biplane fighters operated by Fighter Command, armed with only two machine guns.

BELOW: Large orders for Bristol Blenheims were placed in the late 1930s. In service, the type proved vulnerable to the Luftwaffe's fighters. Blenheim I K7096 was flown by 30 Squadron. Pete West

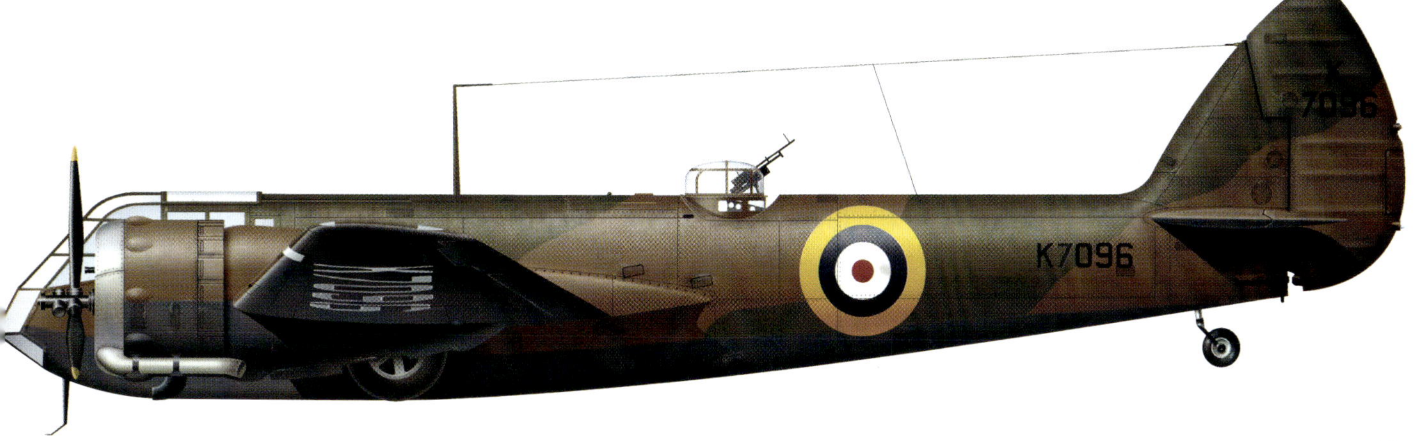

The rate of delivery of modern fighters had risen, with 44 Hurricanes handed over in September 1939, compared with 26 in October 1938. The corresponding figures for the Spitfire was 32 and 13. Frontline strength in the British Isles, including immediate reserves, was 1,978 in September 1939, a slight increase on the 1,854 one year before. In addition, the RAF had 2,200 aircraft in reserve. However, numbers only revealed half the story, as the quality of the aircraft in service had also improved. Fighter Command had 26 squadrons equipped with monoplane fighters, which had replaced obsolete biplanes previously flown by the units, up from six 12 months earlier.

On September 9, 1939, the governing body of the RAF, the Air Council, decided that the target for wartime output needed to be increased by 50% to 3,000 aircraft a month. This target was subsequently reduced to 2,550 per month to be delivered by the middle of 1942, with the assumption that a further 240 aircraft a month could be acquired from the British Dominions, including Canada and Australia. The target, which became known as the Harrogate Programme, formed the basis of wartime planning.

SHADOW SCHEME

None of the planned expansion would have been possible without major investments in the aeronautical industry. In addition to the funds provided by the companies, the government also instigated several schemes to expand the base and scope of the industry.

Britain's aeronautical industry was thankful for the work, as it had been starved of large orders in the 1920s and early 1930s. Contracts helped several famous companies survive to play a major role during World War Two. Hawker Aircraft was revived by orders for the Hart bomber. Orders for the Kestrel engine prevented Rolls-Royce ceasing work on aircraft engines. As targets for production increased during the second half of the 1930s, many companies were operating at full stretch and some work was sub-let. An example is the award of a contract to build 89 Fury II biplane fighters to General Aviation, which helped keep the company afloat.

During 1935, the government devised a plan to expand the aviation industry to meet potential wartime requirements. At that point, most aircraft manufacturers did not have the facilities to fulfil the large orders being placed by the Air Ministry. The government scheme proposed co-opting British motor companies to produce components – especially engines – for the aviation industry, making use of its skilled workforce. It was known as the Shadow Scheme because it 'shadowed' the aircraft industry. The Directorate of Aeronautical Production was formed within the Air Ministry in March 1936 with responsibility for the production of airframes, engines, armament and associated equipment.

Nine new factories were planned and equipped for engine production, initially to build the Bristol Mercury used in that company's Blenheim bomber, although other types were also assembled. Other sites were expanded to make it easier for them

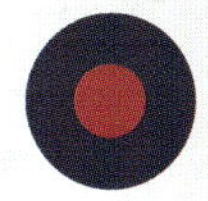

"in early 1938 it was realised that changes had to be made if the targeted output of new aircraft was to be met"

to switch over to aviation production. Most of the facilities created during the initial Shadow Scheme in 1936-37 were built next to existing sites. The initial motor manufacturers chosen to participate in the plan were the Austin Motor Company, Daimler Company, Rootes (Humber, Hillman and Sunbeam), and Rover Cars and Standard/Triumph Motor Company, while Singer and Wolseley originally due to participate pulled out.

By the time of Scheme L in early 1938, it was realised that changes had to be made if the targeted output of new aircraft was to be met. A second phase of building in 1938-39 primarily involved the

BATTLES AND BLENHEIMS

As orders increased, some of the Shadow facilities began to assemble whole aircraft, production starting at an initial two sites in 1938. The first aircraft completed by a Shadow Scheme factory was a Fairey Battle I produced by the Austin Motor Company at Cofton Hackett, the East Works at Longbridge outside Birmingham. The company entered an agreement with Fairey to build the bomber after discussions between the Air Ministry and its owner, Sir Herbert Austin, in February 1936, receiving an order for 863 Battles two years later. The first, Battle I L4935, flew in July 1938 and deliveries to the squadrons started that October.

The second facility to build complete aircraft was Rootes Securities at Blythe Bridge in Staffordshire, which received an initial order for 250 Blenheim Is in October 1936. The first (L8362) was delivered in November 1938. Other Shadow Scheme factories were equipped to build completed aircraft when the war started.

A total of 31 Shadow factories were under construction or finished by June 1939. They were camouflaged at the start of the war, although by then all car factories in Britain had been located and identified by German intelligence.

In addition to the Shadow Scheme, much effort was expended creating satellite plants during the late 1930s. The additional facilities dispersed or duplicated work so that the destruction of any individual site would not bring production to a halt.

On March 22, 1938, the British government decided to centralise the operations of the aviation industry. This laid the groundwork for the creation of the Ministry of Aircraft Production under Lord Beaverbrook from May 1940, permitting government to control planning and allocate resources as it saw fit.

construction of sites on the outskirts of big manufacturing centres or areas with high unemployment. The latter criteria were important not only for social reasons, but also because finding a sufficiently skilled workforce was becoming the limiting factor to growth. Finance was available, factory space was increasing and plant or machinery could be acquired, but the economic depression of the 1930s had reduced the number of apprenticeships available, placing a premium on those who had undergone such training.

Identifying
'THE FEW'

Pilots and aircrew of 14 nations flew with the RAF in the Battle of Britain. Although many became household names during the conflict and after the war, it was not until the early 1960s that a list of those who flew with Fighter Command entered the public domain.

No list of those Winston Churchill labelled 'the few' was kept at the time of the Battle of Britain, and it was only in 1942 that the Air Ministry decided to compile a record of those who had lost their lives, for incorporation into a national memorial. At that point, the campaign was deemed to have taken place between August 7 and October 31, 1940, with the list identifying 449 who had made the ultimate sacrifice.

A Roll of Honour was announced in March 1947 with 1,495 names of those killed, which was placed in the Battle of Britain Memorial at Westminster Abbey in London. It included all those who played a role in the outcome of the campaign, listing not only 449 from Fighter Command, but also 718 of Bomber Command, 280 in Coastal Command and 14 from other RAF commands, as well as 34 of the Fleet Air Arm.

Battle of Britain Aircrew	
Great Britain	2,342
Australia	32
Barbados	1
Belgium	28
Canada	113*
Czechoslovakia	88
France	13
Ireland	10
Jamaica	1
New Zealand	137
Poland	145
Rhodesia	3
South Africa	25
United States	9
Total	2,947

* Includes Pilot Officer Richard A Howley from the Dominion of Newfoundland, which joined Canada as a province on March 31, 1949

The Admiralty offered the Air Ministry the loan of naval pilots then undergoing training following the fall of France and 23 were eventually assigned, serving in 12 Fighter Command units, retaining their naval uniforms while with the RAF units. Four of the pilots became aces during the Battle of Britain. They include Sub-Lieutenant Richard J Cork, RN, who often flew as the wingman of Squadron Leader Douglas Bader with 242 Squadron. Sub-Lieutenant Richard E Gardner, one of the three naval pilots who joined the squadron, was the first to down an enemy aircraft on July 10. The survivors departed their RAF squadrons on return to the Admiralty in December 1940. In addition to those loaned to the RAF, a further 33 naval aviators served with 804 and 808 Squadrons (22 and 11, respectively) during the Battle of Britain.

"A total of 2,937 British and Allied airmen were awarded the Battle of Britain clasp"

BELOW: Hurricane I P3579 of 249 Squadron, the aircraft flown by Flt Lt James Nicolson on August 16, 1940. Pete West

DEFINING THE CRITERIA

On November 9, 1960, the Air Ministry published the exact criteria for the award of the Battle of Britain bar – the gold rosette worn on the ribbon of the 1939-1945 Star. Recipients had to have flown at least one operational sortie with the 71 accredited RAF squadrons or units (omitting the two of the Fleet Air Arm) between July 10 and October 31. A total of 2,937 British and Allied airmen were awarded the Battle of Britain clasp.

The official extension of the period of the battle, plus later research, came to a figure of at least 544 within Fighter Command who were killed or died of their wounds, and a further 795 who did not survive the war.

It was only through the hard work of Flight Lieutenant John H Holloway that a list of 'the few' was created. His desire to collect the autographs of the surviving veterans led him to seek out the identity of all those who took part in the campaign. On his own initiative, from 1955 he compiled the details of 2,937 airmen. The list was first published in 1961 in Derek Dempster's book *The Narrow Margin*. Research since has refined the total slightly, with 2,947 now understood to have fought in the Battle of Britain.

Fighter VC

Flight Lieutenant James B Nicolson of 249 Squadron became the only recipient of the Victoria Cross to be awarded to a Fighter Command pilot during the war. At around 1305hrs on August 16, 1940, while leading a patrol between Poole in Dorset and Romsey, Hampshire, by the three Hurricanes of Red Section from Boscombe Down, Wiltshire, they were 'bounced' by the Luftwaffe.

All three RAF fighters were hit and Nicolson injured by shrapnel in his left foot, while his Hurricane was set on fire, with flames reaching into the cockpit. While preparing to bale out of his crippled aircraft, he was passed by a Messerschmitt Bf 110, which he proceeded to engage, resulting in severe burns on his hands and other parts of his body. He finally departed the blazing cockpit after losing sight of the Bf 110. On landing by parachute, he was immediately rushed to a hospital in Southampton, Hampshire. Doctors initially did not believe he would survive his injuries, but he did and three weeks later was transferred to the RAF Hospital at Halton, Buckinghamshire.

The display commemorating Flt Lt Nicolson at the Tangmere Military Aviation Museum. David Willis

He learned that he had been awarded the Victoria Cross while convalescing at the Palace Hotel in Torquay, Devon. The medal was presented to him at Buckingham Palace by King George VI on November 25, 1940.

Sadly Nicolson, by then a Wing Commander, was killed on May 2, 1945, while flying as a passenger in a 355 Squadron Consolidated Liberator during a raid on Rangoon, Burma. One of the bomber's engines caught fire and it came down in the Bay of Bengal.

The burnt uniform and 'Mae West' life vest worn by Flight Lieutenant Nicolson and other artefacts relating to his career are displayed at the Tangmere Military Aviation Museum on the former airfield in West Sussex.

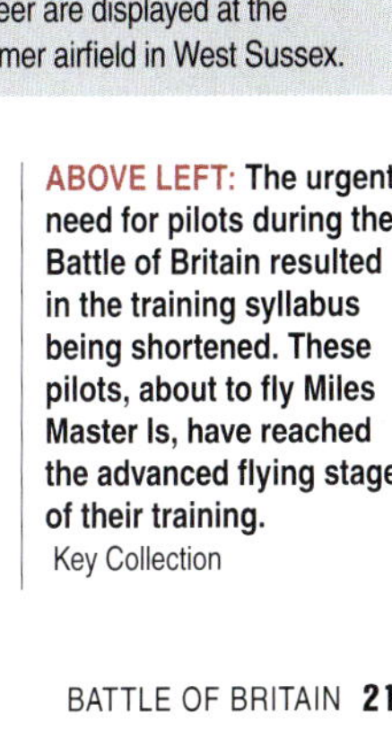

ABOVE LEFT: The urgent need for pilots during the Battle of Britain resulted in the training syllabus being shortened. These pilots, about to fly Miles Master Is, have reached the advanced flying stage of their training. Key Collection

Magnificent in MONOCHROME

During the Battle of Britain, artist Cuthbert Orde was commissioned to immortalise many of the pilots involved, as **Andrew Thomas** reveals.

In the summer of 1940, when the Battle of Britain was at its height, artist Cuthbert Orde was offered access to Fighter Command to capture its aviators at the behest of the Air Ministry's director of RAF Public Relations, Air Cdre Harald Peake. Agreeing enthusiastically, Orde spent the next year travelling to and living with the men he was to depict, resulting in him producing more than 160 monochromatic portraits using charcoal and white chalk. These remarkable drawings were made in situ and often between sorties, so reflect not just the strain of operational flying on the pilots' faces, but also the youth of many of them.

In 1943, the Air Ministry approved the publication of a selection of the depictions, together with brief personal comments on the men by Orde himself, who had spent an hour or two with each. Titled *Pilots of Fighter Command: Sixty Four Portraits*, assistant chief of the air staff AVM John Slessor observed in the foreword: "I think in these drawings he has caught something of their characters, something of the essential selves of the men." Born on December 18, 1888, Cuthbert Orde joined the British Army at the outbreak of war in August 1914, later transferring to the Royal Flying Corps. Initially an observer with 17 Squadron, he served alongside John Slessor. Qualifying as a pilot in June 1916, Orde joined the Testing Squadron at Upavon in Wiltshire, which later moved to Martlesham Heath, Suffolk, and was appointed a flight commander the following year. Having married the daughter of Arthur Wellesley, 4th Duke of Wellington, he was promoted to acting major in August 1918. However, due to ill health, Cuthbert Orde relinquished his commission in January 1919 (although he retained the rank of captain) to embark on a career as an artist.

'TOP BRASS' DECISIONS

Of Orde's commission by the Air Ministry to sketch the portraits of RAF flyers, it was station and squadron

commanders, and occasionally Group Headquarters staff, who selected the subjects, usually four or five individuals from each unit. Some of those nominated were lost before they could sit for him, while others were subsequently killed in action. Orde's collection left a wonderful contemporary archive and many of his works later decorated the corridors of RAF messes and countless headquarters buildings. Known around the stations as 'The Captain', doubtless because he was a former aviator, Cuthbert Orde established a real empathy with those he drew. He closed his introduction to his book with the toast: "To the reader I present the chaps. To the chaps I raise my glass."

These are just *some* of 'his chaps':

FLT LT GEOFFREY 'SAMMY' ALLARD DFC, DFM, 85 SQUADRON – DRAWN SEPTEMBER 13, 1940

Allard was a 28-year-old former RAF Halton apprentice who, after qualifying as an aircraft mechanic, applied for flying training and became a sergeant pilot in 1937. Posted to 85 Squadron, he was thrown into action with the unit over France. By the time Orde met Allard at RAF Church Fenton, North Yorkshire, he had been credited with ten 'kills' and five shared during the Battle of Britain. Orde said: "I can tell you that everyone without exception held the very highest opinion of him. Within a very few weeks he had gained the DFM, a Bar to it, his commission, promotion to flight lieutenant, and the DFC. He was the inspiration of his squadron."

FG OFF WITOLD URBANOWICZ, 303 (POLISH) SQUADRON – DRAWN SEPTEMBER 20, 1940

At 32, Witold Urbanowicz was one of the oldest operational pilots of the battle, having already fought over his native Poland before escaping to Britain via Rumania. After briefly flying with an RAF unit, he was posted to the newly formed 303 (Polish) Squadron equipped with Hurricanes at Northolt, West London, as a flight commander. During a scramble on September 6, he shot down a Messerschmitt Bf 109 near Sevenoaks, Kent, and by the time Orde met with him on the 20th, he had added three Dorniers to his tally. The day before he sat with Orde, they were in the officers' mess and the artist recounted: "I was studying Urbanowicz across the room by the door. Just then the loudspeaker came to life and a steady, monotonous voice announced, 'Escadra Polska… readiness!' Urbanowicz raised both hands, fists clenched above his head and brought them down with a jerk to his sides. He had a look of almost ecstasy on his face."

SGT JAMES HARRY 'GINGER' LACEY DFM, 501 SQUADRON – DRAWN SEPTEMBER 29, 1940

Two days before he sat for his drawing at RAF Kenley, Surrey, 'Ginger' Lacey claimed a Bf 109 over Maidstone, Kent.

It was just one of 18 victories credited to the flyer, making him one of the individual top-scoring pilots during the Battle of Britain. He had joined the RAF Volunteer Reserve before the war and undertook his debut action with 501 Squadron over France. Orde noted: "He learned to fly at a civilian school at the age of 18 and he wished to become a professional pilot. His particular line when fighting was wide deflection shots, and he attributed his skill to his having been taught to shoot rabbits when he was very young. I was very much impressed because all this was said without a trace of conceit. He just had complete confidence in himself."

SQN LDR ARCHIBALD ASHMORE MCKELLAR DFC AND BAR, 605 SQUADRON – DRAWN OCTOBER 3, 1940

What the diminutive Scot Archie McKellar lacked in stature (he was just 5ft 3in tall), he made up for in character and skill. Joining 605 Squadron as a flight commander in June 1940, by the time Orde met him at South London's Croydon Aerodrome he was the CO. Orde recalled: "Everyone had a very high opinion and affection for him.

FAR LEFT: Flt Lt Geoffrey 'Sammy' Allard. ALL MINISTRY OF DEFENCE UNLESS STATED

LEFT: Polish pilot Fg Off Witold Urbanowicz.

LEFT: Taken on July 16, 1941, this famous photograph shows 'Ginger' Lacey climbing into a 501 Squadron Spitfire IIa (P7990'/SD-L'), wearing the first parachute manufactured in Australia and a silk scarf signed by the workers. KEY COLLECTION

FAR LEFT: Fg Off 'Sammy' Allard – described as "...the inspiration of his squadron" – was one of the first subjects for the artist's project. Allard flew a distinctively marked Hurricane while with 85 Squadron, which featured an unusual paint line on its lower nose and rear fuselage. He is seen here in the aircraft posing for a publicity photograph. MALCOLM V LOWE COLLECTION

LEFT: Sgt James Harry 'Ginger' Lacey.

RIGHT: Sqn Ldr Archibald Ashmore McKellar.

FAR RIGHT: Flt Lt Robert Wardlow 'Bobby' Oxspring.

RIGHT: Bobby Oxspring with his personal mount, Spitfire Vc AB216/'DL-Z', while commanding 91 Squadron at RAF Hawkinge in 1942.
KEY COLLECTION

I drew him the day he was awarded the Bar to his DFC and he read aloud in the mess his citation in the newspapers. He laughed a great deal while doing so, to cover a certain embarrassment at being described as a 'brilliant tactician' – a very true description I'm told. He was small, very alert, very quick minded and jovial… and a very unstable sitter as he was always jumping up to look at the drawing!" Orde was still with 605 on October 7 and later wrote: "On that morning he attacked four Messerschmitts, one after the other and brought them all down in flames and a few hours later, on a second flight, got yet another. Quick as lightning he was – and knew precisely what to do and the best way of doing it."

FAR RIGHT: Sqn Ldr John Alexander 'Johnny' Kent.

BELOW: Supermarine Spitfire I R6800/'LZ-N' was the personal mount of 66 Squadron's CO, Sqn Ldr Rupert Leigh, when Orde visited 'Bobby' Oxspring at RAF Gravesend, Kent.
C REILLEY

FLT LT ROBERT WARDLOW 'BOBBY' OXSPRING, 66 SQUADRON – DRAWN OCTOBER 9, 1940

By the time he sat for Orde, 22-year-old Bobby Oxspring had been in action solidly for two months and credited with seven confirmed and one shared victory. While Orde spent the briefest of

time with him, he recollected: "I had hardly any opportunity of getting to know Oxspring as I went over to Gravesend for the day only to draw him and Sergeant [Matthew] Cameron. I remember well our working in the control tower building and how infernally cold and draughty it was, and his telling me that it was his ambition to command 66 Squadron one day, as his father commanded it in the last war."

SQN LDR JOHN ALEXANDER 'JOHNNY' KENT DFC, AFC, 92 SQUADRON – DRAWN OCTOBER 1940

Johnny Kent was a 26-year-old Canadian who had joined the RAF in 1935. During the battle, he served initially as a flight commander with 303 (Polish) Squadron, claiming four enemy aircraft. As Orde revealed: "When I first met him, he was a flight lieutenant in [Ronald Gustave] Kellett's Polish squadron, and he led it in action on many occasions. He is in appearance tall, lean and wiry. In action he has the reputation of being cool, ruthless and undismayed by the strength of the enemy. On one occasion having become separated from his squadron, he looked around

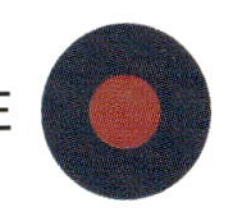

for something to attack. He found it – a formation of 40 Germans who he proceeded to charge, and when he had brought down one and damaged another returned home only because he had used up all his ammunition."

Orde later met with Kent when he became one of 'his chaps': "He was promoted to squadron leader and took over the famous 92 Squadron then at Biggin Hill and had a wonderful record. Kent was the ideal chap for that riotous outfit, for besides being tough, calculating and inspiring in the air he is an extremely amusing chap ready to cap any story."

PLT OFF JOHN RONALD 'JACK' URWIN-MANN, 238 SQUADRON – DATE UNKNOWN

Twenty-year-old Jack Urwin-Mann hailed from Vancouver, Canada, and flew with 238 Squadron throughout the battle, claiming eight 'kills' and two shared. He was portrayed by Orde at RAF Chilbolten, Hampshire. As the artist recollected: "I went to a camp near Andover to do this drawing – the muddiest and most windswept place I was ever in. We worked in the squadron office to the clicking of typewriters, and the

incessant opening and shutting of the door. We both survived and it was rather an amusing experience. Urwin-Mann is a particularly good pilot and was terrific at Hurricane aerobatics. He is a very good leader and definitely comes in the category of inherently tough, I think. He was very quick, and I should think quite imperturbable. They were extremely kind hosts to me each day I went over."

FLT JOHN CHARLES DUNDAS DFC, 609 SQUADRON – DATE UNKNOWN

John Dundas was an original member of 609 Squadron having operated over Dunkirk. Meeting the pilot at RAF Middle Wallop, Hampshire, Orde clearly admired the 25-year-old, who was his unit's top-scoring pilot of the Battle of Britain: "He had a first class honours degree at Oxford. Besides a brilliant mind, he had a most delightful and amusing personality. He and his squadron commander understood and admired each other and would spend hours in the evenings arguing and discussing fighter tactics. Next day the squadron would take to the air to try out the new theory. This quickness of perception no doubt made him a very tricky adversary in battle, and I can well imagine him as he waded into a Hun. With his tall, spare figure his collar would never stay flat, and eternal pipe, he didn't give the impression of toughness. I can't think why he was such a good pilot and fighter, for he was apparently a very poor car driver." »

LEFT: Flt John Charles Dundas.

ABOVE: Flt Lt Robert Finlay Boyd.

ABOVE RIGHT: A Hurricane I (P3462/'VK-G') from 238 Squadron sits on readiness at RAF Middle Wallop during August 1940. Canadian 'Jack' Urwin-Mann was awarded the first of his two DFCs for actions during the Battle of Britain while serving with this unit. R C B ASHWORTH

FLT LT ROBERT FINLAY BOYD DFC, 602 SQUADRON – DRAWN OCTOBER 21, 1940

Credited with nine confirmed 'kills' and six shared, Boyd was a pre-war auxiliary. Having worked as a mining engineer, he served with 602 Squadron throughout the Battle of Britain. Orde recalled Boyd, who helped destroy a Junkers Ju 88 that same day, was "verra Scotch" when he met him at RAF Westhampnett, West Sussex. The artist noted: "He had a tremendous lot of fighting experience and keeps on shooting down Huns. They operate from a satellite aerodrome that was strictly a wartime site. The Spitfires were parked under immense elm trees and all was set in the beautiful South Downs landscape. The squadron were a very 'civil lot o' boys' as they say. Finlay Boyd is younger than he looks. He was 24 when I made this drawing. He is a very good pilot, a very good shot, and, of course, as dour and tenacious as he can be and would never let go once he was on the track of a Hun."

SQN LDR ADRIAN HOPE BOYD DFC & BAR, 145 SQUADRON – DRAWN OCTOBER 27, 1940

By the start of the campaign, Adrian Boyd was an experienced fighter pilot flying Hurricanes with 145 Squadron. When Orde met him at RAF Tangmere, West Sussex, he was CO and had claimed nine enemy aircraft downed, including five in one day on August 8. Orde wrote:

" 'Boydy' I met just as he was giving up his squadron. He was one of the greatest successes in the Battle of Britain. He has got an inherent toughness that seems to have come out in the drawing. I have an entertaining recollection of Boydy the night before he left, sitting on a table with a large whisky and soda in his hands, extolling with much force and sentimentality the advantages and happiness of married life."

RIGHT: Sqn Ldr Adrian Hope Boyd.

BELOW: Taken at the end of the Battle of Britain, pilots from 501 Squadron pose with one of the unit's Hurricanes. Three of those pictured were Cuthbert Orde's 'chaps': the CO, Sqn Ldr Henry Hogan (standing 7th from left), Flt Lt Eustace 'Gus' Holden (on Hogan's left) and 'Ginger' Lacey (seated right). 501 SQN ASSOCIATION

The Luck of the IRISH

Before he passed away in March 2025 aged 105, John Hemingway was the last surviving Battle of Britain pilot. In 2020 he told his story to **Jonny Cracknell**

There has always been a strong sense of admiration for 'The Few' who gallantly took to the skies during the Battle of Britain. With countless growing up idolising them as heroes, some even aspired to follow in their footsteps. However, it's a sobering thought that of the almost 3,000 recognised Allied airmen who flew between July 10 and October 31, 1940, all are now passed.

History narrates how The Few – as a small band of courageous young men, from all walks of life – refused to wilt in the face of Nazi tyranny, despite seemingly insurmountable odds.

Spitfires and Hurricanes still grace the skies as the irreplaceable sound of their Merlin engines perpetuate the tale, but it's the individual stories that truly capture the human sacrifice, significance and reality of the conflict.

HIS FIGHT; OUR FORTUNE

The last known survivor was the remarkable 105-year-old Gp Capt John Allman 'Paddy' Hemingway DFC. Not only did he take part in the Battle of Britain (BoB), he also fought during the Battle of France and across Italy. It is with a huge amount of fortune that John's presence is known today – until early 2018, his whereabouts and fate had been unknown. With the BoB highlighted during the RAF100 commemorations in 2018, John's family came forward and confirmed his wellbeing in Ireland.

Like so many veterans, John didn't feel his involvement deserved special acclamation, saying: "Everyone played their part, so I never regarded myself as a history maker, as it were. Or that every move we made would become the subject of prolonged interest and study. Rather, with the likelihood I wouldn't last long, each day and flight became a unity in itself and no more important than any other part of my life so far, or indeed, since. Hence my almost solid refusal to partake in

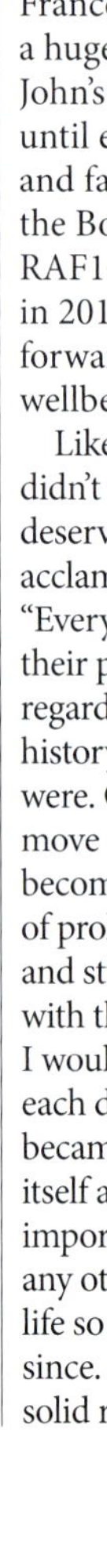
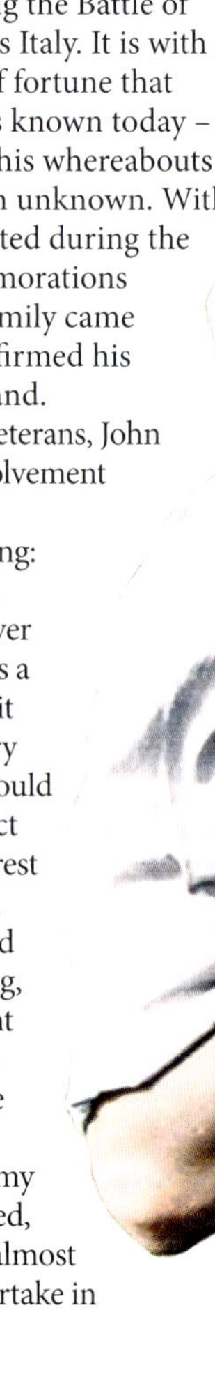

"In those few moments I realised I needed to shrug off sentimentality"

LEFT: Following intensive action with 11 Group during the Battle of Britain, 85 Squadron was withdrawn north to Church Fenton, Yorkshire, in early September 1940. The unit is seen here being led by Peter Townsend on October 5 as it prepared for its then new role… night-fighting. KEY COLLECTION

BELOW: Posed with his logbook, John's service medals – from left: Distinguished Flying Cross, 1939-1945 Star with Battle of Britain clasp, Aircrew Europe Star, Italy Star and War Medal 1939-1945. JONNY CRACKNELL

many programmes and studies." Some never had the chance to describe their fight – more than 500 Allied airmen perished during the battle, while another 800 or so would not survive the war. One of the lucky ones, in his final interview, John admitted his story is amazing: "Given that I was shot down four times, lived when my parachute didn't open properly and survived when many didn't, you could say I'm a lucky Irishman!"

Born in Dublin on July 17, 1919 John joined the RAF in March 1938 and started flying training at Brough in East Yorkshire. Having successfully gained his 'wings', he was granted a short-service commission and joined his first operational squadron. He said: "I was posted to 85 Squadron at Debden [Essex] flying Hurricanes in December 1938. I hadn't flown the Hurricane, but they must have thought I wouldn't break one."

Settling into a life of pre-war flying, John explained: "I was in the mess when we heard Prime Minister Neville Chamberlain announce we were going to war.

"At about midnight on September 3, 1939 I was woken and ordered to get to my aircraft ready for action." Dressing quickly, John rushed for his machine: "I remember looking around as I ran to the dispersal thinking how cold and indifferent the once-familiar buildings seemed. In those few moments I realised I needed to shrug off sentimentality and cope entirely on my own at all levels – no matter what.

"I was [in] one of three Hurricanes ordered to launch – we were certainly Debden's first flight of the war, and probably one of the first defensive sorties launched. We saw nothing and landed about 50 minutes later. I returned to bed knowing everything ❯

RIGHT: A wonderful colourised photograph of 85 Squadron pilots – including John, second from left – posing with CO Peter Townsend (centre with walking stick) at Church Fenton in early September 1940. Townsend had just returned to the unit after being shot down and injured by a Messerschmitt Bf 110 on August 31, 1940.

RIGHT: John (second from right) relaxing in the crew room following another defensive patrol from Church Fenton sometime in September 1940.

BELOW: Scramble! Pilots from 85 Squadron run for their Hurricanes during the Battle of Britain – John Hemingway is in short sleeves second from right. On the far left is Sgt John Ellis who was killed flying Hurricane I P2673/'VY-E' soon after this image was taken.

had definitely changed and feeling doubtful about the future. Despite the feeling of isolation and uncertainty I slept like a log as usual."

FIRST 'KILL'

Just days later, 85 Squadron was dispatched to northern France where John's 'luck of the Irish' struck – he won a raffle to spend Christmas at home.

Returning to the unit at Lille-Seclin during January 1940, he was assigned to Flt Lt Richard 'Dickie'

Lee's B Flight; Lee – godson of the so-called Father of the RAF, Viscount (Hugh) Trenchard – had claimed 85's first victory. Thrown into action supporting the British Expeditionary Force (BEF) as it faced defeat, John was in the thick of the action.

On May 10, John flew four patrols between Louvain and Hasselt in Belgium, as German forces swept through the Low Countries into France.

"I saw nothing on the first, second or fourth sorties… but on the third I spotted a formation of nine Heinkel

111s flying in three vics of three – an ideal formation to attack… or so I thought" explained John. "I dived, settled behind the lead bomber of the rear vic, and opened fire. In my innocence, I was sure the Heinkels on either side wouldn't fire at me in fear of hitting each other. It seemed that no-one was firing back – I couldn't see any tracer and I wasn't hit as I half expected. Strange to say though, I pulled up and away – but only momentarily. I dived back again and emptied my guns into the same bomber. It faltered and crashed – it was later confirmed as destroyed.

"Even under favourable circumstances, it had taken all of my ammunition to down a He 111 from behind. We had heard the Germans were fitting armour plating in their bombers, which might have explained it. However, it was obvious we had to devise another means of attacking them from the beam or head on."

The following day, John flew another three sorties and shared in the destruction of a Dornier Do 17, before being shot down over Maastricht in the Netherlands while flying Hurricane L1979/'VY-X'. John said: "On my third flight, I spotted a low-flying Fieseler Storch and dived to attack it. The pilot must have seen me coming though as he turned below me, before diving towards the ground and staying there – all the time it was leading me towards the guns it was spotting for." The anti-aircraft guns opened up, as John recalled: "I heard the shells going by and felt one or two clobber the aeroplane, but I was too 'green' to realise it was serious and continued attacking. Suddenly there was a hell of bang and the needles in the cockpit went all over the place as it filled with smoke. I was furious that the Germans should do this to me – I was going to fly down the barrel of the gun and blow the whole lot to blazes. Then I thought that would apply to me too. So I turned west, and crash-landed in a field before getting away as quickly as possible."

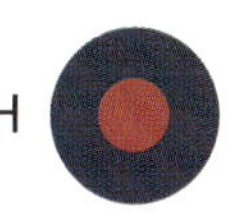

"...the Dornier gunners rattled away at me and that was it – BANG!"

Heading west, John met a British armoured car – the crew of which wouldn't believe that the Germans had crossed the Meuse River. Walking as far as Brussels, he spent several hours on a bridge waiting for someone to pass – eventually a little black Citroen appeared. John remembered: "We drove west to Lille and I returned to the squadron soon after. When I got back to the base it had been bombed and a lot of pilots were no longer there… most had been shot down and killed or taken prisoner. A lot of our aeroplanes had been damaged too – I think 19 were destroyed in just ten days."

After near constant combat, the pilots were red-eyed with tiredness. On May 17, exhausted, John was sent home with 'Dickie' Lee and Sgt Geoffrey 'Sammy' Allard; the rest of 85 was evacuated a week or so later. "The day before, everyone thought Sammy was dead" revealed John: "He flew four sorties on about an hour's sleep… and even fell asleep while flying over enemy territory. As he taxied in from his last patrol, the groundcrew were surprised he didn't jump out of his Hurricane after he shut down. Hesitantly, a mechanic opened the canopy only to find Sammy had succumbed to sleep in the cockpit. He slept there for 30 hours…"

Posted briefly to 253 Squadron at RAF Kirton in Lindsey, Lincolnshire the following month, as a deputy flight commander, John was soon back in action over France, flying offensive patrols around Dunkirk just before the British Expeditionary Force's mass withdrawal. He recalled: "Although we were covering the town, we didn't actually see Dunkirk. We were operating further into Northern France looking for Huns to prevent – in theory – attacks getting through to the retreating forces. At the time we didn't know the importance of what was happening there."

With the BoB imminent, 85 Squadron was quickly re-equipped at Debden under the leadership of Sqn Ldr Peter Townsend; John re-joined the unit on June 15. On August 18 – dubbed 'The Hardest Day' – John was shot down in Hurricane V7249 following a skirmish with a Junkers Ju 88 near the Thames estuary. He explained: "We vectored south from Debden and then out over the North Sea – climbing all the time. While the squadron got you into the battle, you fought alone during it. As we closed, I broke away to continue climbing towards the circling bombers… I thought they presented the ideal target. If I circled inside them, but in the opposite direction, my attacks would be well forward of them.

"The bombers, by firing at me, would risk hitting each other. Alas, they must have gained height as I was still climbing when I reached them. I tried to get a good aim inside, but they were approaching too fast – instead, I decided to choose one that would cross my sights. Almost stalling, I saw two aircraft firing at me. Hitting me, it knocked the Hurricane over and I entered an inverted spin."

INTO THE SEA

With the cockpit covered in oil, John released the canopy and managed to regain control at about 9,000ft: "Thankfully, the hood opened. We were often warned to enter a fight with it open because they had been known to jam. As I set course for home, the engine stopped. I had no wish to bale out… but I remembered that Hurricanes often tipped up and sank when ditching. I tried to climb out on to the wing while holding the stick and hoped to crash like that, but it was so slippery that I was blown off. In retrospect, had I landed that way I'm sure I'd have died… I'd have been thrown forward into the sea at 70mph. Thankfully, my parachute opened. I landed in the sea, before getting rid of the 'chute and as much clothing as possible… I was frightened I'd be dragged under."

Surrounded by jellyfish, John swam for the shore before being rescued, through good fortune: "The crew of a Lightship about 12 miles off Clacton [Essex] had seen me glide overhead before baling out. They immediately launched a lifeboat towards where they had thought I'd landed." After searching for nearly two hours and knowing there was no chance the stricken pilot could survive in the harsh North Sea, the lifeboat turned back toward the ship. However, they heard an unusual noise and rowed towards it. John recalled: "They literally bumped into me. Once they hauled me on board, I insisted on taking an oar. While rowing, I asked if it had been the sound of me swimming they heard, they said 'no'… apparently I hadn't been swimming – just rolling in the waves."

»

LEFT: On July 14, 1940 John flew a 45-minute patrol in Hurricane I P3408/'VY-K' – the aircraft is seen here sometime in October 1940. The regular mount of Sgt Geoffrey 'Sammy' Allard, note the unusual demarcation line below the engine exhaust separating the Dark Earth/Dark Green upper surfaces and Sky undersides. VIA ANDREW THOMAS

LEFT: A trio of 85 Squadron Hurricanes – P3854/'VY-Q' (left), V6611/'VY-U' (closest) and V7240/'VY-M' – in flight. John scrambled after an enemy raid in V6611 on September 5, 1940. VIA ANDREW THOMAS

BELOW: Taking a break between night sorties, aircrew from 85 Squadron pose with Hurricane P3118/'VY-X' at RAF Church Fenton during 1941. From left: John (then a flying officer), Plt Off Geoffrey Howitt, Fg Off James Marshall, Sqn Ldr Peter Townsend with the squadron's mascot Kim, and Fg Off William Carnaby. Note Carnaby is leaning on the unit's scoreboard displaying more than 100 'kills'.

ABOVE: A Douglas Havoc similar to the machine from which John managed to escape. KEY COLLECTION

RIGHT: The last of 'The Few' – John Allman 'Paddy' Hemingway DFC at home in Ireland during October 2019. As he said: "The only advice I can give to people is to be Irish!" JONNY CRACKNELL

BELOW: John's logbook entries from August 1940 showing he was shot down twice within the space of just eight days – first by a Ju 88 on the 18th, and then what he thought was a Bf 109 on the 26th. JONNY CRACKNELL

'Dicky' Lee was also lost that day. Last seen chasing an enemy formation about 30 miles (48km) off the east coast, he was aged just 23. John had huge respect for Lee, regarding him as the most fearless and capable pilot. He fondly recalled the time Lee flew a Hurricane inverted at Castle Camps in Cambridgeshire, so low that the groundcrew had to remove grass from the radio mast when he landed. John said: "He was a wonderful person – I still say and think it. I just didn't want to believe it; he was going to turn up, something had happened, but he was going to turn up. But of course, he never did."

Just eight days later, on August 26, John was shot down for the third time. Flying Hurricane P3966, he engaged a formation of 15 Dorniers and 30 Messerschmitt Bf 109s looming on the Kent coast.

'THE SILLIEST THING'

He said: "Peter Townsend was absolutely convinced the best way to attack bombers was head on. We scrambled after a formation coming up the Thames Estuary and Townsend

arranged our approach so we were in front of and above them. I remember the first couple of Hurricanes shot straight under them as we attacked.

"Diving ever steeper, I managed to get a Dornier 215 in my sights and fire the briefest of bursts before scudding under the blue belly of another. I fired another split-second squirt and then started the silliest thing I've ever done I suppose… I started to pull around to have another go. Of course, as soon as I did, the Dornier gunners rattled away at me and that was it – BANG!"

With the cockpit filling with smoke, John thought his aeroplane was on fire: "It certainly felt like it was. Luckily, the hood opened. We'd heard tales that German fighters were shooting down parachutists in the air, so I decided to dive into the cloud before jumping. I landed in Pitsea Marshes and the local Home Guard quickly got me back to the squadron. I was OK, but soon paid for it – for four days my sinuses just about killed me. By then we'd lost so many pilots we were withdrawn north." Incredibly, the wreckage of John's Hurricane was recovered in March 2019. Viewing a live feed from his home in Ireland,

John watched as they recovered the likes of the control column – the gun-button still set to 'Fire' – the tailwheel, the machine's data plate and the engine block.

By late September 1940, 85 Squadron had moved to Church Fenton in Yorkshire to rest. While there, both John and the unit predominantly switched to flying nocturnal defensive patrols (see panel on the right).

Recognising John's continuous combat since early 1940, Townsend soon re-assigned him to light duties. John held him in great esteem: "Peter was an incredibly successful fighter pilot, an absolutely wonderful CO and a first-class wartime leader. He would listen, was very quietly spoken and, despite what was later said in the newspapers regarding his romance with Princess Margaret, my view of him has never changed."

In one of his subsequent roles as a flight controller, John directed aircraft during the Normandy landings in June 1944. However, he soon became restless and wanted to fly in combat again.

ITALIAN INCIDENT

With the Allies turning the tide of the war, John – then a squadron leader – joined 43 Squadron's B Flight at Ravenna in northern Italy during February 1945, flying Spitfire LF.IXs. He remarked: "I learnt to fly the Spitfire in the north of England and was then sent out to Italy, where we learned to dive bomb. We were quickly taught to trim forward – there was always a danger of blacking out. Shortly after I arrived, the CO [acting Sqn Ldr Arthur Harry Jupp] was tour expired and I took over the squadron. At the time we were dive bombing anything we could find – the Germans were retreating and we were helping them do it!"

Flying almost daily through March and April on bomber escort and reconnaissance missions, John also carried out several strikes on key targets including railways and communications positions. On April 23, he was shot down for the fourth time while flying his then regular mount – Spitfire LF.IX PT836/'FT-A', near Copparo.

He said: "I was attacking what I thought was ordinary Germans on the ground when suddenly this ack-ack opened up and hit me – knocking out my engine" recalled John: "I wanted to bale out as I was at about 3,000ft, but they must have hit the aeroplane again as I suddenly shot out of it. Tumbling over and over; my parachute harness stripped the skin off my legs and crotch.

"I landed and left my parachute where it was before some local farm

YEAR 1940		AIRCRAFT		PILOT, OR	2ND PILOT, PUPIL	DUTY
MONTH	DATE	Type	No.	1ST PILOT	OR PASSENGER	(INCLUDING RESULTS AND REMARKS)
—	—	—	—	—	—	— TOTALS BROUGHT FORWARD
AUGUST						
"	12.	HURRICANE	V7249.	SELF.		KIWI6 – MARTLESHAM.
"	12.	ditto.	V7249.	SELF.		OPERATIONAL PATROL.
"	12.	ditto.	V7249.	SELF.		ditto.
"	12.	ditto.	V7249.	SELF.		ditto.
"	12.	ditto.	V7249.	SELF.		MARTLESHAM – KIWI6.
"	15.	ditto.	V7249.	SELF.		BALBO.
"	15.	ditto.	V7249.	SELF.		AIR TEST.
"	16.	ditto.	V7249.	SELF.		BALBO.
"	16.	ditto.	P3966.	SELF.		FLAP.
"	16.	ditto.	P3966.	SELF.		ditto.
"	18.	ditto.	V7249.	SELF.		ditto.
"	18.	ditto.	V7249.	SELF.		SHOT DOWN BY JU88. BALED OUT
"	20.	ditto.	L1915.	SELF.		INTO SEA. 12 MLS. OFF CLACTON.
"	20.	ditto.	L1915.	SELF		DEBDEN – CROYDON.
"	21.	ditto.	L2071.	SELF.		FLAP.
"	24.	ditto.	P3966.	SELF.		PATROL DOVER 15000'.
"	24.	ditto.	P3966.	SELF.		AERODROME PATROL.
"	25.	ditto.	V6580.	SELF.		ENGINE AND RADIO TEST.
"	25.	ditto.	P3966.	SELF.		OPERATIONAL PATROL
"	26.	ditto.	P3966.	SELF		ditto.
"	26.	ditto.	P3966.	SELF		SHOT DOWN IN FLAMES BY ME109
"	28.	ditto.	V7349.	SELF.		OPERATIONAL PATROL
"	29.	ditto.	V7349.	SELF.		ditto.

GRAND TOTAL [Cols. (1) to (10)] .....488.....Hrs.....40.....Mins.   TOTALS CARRIED FORWARD

Lucky

Escape

By April 1941, 85 Squadron had re-equipped with Douglas Havocs. Damaging several He 111s during early May, John found himself needing to bale out again, this time owing to technical issues. He recalled: "In May 1941, I was flying Havoc night-fighters – they were wonderful machines. After a two-hour patrol on the 13th in bad weather, we were letting down to Debden through 600ft when the instruments failed. I'd experienced this before and knew there was no chance. I was aware no pilot had ever successfully baled out of a Havoc because of its high tail assembly. So, I tried to improve my chances by crawling back over the oxygen bottles behind me, but was blown out of the aircraft almost immediately. My right hand hit the tail, breaking two fingers – causing it to go numb. I couldn't feel to pull the rip cord, but I managed to use my left hand and hit a tree just before the 'chute fully opened. Thankfully, it got tangled enough in the tree to break my fall while the soft midden did the rest. As well as my hand, I'd hurt both ankles." Gazetted on July 1, John was awarded the DFC and mentioned in dispatches. He was just 21 years old.

workers hid me and gave me some clothes – so I quickly changed. Suddenly, a voice rang out. I don't know what was said, but he was running so I chased after him along a ditch. At the end of it, I settled down and saw two armed German soldiers running towards the hole I'd just been in! As soon as they vanished into it I ran into an orchard. I remember gunfire – I imagine they were shooting at me." Managing to get away, John put it down to being dressed as an Italian peasant.

He remembered: "Eventually my crotch was so painful that I went to a farmhouse, knocked on the door and in my best pidgin said 'Me English' – thankfully, they didn't shoot and took me in.

"They put me down another hole in the middle of a field, gave me a bottle of wine and some chicken and told me to stay there until they came back for me. They did, about ten hours later – or something like that – and took me to another farmhouse. A lot of talking and gesticulating went on and I was introduced to a young girl of about six or seven.

"She took me by the hand and we wandered south past scores of German troops. I was terrified – more for that young girl than I think you can possibly imagine. We carried on to another farmhouse and I didn't look at them again." He was met there by members of the Italian Resistance. John recollected: "Despite my sore crotch, they marched me as fast as they could south until we met the advanced column of the 16th/5th Lancers. I had a damn good meal and soon returned to the squadron."

THE LAST OF 'THE FEW'

With the unconditional surrender of Germany in May 1945 and Japan four months later, John was promoted to wing commander on December 6 that year. Leaving 43 Squadron, then based at Klagenfurt in Austria, he went on to command 244 Wing. He later served with the RAF in the Middle East, the Air Ministry in London and as a senior staff officer at NATO Headquarters in France, before becoming station commander at RAF Leconfield, East Yorkshire in 1966. He retired from the RAF in September 1969 with the rank of group captain.

John had three children – Brian, Michael and Susan and, following the death of his wife Bridget in 1998, he moved to Canada to live with his daughter.

He returned to Ireland in 2011 and a peaceful life in south Dublin. At the time, his son Brian revealed: "He sees himself as a symbol of everyone's heroism and commitment to the war. He is also very mindful of the thousands of other pilots no longer with us any more. If people feel proud to be British because of the part he played in the Battle for Britain, then he is proud."

During this interview around the time of his 101st birthday, John explained: "I was just one of 3,000 pilots and 200,000 RAF personnel who won the Battle of Britain and I feel privileged to have met so many amazing young men and pilots – many of whom perished. The battle should not be about me, but all who served."

Having survived everything a determined enemy could throw at him, John jovially put the reason for his long and lucky life down to his heritage, as he summed up: "I can't say don't drink, or don't fool about with people or don't fly and get shot at – I've done everything... and I'm an Irishman. The only advice I can give to people is to be Irish!"

ABOVE: The data plate from Hurricane P3966 was recovered from Fobbing Marshes, Essex in March 2019 – 78 years after John was shot down flying the aircraft. KENT BOB MUSEUM TRUST

BELOW: Pilots run for their machines at Castle Camps in late July 1940. South African ace Plt Off Albert G Lewis (third from right) can be seen heading for Hurricane P2923/'VY-R'. Hemingway flew almost 30 sorties in the last two weeks of July. VIA ANDREW THOMAS

"I was furious that the Germans should do this to me"

Offence
DEFENCE

Fighter Command was Britain's primary defence during the Battle of Britain. From its small beginnings, it grew into a force capable of blunting the Luftwaffe onslaught in 1940.

Order of battle of Fighter Command's air defence squadrons on August 8, 1940, the day before 9 (Fighter) Group formed		
Fighter Command		HQ Bentley Priory, Stanmore, Middlesex
10 (FIGHTER) GROUP HQ Rudloe Manor, Box, Wiltshire		
Filton Sector		
87 Squadron	Hurricane I	Exeter, Devon
92 Squadron	Spitfire I	Pembrey, Carmarthenshire
213 Squadron	Hurricane I	Exeter, Devon
234 Squadron	Spitfire I	St Eval, Cornwall
247 Squadron	Gladiator II	Roborough, Devon
Middle Wallop Sector		
152 Squadron	Spitfire I	Warmwell, Dorset
238 Squadron	Hurricane I	Middle Wallop, Hampshire
604 Squadron	Blenheim If	Middle Wallop, Hampshire
609 Squadron	Spitfire I	Middle Wallop, Hampshire
11 (FIGHTER) GROUP HQ Uxbridge, Greater London		
Biggin Hill Sector		
32 Squadron	Hurricane I	Biggin Hill, Greater London
501 Squadron	Hurricane I	Gravesend, Kent
600 Squadron	Blenheim If	Manston, Kent
610 Squadron	Spitfire I	Biggin Hill, Greater London
Debden Sector		
17 Squadron	Hurricane I	Debden, Essex

The Air Defences of Great Britain command was formed on the first day of 1925 at the Air Ministry in London, dropping the 's' in 'Defences' upon moving to Hillingdon House at Uxbridge in London, on June 1, 1926. In the late 1920s, RAF fighter squadrons were assigned to the Fighting Area, a subordinate organisation within Air Defence of Great Britain. Fighting Area's original headquarters were at Kenley, Surrey, but moved to Hillingdon House in August 1926, to co-locate with those of Air Defence of Great Britain.

During the austere years of the late 1920s and early 1930s, the RAF received little in the way of new equipment. This started to change when Germany began to rearm and, when the Luftwaffe was revealed in March 1935, the need to expand and reorganise the RAF to counter the perceived threat became clearer. In 1936, the RAF reorganised along functional lines, with operational squadrons in the British Isles being assigned to Bomber, Coastal and Fighter Commands.

NEW COMMAND

Fighter Command was formed on July 14, 1936, with headquarters at Bentley Priory at Stanmore, Middlesex, under the leadership of Air Chief Marshal Hugh C T Dowding. The new organisation – with the motto Offence, Defence – was responsible for all fighter units based in Great Britain, comprising nine airfields with 17 fighter squadrons, plus five

MAIN PICTURE: Three Hurricane Is of 257 Squadrons get airborne. The nearest aircraft, 'DT-G', remained in service until it crashed on landing on January 4, 1945.

ABOVE RIGHT: RAF Fighter Command was created in July 1936, becoming Air Defence of Great Britain in November 1943. David Willis Collection

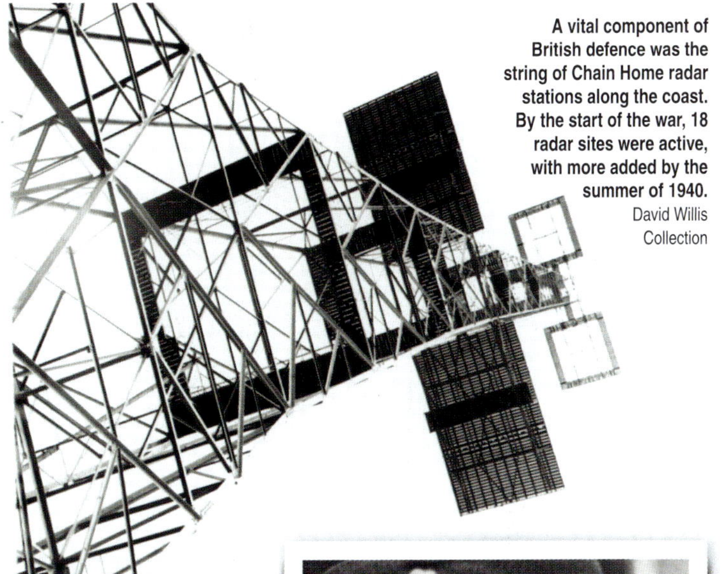

A vital component of British defence was the string of Chain Home radar stations along the coast. By the start of the war, 18 radar sites were active, with more added by the summer of 1940. David Willis Collection

army co-operation squadrons. London was the centre of focus for the new command, with its assets radiating outwards from the city. Dowding considered the force was sufficient to provide an adequate defence as far north as York in Yorkshire and the Solent in Hampshire.

Just before the creation of Fighter Command, Fighting Area was redesignated 11 (Fighter) Group on May 1, 1936. The command's second group was established to defend the industry and population centre in the Midlands, as well as covering the eastern counties and north up to York. No. 12 (Fighter) Group formed at Uxbridge on April 1, 1937, moving to Hucknall in Nottinghamshire on May 18 the same year. It relocated its headquarters to Watnall, also in ›

ABOVE: Air Chief Marshal Sir Hugh Dowding was responsible for turning Fighter Command into an effective air defence organisation. He was its commander from July 1936 until November 1940. Key Collection

Squadron	Aircraft	Location
85 Squadron	Hurricane I	Debden, Essex
Hornchurch Sector		
41 Squadron	Spitfire I	Hornchurch, Essex
54 Squadron	Spitfire I	Hornchurch, Essex
65 Squadron	Spitfire I	Hornchurch, Essex
74 Squadron	Spitfire I	Hornchurch, Essex
Kenley Sector		
64 Squadron	Spitfire I	Kenley, Surrey
111 Squadron	Hurricane I	Croydon, Greater London
615 Squadron	Hurricane I	Kenley, Surrey
1 Squadron, RCAF	Hurricane I	Croydon, Greater London
North Weald Sector		
25 Squadron	Blenheim If	Martlesham Heath, Suffolk
56 Squadron	Hurricane I	North Weald, Essex
151 Squadron	Hurricane I	North Weald, Essex
Northolt Sector		
1 Squadron	Hurricane I	Northolt, Greater London
257 Squadron	Hurricane I	Northolt, Greater London
303 Squadron	Hurricane I	Northolt, Greater London
Tangmere Sector		
43 Squadron	Hurricane I	Tangmere, West Sussex
145 Squadron	Hurricane I	Westhampnett, West Sussex
601 Squadron	Hurricane I	Tangmere, West Sussex
Fighter Interception Unit	various, including Blenheim If, I Hurricane I	Tangmere, West Sussex
12 (FIGHTER) GROUP HQ Watnall, Nottinghamshire		
Coltishall Sector		
66 Squadron	Spitfire I	Coltishall, Norfolk
242 Squadron	Hurricane I	Coltishall, Norfolk
Digby Sector		
29 Squadron	Blenheim If	Digby, Lincolnshire
46 Squadron	Hurricane I	Digby, Lincolnshire
611 Squadron	Spitfire I	Digby, Lincolnshire
Duxford Sector		
19 Squadron	Spitfire I	Duxford, Cambridgeshire
310 Squadron	Hurricane I	Duxford, Cambridgeshire
312 Squadron	Hurricane I	Duxford, Cambridgeshire
Kirton-in-Lindsey Sector		
222 Squadron	Spitfire I	Kirton-in-Lindsey, Lincolnshire
264 Squadron	Defiant I	
A Flight		Ringway, Cheshire
B Flight		Kirton-in-Lindsey, Lincolnshire
Wittering Sector		
23 Squadron	Blenheim If	Collyweston, Lincolnshire
229 Squadron	Hurricane I	Wittering, Cambridgeshire
266 Squadron	Spitfire I	Wittering, Cambridgeshire
13 (FIGHTER) GROUP HQ Newcastle-on-Tyne, Tyne and Wear		
Church Fenton Sector		
73 Squadron	Hurricane I	Church Fenton, North Yorkshire
249 Squadron	Hurricane I	Church Fenton, North Yorkshire
302 Squadron	Hurricane I	Leconfield, Yorkshire
616 Squadron	Spitfire I	Leconfield, Yorkshire
Catterick Sector		
219 Squadron	Blenheim If	Catterick, North Yorkshire
Dyce Sector		
263 Squadron	Hurricane I	Grangemouth, Stirlingshire
Turnhouse Sector		
253 Squadron	Hurricane I	Turnhouse, Edinburgh
602 Squadron	Spitfire I	Drem, East Lothian
603 Squadron	Spitfire I	Turnhouse, Edinburgh
605 Squadron	Hurricane I	Drem, East Lothian
Usworth Sector		
72 Squadron	Spitfire I	Acklington, Northumberland
79 Squadron	Hurricane I	Acklington, Northumberland
607 Squadron	Hurricane I	Usworth, Tyne and Wear
Wick Sector		
3 Squadron	Hurricane I	Wick, Highland
141 Squadron	Defiant I	Prestwick, South Ayrshire
232 Squadron	Hurricane I	Sumburgh, Shetland Islands
504 Squadron	Hurricane I	Castletown, Caithness
804 Squadron	Sea Gladiator	Hatston (HMS *Sparrowhawk*), Orkney Islands
HQ RAF NORTHERN IRELAND, HQ Fort William Park, Belfast, Northern Ireland		
245 Squadron	Hurricane I	Aldergrove, County Antrim

Excluded are various training and other second line units (such as communication flights).

EXPANDING NORTH

Defence of northern England, Scotland and Northern Ireland was assigned to 13 (Fighter) Group, which formed at Hucknall, on March 15, 1939, and became operational on May 25 that year under the command of Air Vice-Marshal Richard Saul. Its headquarters moved to Kenton Bar in Newcastle-on-Tyne, Tyne and Wear, on July 29, and with the start of the war it relocated again to Blakelaw Estate, Ponteland Road in the same city on September 5.

Soon after war was declared, Fighter Command was assigned the task of protecting the coastal convoys operating off the shores of the British Isles. Defence of the Royal Navy's anchorage at Scapa Flow in the Orkneys was also added to 13 (Fighter) Group's tasks. As the number of squadrons within Fighter Command increased, it became possible to add new groups to expand the air defence network.

Formed on June 1, 1940, 10 (Fighter) Group became operational on July 8. It was headquartered at Rudloe Manor at Box in Wiltshire, and was responsible for the defence of the West Country, including the important naval facilities at Plymouth, the southwest ports and other naval dockyards, in addition to providing cover for Channel convoys. A

constructed at strategic locations close to the coast to provide early warning of unidentified aircraft approaching Britain. Overland reporting of aircraft was the responsibility of the Observer Corps, a civil defence organisation formed in late 1925. The Chain Home radar detection and tracking units were assigned to 60 (Signals) Group on April 18, 1940. They played a major role in the Battle of Britain.

TOP: Plotters created a visual representation of the air battle on a table at the Sector or Group Control Rooms.

ABOVE: Heavily censored image of the Sector Operations Room at Duxford, Cambridgeshire. AHB/UK MoD Crown

Nottinghamshire, on July 8, 1940. Creation of the new group left 11 (Fighter) Group to concentrate on the defence of London and the southeast.

A Command Operations Room was created to control the force. Experience gained during exercises showed that it was prudent to delegate as much responsibility to the groups as possible, resulting in each establishing an Operations Centre to control operations in their area of responsibility. Radar stations were

No. 72 Squadron markings, as worn on its Spitfire Is. David Willis

"RAF squadrons usually had an authorised establishment of 16 aircraft, plus two more in an immediate reserve"

LEFT: A 85 Squadron Hurricane I landing at Castle Camps in Cambridgeshire in September 1940.

The Czechoslovakian pilots of 310 Squadron gather in front of Hurricane I P3143 'NN-D' at Duxford, Cambridgeshire, on September 7, 1940, one month after becoming operational during the Battle of Britain. All Key Collection unless stated

separate organisation to defend the North West, 9 (Fighter) Group, was established on August 9, 1940, with headquarters at Barton Hall, Preston in Lancashire.

TACTICAL STRUCTURE

Within each group the main fighter airfields were designated as Sector Stations, each with a Sector Control Room able to control RAF fighter formations in the local area during the fighting. Sector Stations usually had associated satellite airfields, on which additional squadrons were based and also allowing the fighter force to be dispersed, to reduce the probability of an attack on one airfield destroying all aircraft in that area.

Two or three squadrons based at the same airfield were generally known as Wings, which were temporary tactical groupings. During the Battle of Britain, squadrons were moved at short notice to react to threats, while 'battle weary'

units were withdrawn to quieter areas, usually within 13 (Fighter) Group's region, to rest and regroup.

RAF fighter squadrons usually had an authorised establishment of 16 aircraft, plus two more in an immediate reserve. During the Battle of Britain, with frequent losses and accidents, and deliveries of new

aircraft when they became available, the actual number on strength at any one point varied greatly. Each squadron typically had two operational flights ('A' and 'B') of six to eight aircraft. The flights were divided into sections for command in the air, identified by different colours (such as 'Red', 'Blue' or 'Green').

ABOVE: Beaufighter If R2186 served with the Fighter Interception Unit at Shoreham in West Sussex.

BELOW: Hurricane I P3886 'UF-K' of 601 'County of London' Squadron. Pete West

BATTLE OF BRITAIN SQUADRONS AND UNITS

The following lists all the squadrons and units involved in the defence of Britain during the Battle of Britain, from July 1 to October 31, 1940. It includes all the squadrons deemed to have fought under the control of Fighter Command as outlined by the official Air Ministry list released on November 9, 1960, plus three Coastal Command units. Although it was not recorded in the official list, details of the Fighter Flight, Sumburgh (which became 247 Squadron) are given. Each entry covers the aircraft operated during the Battle of Britain, with dates when that type was flown by the unit and the code allocated to it, the airfields they operated from, plus the commanding officer/s (C/O) during the period.

1 Squadron Code JX

Aircraft	Hurricane I	Oct 38	Feb 41
Based at	Tangmere, West Sussex	23 Jun 40	1 Aug 40
	Northolt, Greater London	1 Aug 40	9 Sep 40
	Wittering, Cambridgeshire	9 Sep 40	15 Dec 40
C/O	S/Ldr David A Pemberton	May 40	Nov 40

3 Squadron Code QO

Aircraft	Hurricane I	Jul 39	Apr 41
Based at	Wick, Highland	23 May 40	2 Sep 40
	Castletown, Caithness	2 Sep 40	14 Sep 40
	Turnhouse, Edinburgh	14 Sep 40	9 Oct 40
	Dyce, Aberdeenshire	9 Oct 40	12 Oct 40
	Castletown, Caithness	12 Oct 40	7 Jan 41
C/O	S/Ldr Stephen F Godden	Jun 40	Sep 40
	S/Ldr George F Chater	Sep 40	Nov 40

17 Squadron Code YB

Aircraft	Hurricane I	Jun 39	Feb 41
Based at	Debden, Essex	19 Jun 40	19 Aug 40
	Tangmere, West Sussex	19 Aug 40	2 Sep 40
	Debden, Essex	2 Sep 40	8 Oct 40
	Martlesham Heath, Suffolk	8 Oct 40	28 Feb 41
C/O	S/Ldr Ralph I G MacDougall	Jun 40	Jul 40
	S/Ldr Cedric W Williams	Jul 40	Aug 40
	S/Ldr Anthony G Miller	Aug 40	Jul 41

19 Squadron Code QV

Aircraft	Spitfire I	Aug 38	Sep 40
	Spitfire IIa	Sep 40	Oct 41
Based at	Fowlmere, Hertfordshire	25 Jun 40	3 Jul 40
	Duxford, Cambridgeshire	3 Jul 40	24 Jul 40
	Fowlmere, Hertfordshire	24 Jul 40	30 Oct 40
C/O	S/Ldr Philip C Pinkham	May 40	Sep 40
	S/Ldr Brian J Lane	Sep 40	Jun 41

23 Squadron Code YP

Aircraft	Blenheim If	Dec 38	Apr 41
Based at	Collyweston, Lincolnshire	31 May 40	12 Sep 40
	Ford, West Sussex	12 Sep 40	6 Aug 42*
C/O	S/Ldr Leslie C Bicknell	Jan 40	Aug 40
	S/Ldr George F W Heycock	Aug 40	Nov 40

* det at Middle Wallop, Hampshire, 12 Sep 40 to 25 Sep 40

25 Squadron Code ZK

Aircraft	Blenheim If	Dec 38	Jan 41
	Beaufighter If	Oct 40	Jan 43
Based at	Martlesham Heath, Suffolk	19 Jun 40	1 Sep 40
	North Weald, Essex	1 Sep 40	8 Oct 40
	Debden, Essex	8 Oct 40	27 Nov 40
C/O	S/Ldr William W Loxton	Jun 40	Sep 40
	S/Ldr Henry M Mitchell	Sep 40	Jan 41

29 Squadron Code RO

Aircraft	Blenheim If	Dec 38	Feb 41
	Hurricane I	Aug 40	Dec 40
Based at	Digby, Lincolnshire	Jun 40	8 Jul 40
	Wellingore, Lincolnshire	8 Jul 40	27 Apr 41
C/O	S/Ldr John S McLean	Apr 40	Jul 40
	S/Ldr Ernest R Bitmead	Jul 40	Jul 40
	S/Ldr Stanley C Widdows	Jul 40	Jul 41

32 Squadron Code GZ

Aircraft	Hurricane I	Oct 38	Jul 41
Based at	Biggin Hill, Greater London	4 Jun 40	28 Aug 40
	Acklington, Northumberland	28 Aug 40	15 Dec 40
C/O	S/Ldr John Worall	May 40	Aug 40
	S/Ldr Michael N Crossley	Aug 40	Apr 41

41 Squadron Code EB

Aircraft	Spitfire I	Jan 39	Nov 40
Based at	Catterick, North Yorkshire	8 Jun 40	26 Jul 40
	Hornchurch, Essex	26 Jul 40	8 Aug 40
	Catterick, North Yorkshire	8 Aug 40	3 Sep 40
	Hornchurch, Essex	3 Sep 40	23 Feb 41
C/O	S/Ldr Hilary R L Hood	Apr 40	Sep 40
	S/Ldr Robert C F Lister	Sep 40	Sep 40
	S/Ldr Donald O Finlay	Sep 40	Aug 41

43 Squadron Code FT

Aircraft	Hurricane I	Nov 38	Apr 41
Based at	Tangmere, West Sussex*	31 May 40	8 Sep 40
	Usworth, Tyne and Wear	8 Sep 40	12 Dec 40
C/O	S/Ldr Charles G Lott	Oct 39	Jul 40
	S/Ldr John V Badger	Jul 40	Sep 40
	S/Ldr Caesar B Hull	Sep 40	Sep 40
	S/Ldr Thomas F Dalton-Morgan	Sep 40	Jan 42

* det at Northolt, Greater London, 23 Jul 40 to 1 Aug 40

46 Squadron Code PO

Aircraft	Hurricane I	Feb 39	Dec 40
Based at	Digby, Lincolnshire	13 Jun 40	18 Aug 40
	Duxford, Cambridgeshire	18 Aug 40	19 Aug 40
	Digby, Lincolnshire	19 Aug 40	1 Sep 40
	Stapleford Tawney, Essex	1 Sep 40	8 Nov 40
C/O	S/Ldr James R MacLachlan	Jun 40	Oct 40
	S/Ldr Anthony R Collins	Oct 40	Oct 40
	S/Ldr Lionel M Gaunce	Oct 40	Dec 40

54 Squadron Code KL

Aircraft	Spitfire I	May 1939	Feb 1941
Based at	Rochford, Essex	25 Jun 40	24 Jul 40
	Hornchurch, Essex	24 Jul 40	28 Jul 40
	Catterick, North Yorkshire	28 Jul 40	8 Aug 40
	Hornchurch, Essex	8 Aug 40	3 Sep 40
	Catterick, North Yorkshire	3 Sep 40	23 Feb 41
C/O	S/Ldr James A Leathart	May 40	Aug 40
	S/Ldr Donald O Finlay	Aug 40	Sep 40
	S/Ldr Felix P R Dunworth	Sep 40	Dec 40

56 Squadron Code US

Aircraft	Hurricane I	May 38	Feb 41
Based at	North Weald, Essex	4 Jun 40	1 Sep 40
	Boscombe Down, Wiltshire	1 Sep 40	29 Nov 40
C/O	S/Ldr Edward V Knowles	Jun 39	Jul 40
	S/Ldr Graham A L Manton	Jul 40	Aug 40
	S/Ldr Herbert M Pinfold	Sep 40	Jan 41

64 Squadron Code SH

Aircraft	Spitfire I	Apr 40	Feb 41
Based at	Kenley, Surrey	16 May 40	19 Aug 40
	Leconfield, Yorkshire	19 Aug 40	13 Oct 40
	Biggin Hill, Greater London	13 Oct 40	15 Oct 40
	Coltishall, Norfolk	15 Oct 40	10 Nov 40
C/O	S/Ldr Norman C Odbert	Jun 40	Jul 40
	S/Ldr Aeneas R D MacDonnell	Jul 40	Mar 41

65 Squadron Code YT

Aircraft	Spitfire I	Mar 39	Mar 41
Based at	Hornchurch, Essex	5 Jun 40	28 Aug 40
	Turnhouse, Edinburgh	28 Aug 40	29 Nov 40
C/O	S/Ldr Desmond Cooke	Oct 37	Jul 40
	S/Ldr Henry C Sawyer	Jul 40	Aug 40
	S/Ldr Arthur L Holland	Aug 40	Oct 40
	S/Ldr Gerald A W Saunders	Oct 40	Sep 41

66 Squadron Code LZ

Aircraft	Spitfire I	Nov 38	Nov 40
Based at	Coltishall, Norfolk	29 May 40	3 Sep 40
	Kenley, Surrey	3 Sep 40	11 Sep 40
	Gravesend, Kent	11 Sep 40	30 Oct 40
C/O	S/Ldr Rupert H A Leigh	Apr 40	Oct 40
	S/Ldr Athol S Forbes	Oct 40	Oct 41

72 Squadron Code RN

Aircraft	Spitfire I	Apr 39	Apr 41
Based at	Acklington, Northumberland	6 Jun 40	31 Aug 40
	Biggin Hill, Greater London	31 Aug 40	1 Sep 40
	Croydon, Greater London	1 Sep 40	14 Sep 40
	Biggin Hill, Greater London	14 Sep 40	13 Oct 40
	Coltishall, Norfolk	13 Oct 40	30 Oct 40
	Matlask, Norfolk	30 Oct 40	2 Nov 40
C/O	S/Ldr Ronald B Lees	Dec 38	Jul 40
	S/Ldr Anthony R Collins	Jul 40	Sep 40
	S/Ldr Edward Graham	Sep 40	Apr 41

73 Squadron Code TP

Aircraft	Hurricane I	Jul 38	Jan 42
Based at	Church Fenton, North Yorkshire	18 Jun 40	5 Sep 40
	Castle Camps, Cambridgeshire	5 Sep 40	13 Nov 40
C/O	S/Ldr James W C More	Apr 40	Aug 40
	S/Ldr Maurice W S Robinson	Aug 40	Sep 40
	S/Ldr Alan D Murray	Sep 40	Apr 41

74 Squadron Code ZP

Aircraft	Spitfire I	Feb 39	Sep 40
	Spitfire IIa	Sep 40	May 41
Based at	Hornchurch, Essex	25 Jun 40	14 Aug 40
	Wittering, Cambridgeshire	14 Aug 40	21 Aug 40
	Kirton-in-Lindsey, Lincolnshire	21 Aug 40	9 Sep 40
	Coltishall, Norfolk	9 Sep 40	15 Oct 40
	Biggin Hill, Greater London	15 Oct 40	20 Feb 41
C/O	S/Ldr Francis L White	Mar 40	Aug 40
	S/Ldr Adolph G Malan	Aug 40	Mar 41

79 Squadron Code NV

Aircraft	Hurricane I	Nov 38	Jun 41
Based at	Biggin Hill, Greater London	5 Jun 40	2 Jul 40
	Hawkinge, Kent	2 Jul 40	11 Jul 40
	Sealand, Flintshire	11 Jul 40	13 Jul 40
	Acklington, Northumberland	13 Jul 40	27 Aug 40
	Biggin Hill, Greater London	27 Aug 40	8 Sep 40

	Pembrey, Carmarthenshire	8 Sep 40	14 Jun 41
C/O	S/Ldr J D C Joslin	May 40	Jul 40
	S/Ldr Geoffrey D L Haysom	Jul 40	Jul 40
	S/Ldr John H Hayworth	Jul 40	Jun 41

85 Squadron Code VY

Aircraft	Hurricane I	Sep 38	Jul 41
Based at	Debden, Essex	22 May 40	19 Aug 40
	Croydon, Greater London	19 Aug 40	3 Sep 40
	Castle Camps, Cambridgeshire	3 Sep 40	5 Sep 40
	Church Fenton, North Yorkshire	5 Sep 40	23 Oct 40
	Kirton-in-Lindsey, Lincolnshire	23 Oct 40	23 Nov 40
C/O	S/Ldr Peter W Townsend	May 40	Jun 41

87 Squadron Code LK

Aircraft	Hurricane I	Jul 38	Jun 41
Based at	Church Fenton, North Yorkshire	26 May 40	5 Jul 40
	Exeter, Devon	5 Jul 40	29 Nov 40
C/O	S/Ldr John S Dewar	Dec 39	Jul 40
	S/Ldr Robert Lovatt-Gregg	Jul 40	Aug 40
	S/Ldr Randolph S Mills	Aug 40	Dec 40

92 Squadron Code QJ

Aircraft	Spitfire I	Mar 40	Mar 40
Based at	Pembrey, Carmarthenshire	18 Jun 40	8 Sep 40
	Biggin Hill, Greater London	8 Sep 40	9 Jan 41
C/O	S/Ldr Phillip J Sanders	May 40	Sep 40
	S/Ldr Alan M MacLachlan	Sep 40	Oct 40
	S/Ldr John A Kent	Oct 40	Feb 41

111 Squadron Code JU

Aircraft	Hurricane I	Jan 38	Apr 41
Based at	Croydon, Greater London	4 Jun 40	19 Aug 40
	Debden, Essex	19 Aug 40	3 Sep 40
	Croydon, Greater London	3 Sep 40	8 Sep 40
	Drem, East Lothian	8 Sep 40	12 Oct 40
	Dyce, Aberdeenshire*	12 Oct 40	20 Jul 41
C/O	S/Ldr John M Thompson	Jan 40	Oct 40
	S/Ldr Arthur J Biggar	Oct 40	Feb 41

* det at Montrose, Forfarshire (Angus), 12 Oct 40 to 5 Apr 41

141 Squadron Code TW

Aircraft	Defiant I	Apr 40	Aug 41
Based at	Turnhouse, Edinburgh	28 Jun 40	12 Jul 40
	West Malling, Kent	12 Jul 40	21 Jul 40
	Prestwick, South Ayrshire	21 Jul 40	22 Aug 40
	Dyce, Aberdeenshire *	22 Aug 40	30 Aug 40
	Turnhouse, Edinburgh +	30 Aug 40	15 Oct 40
	Drem, East Lothian	15 Oct 40	3 Nov 40
C/O	S/Ldr William A Richardson	Oct 39	Sep 40
	S/Ldr Edward C Wolfe	Sep 40	Jul 41

* det at Montrose, Forfarshire (Angus)

+ dets at Biggin Hill, Greater London, 13 Sep 40 to 18 Sep 40; Gatwick, West Sussex, 18 Sep 40 to 22 Oct 40

145 Squadron Code SO

Aircraft	Hurricane I	Mar 40	Feb 41
Based at	Tangmere, West Sussex	10 May 40	31 Jul 40
	Westhampnett, West Sussex	31 Jul 40	14 Aug 40
	Drem, East Lothian	14 Aug 40	31 Aug 40
	Dyce, Aberdeenshire	31 Aug 40	9 Oct 40
	Tangmere, West Sussex	9 Oct 40	7 May 41
C/O	S/Ldr John R A Peel	Jun 40	Jan 41

151 Squadron Code DZ

Aircraft	Hurricane I	Dec 38	Feb 42
Based at	North Weald, Essex	20 May 40	29 Aug 40
	Stapleford Tawney, Essex	29 Aug 40	1 Sep 40
	Digby, Lincolnshire	1 Sep 40	28 Nov 40
C/O	S/Ldr Edward M Donaldson	Dec 38	Aug 40
	S/Ldr John A G Gordon	Aug 40	Sep 40
	S/Ldr Hamish West	Sep 40	Dec 40

152 Squadron Code UM

Aircraft	Spitfire I	Jan 40	Apr 41
Based at	Acklington, Northumberland	1 Oct 39	12 Jul 40
	Warmwell, Dorset	12 Jul 40	9 Apr 41
C/O	S/Ldr Peter K Devitt	Mar 40	Nov 40

213 Squadron Code AK

Aircraft	Hurricane I	Jan 39	Feb 42
Based at	Biggin Hill, Greater London	9 Jun 40	18 Jun 40
	Exeter, Devon	18 Jun 40	7 Sep 40
	Tangmere, West Sussex	7 Sep 40	29 Nov 40
C/O	S/Ldr Henry McGregor	Jun 40	Sep 40
	S/Ldr Duncan S MacDonald	Sep 40	Oct 41

219 Squadron Code FK

Aircraft	Blenheim If	Oct 39	Dec 40
Based at	Catterick, North Yorkshire	4 Oct 39	12 Oct 40
	Redhill, Surrey	12 Oct 40	10 Dec 40
C/O	S/Ldr James H Little	May 40	Feb 41

222 Squadron Code ZD

Aircraft	Spitfire I	Mar 40	Mar 41
Based at	Kirton-in-Lindsey, Lincolnshire	4 Jun 40	29 Aug 40
	Hornchurch, Essex	29 Aug 40	11 Nov 40
C/O	S/Ldr Herbert W Mermagen	Oct 39	Jul 40
	S/Ldr John H Hill	Jul 40	Jan 41

229 Squadron Code RE

Aircraft	Hurricane I	Mar 40	Sep 41
Based at	Wittering, Cambridgeshire	26 Jun 40	9 Sep 40
	Northolt, Greater London	9 Sep 40	15 Dec 40
C/O	S/Ldr Harold J Maguire	Oct 39	Sep 40
	S/Ldr Arthur J Banham	Sep 40	Oct 40
	S/Ldr Frederick E Rosier	Oct 40	Oct 41

232 Squadron Code EF

Aircraft	Hurricane I	Jul 40	Aug 41
Based at	Sumburgh, Shetland Islands	17 Jul 40	18 Sep 40
	Castletown, Caithness	18 Sep 40	13 Oct 40
	Skitten, Caithness	13 Oct 40	24 Oct 40
	Drem, East Lothian	24 Oct 40	11 Nov 40
C/O	F/Lt Maurice M Stephens	Jul 40	Oct 40
	F/Lt Alan W Pennington-Legh	Oct 40	May 41

234 Squadron Code AZ

Aircraft	Spitfire I	Mar 40	Nov 40
Based at	St Eval, Cornwall	18 Jun 40	13 Aug 40
	Middle Wallop, Hampshire	13 Aug 40	11 Sep 40
	St Eval, Cornwall	11 Sep 40	25 Feb 41
C/O	S/Ldr William A J Satchell	Oct 39	Aug 40
	S/Ldr Joseph S O'Brien	Aug 40	Sep 40

235 Squadron Code QY (Coastal Command unit)

Aircraft	Blenheim IVf	Feb 40	Dec 41
Based at	Detling, Kent	26 May 40	24 Jun 40
	Bircham Newton, Norfolk	24 Jun 40	4 Jun 41
C/O	Wg Cdr Ronald N Clarke	May 40	Dec 40

236 Squadron Code FA (Coastal Command unit)

Aircraft	Blenheim If	Dec 39	Jul 40
	Blenheim IVf	Jul 40	Mar 42
Based at	Thorney Island, West Sussex	4 Jul 40	8 Aug 40
	St Eval, Cornwall	8 Aug 40	21 Mar 41
C/O	S/Ldr Peter E Drew	30 Oct 39	Aug 40
	S/Ldr George W Montagu	Aug 40	Jan 41

238 Squadron Code VK

Aircraft	Hurricane I	Jun 40	Sep 41
Based at	Middle Wallop, Hampshire	20 Jun 40	14 Aug 40
	St Eval, Cornwall	14 Aug 40	10 Sep 40
	Middle Wallop, Hampshire	10 Sep 40	30 Sep 40
	Chilbolton, Hampshire	30 Sep 40	1 Apr 41
C/O	S/Ldr Cyril E J Baines	May 40	Jul 40
	S/Ldr Harold A Fenton	Jul 40	Oct 41

242 Squadron Code LE

Aircraft	Hurricane I	Jan 40	Feb 41
Based at	Coltishall, Norfolk	18 Jun 40	26 Oct 40
	Duxford, Cambridgeshire	26 Oct 40	30 Nov 40
C/O	S/Ldr Douglas R S Bader	Jun 40	Mar 41

245 Squadron Code DX

Aircraft	Hurricane I	Mar 40	Aug 41
Based at	Turnhouse, Edinburgh	5 Jun 40	20 Jul 40
	Aldergrove, Northern Ireland	20 Jul 40	14 Jul 41
C/O	S/Ldr Eric W Whiteley	Nov 39	Dec 40

247 Squadron Code HP

Aircraft	Gladiator II	Aug 40	Feb 41
Based at	Roborough, Devon*	1 Aug 40	10 Feb 41
C/O	F/Lt George F Chater	Aug 40	Sep 40
	S/Ldr Peter St G O'Brian	Sep 40	May 42

* det at St Eval, Cornwall

248 Squadron Code WR (Coastal Command unit)

Aircraft	Blenheim IVf	Feb 40	Jul 41
Based at	Dyce, Aberdeenshire	22 May 40	20 Jul 40
	Sumburgh, Shetland Islands	20 Jul 40	6 Jan 41
C/O	S/Ldr Victor C F Streatfield	Mar 40	Jan 41

249 Squadron Code GN

Aircraft	Hurricane I	Jun 40	Feb 41
Based at	Leconfield, Yorkshire	18 May 40	8 Jul 40
	Church Fenton, North Yorkshire	8 Jul 40	14 Aug 40
	Boscombe Down, Wiltshire	14 Aug 40	1 Sep 40
	North Weald, Essex	1 Sep 40	May 41
C/O	S/Ldr John Grandy	May 40	Dec 40

253 Squadron Code SW

Aircraft	Hurricane I	Feb 40	Aug 41
Based at	Kirton-in-Lindsey, Lincolnshire	24 May 40	21 Jul 40
	Turnhouse, Edinburgh	21 Jul 40	23 Aug 40
	Prestwick, South Ayrshire	23 Aug 40	29 Aug 40
	Kenley, Surrey	29 Aug 40	3 Jan 41
C/O	S/Ldr Thomas P Gleave	Jun 40	Aug 40
	S/Ldr Harold M Starr	Aug 40	Sep 40
	S/Ldr Gerald R Edge	Sep 40	Sep 40
	F/Lt Raymond M B Duke-Woolley	Sep 40	Nov 40

257 Squadron Code DT

Aircraft	Hurricane I	Jun 40	Jul 41
Based at	Hendon, Greater London	17 May 40	4 Jul 40
	Northolt, Greater London	4 Jul 40	15 Aug 40
	Debden, Essex	15 Aug 40	5 Sep 40
	Martlesham Heath, Sfk	5 Sep 40	8 Oct 40
	North Weald, Essex	8 Oct 40	7 Nov 40
C/O	S/Ldr David W Bayne	May 40	Jul 40
	S/Ldr Hill Harkness	Jul 40	Sep 40
	S/Ldr Robert S Tuck	Oct 40	Jul 41

263 Squadron Code HE

Aircraft	Hurricane I	Jun 40	Nov 40
	Whirlwind I	Jul 40	Dec 43
Based at	Drem, East Lothian	10 Jun 40	28 Jun 40
	Grangemouth, Stirlingshire	28 Jun 40	2 Sep 40
	Drem, East Lothian	2 Sep 40	28 Nov 40
C/O	S/Ldr Henry Eeles	Jun 40	Dec 40

264 Squadron Code PS

Aircraft	Defiant I	Dec 39	Sep 41
Based at	Duxford, Cambridgeshire	10 May 40	23 Jul 40
	Kirton-in-Lindsey, Lincolnshire*	23 Jul 40	22 Aug 40
	Hornchurch, Essex	22 Aug 40	27 Aug 40
	Rochford, Essex	27 Aug 40	28 Aug 40
	Kirton-in-Lindsey, Lincolnshire +	28 Aug 40	29 Oct 40
	Rochford, Essex	29 Oct 40	27 Nov 40
C/O	S/Ldr Philip A Hunter, DSO	Mar 40	Aug 40
	S/Ldr George D Garvin	Aug 40	Nov 40

* dets at Coleby Grange, Lincolnshire, and Ringway, Cheshire

+ dets at Northolt, Greater London; Luton and Martlesham Heath, Suffolk

266 Squadron Code UO

Aircraft	Spitfire I	Jan 40	Sep 40
	Spitfire IIa	Sep 40	Oct 40
	Spitfire I	Oct 40	Apr 41
Based at	Wittering, Cambridgeshire	14 May 40	9 Aug 40
	Tangmere, West Sussex	9 Aug 40	12 Aug 40
	Eastleigh, Hampshire	12 Aug 40	14 Aug 40
	Hornchurch, Essex	14 Aug 40	21 Aug 40
	Wittering, Cambridgeshire	21 Aug 40	28 Sep 41
C/O	S/Ldr John W A Hunnard	Oct 39	Jul 40
	S/Ldr Rodney L Wilkinson	Jul 40	Aug 40
	S/Ldr Desmond G H Spencer	Aug 40	Sep 40
	S/Ldr Patrick G Jameson	Sep 40	Jun 41

302 'Poznański' Squadron Code WX (from at least Oct 41)

Aircraft	Hurricane I	Jul 40	Mar 41
Based at	Leconfield, Yorkshire*	13 Jul 40	11 Oct 40
	Northolt, Greater London	11 Oct 40	23 Nov 40
	Westhampnett, West Sussex	23 Nov 40	7 Apr 41
C/O	S/Ldr William A J Satchell	Jul 40	Jan 41

* det at Duxford, Cambridgeshire, from Sep 40

303 'Warsaw-Kościuszko' Squadron Code RF

Aircraft	Hurricane I	Aug 40	Jan 41
Based at	Northolt, Greater London	2 Aug 40	11 Oct 40
	Leconfield, Yorkshire	11 Oct 40	3 Jan 41
C/O	S/Ldr Ronald G Kellett	Aug 40	Jan 41

310 Squadron Code NN

Aircraft	Hurricane I	Jul 40	Mar 41
Based at	Duxford, Cambridgeshire	10 Jul 40	26 Jun 41
C/O	S/Ldr George D M Blackwood	Jul 40	Jan 41

312 Squadron Code DU

Aircraft	Hurricane I	Aug 40	May 41
Based at	Duxford, Cambridgeshire	29 Aug 40	26 Sep 40
	Speke, Merseyside	26 Sep 40	3 Mar 41
C/O	S/Ldr Frank H Tyson	Aug 40	Apr 41

501 'County of Gloucester' Squadron Code SD

Aircraft	Hurricane I	Mar 39	May 41
Based at	Croydon, Greater London	21 Jun 40	4 Jul 40
	Middle Wallop, Hampshire	4 Jul 40	25 Jul 40
	Gravesend, Kent	25 Jul 40	10 Sep 40
	Kenley, Surrey	10 Sep 40	17 Dec 40
C/O	S/Ldr Henry A V Hogan	Jun 40	Nov 40

504 'County of Nottingham' Squadron Code TM

Aircraft	Hurricane I	Mar 39	Aug 41
Based at	Castletown, Caithness	21 Jun 40	1 Sep 40
	Catterick, N Yorks	1 Sep	5 Sep
	Hendon, Greater London	5 Sep 40	26 Sep 40
	Filton, South Glos	26 Sep 40	26 Sep 40
	Exeter, Devon	26 Sep 40	21 Jul 41
C/O	S/Ldr John Sample	May 40	Mar 41

600 'City of London' Squadron Code BQ

Aircraft	Blenheim If	Jan 39	Feb 41
	Beaufighter If	Sep 40	Feb 42
Based at	Manston, Kent	20 Jun 40	22 Aug 40
	Hornchurch, Essex	22 Aug 40	12 Sep 40
	Redhill, Surrey	12 Sep 40	12 Oct 40
	Catterick, North Yorkshire	12 Oct 40	14 Mar 41
C/O	S/Ldr David de Brassey Clark	Apr 40	Sep 40
	S/Ldr Hugh L Maxwell	Sep 40	Nov 40

601 'County of London' Squadron Code UF

Aircraft	Hurricane I	May 40	Mar 41
Based at	Tangmere, West Sussex	17 Jun 40	19 Aug 40
	Debden, Essex	19 Aug 40	2 Sep 40
	Tangmere, West Sussex	2 Sep 40	7 Sep 40
C/O	S/Ldr John M W Aitken	Jun 40	Jul 40
	S/Ldr William F C Hobson	Jul 40	Aug 40
	S/Ldr Edward F Ward	Aug 40	Aug 40
	S/Ldr Sir Archibald P Hope	Aug 40	Dec 40

602 'City of Glasgow' Squadron Code LO

Aircraft	Spitfire I	Jan 39	Jun 41
Based at	Drem, East Lothian*	13 Oct 39	13 Aug 40
	Westhampnett, West Sussex	13 Aug 40	17 Dec 40
C/O	S/Ldr George Pinkerton	Mar 40	Jul 40
	S/Ldr Alexander V R Johnstone	Jul 40	Jun 42

* detachments at Dyce, Aberdeenshire and Montrose, Forfarshire

603 'City of Edinburgh' Squadron Code XT

Aircraft	Spitfire I	Sep 39	Nov 40
Based at	Turnhouse, Edinburgh	5 May 40	27 Aug 40
	Hornchurch, Essex	27 Aug 40	3 Dec 40
C/O	S/Ldr Ernest H Stevens	Aug 39	Sep 40
	S/Ldr George L Denholm	Sep 40	Apr 41

604 'County of Middlesex' Squadron Code NG

Aircraft	Blenheim If	Jan 39	Jan 41
	Beaufighter If	Sep 40	Apr 43
Based at	Manston, Kent	16 Jan 40	3 Jul 40
	Gravesend, Kent	3 Jul 40	26 Jul 40
	Middle Wallop, Hampshire	26 Jul 40	7 Dec 42
C/O	S/Ldr Michael F Anderson	Mar 40	Aug 41

605 'County of Warwick' Squadron Code UP

Aircraft	Hurricane I	Aug 39	Dec 40
Based at	Drem, East Lothian	28 May 40	7 Sep 40
	Croydon, Greater London	7 Sep 40	26 Feb 41
C/O	S/Ldr Walter M Churchill	Jun 40	Sep 40
	S/Ldr Archie A McKellar	Sep 40	Nov 40

607 'County of Durham' Squadron Code AF

Aircraft	Hurricane I	Mar 40	Jul 41
Based at	Usworth, Tyne and Wear	5 Jun 40	1 Sep 40
	Tangmere, West Sussex	1 Sep 40	10 Oct 40
	Turnhouse, Edinburgh	10 Oct 40	8 Nov 40
C/O	S/Ldr James A Vick	Jun 40	Oct 40
	S/Ldr A W Vincent	Oct 40	Mar 41

609 'West Riding' Squadron Code PR

Aircraft	Spitfire I	Aug 39	May 41
Based at	Northolt, Greater London	19 May 40	5 Jul 40
	Middle Wallop, Hampshire	5 Jul 40	29 Nov 40
C/O	S/Ldr Horace S Darley	Jun 40	Oct 40
	S/Ldr Michael L Robinson	Oct 40	Jul 41

610 'County of Chester' Squadron Code DW

Aircraft	Spitfire I	Sep 39	Feb 41
Based at	Biggin Hill, Greater London	10 May 40	26 May 40
	Gravesend, Kent	26 May 40	2 Jul 40
	Biggin Hill, Greater London	2 Jul 40	13 Sep 40
	Acklington, Northumberland	13 Sep 40	19 Dec 40
C/O	S/Ldr Andrew T Smith	May 40	Jul 40
	S/Ldr John Ellis	Jul 40	Apr 41

611 'West Lancashire' Squadron Code FY

Aircraft	Spitfire I	May 39	Mar 41
	Spitfire IIa/IIb	Aug 40	Jun 41
Based at	Digby, Lincolnshire	10 Oct 39	14 Dec 40
C/O	S/Ldr James E McComb	Sep 39	Oct 40
	S/Ldr Ernest R Bitmead	Oct 40	May 41

615 'County of Surrey' Squadron Code KW

Aircraft	Hurricane I	Apr 40	Feb 41
Based at	Kenley, Surrey	20 May 40	29 Aug 40
	Prestwick, South Ayrshire	29 Aug 40	10 Oct 40
	Northolt, Greater London	10 Oct 40	17 Dec 40
C/O	S/Ldr Joseph R Kayll	Mar 40	Dec 40

616 'South Yorkshire' Squadron Code YQ

Aircraft	Spitfire I	Oct 39	Feb 41
Based at	Leconfield, Yorkshire	6 Jun 40	19 Aug 40
	Kenley, Surrey	19 Aug 40	3 Sep 40
	Coltishall, Norfolk	3 Sep 40	9 Sep 40
	Kirton-in-Lindsey, Lincolnshire	9 Sep 40	26 Feb 41
C/O	S/Ldr Marcus Robinson	May 40	Sep 40
	S/Ldr Howard F Burton	Sep 40	Sep 41

Fighter Flight, RAF Sumburgh* Code None known

Aircraft	Gladiator II	Jan 40	Jul 40
Bases	Sumburgh, Shetland Islands	5 Jan 40	21 Jul 40
	Roborough, Devon	21 Aug 40	31 Jul 40

* established as Fighter Flight, Shetlands, 18 Dec 39; to Fighter Flight, RAF Sumburgh 5 Jan 40; became 247 Squadron 1 Aug 40

421 (Reconnaissance) Flight Code LZ

Aircraft	Hurricane II	Oct 40	Feb 41
Airfield	Gravesend, Kent	8 Oct 40	31 Oct 40

422 (Fighter Interception) Flight Code None known

Aircraft	Hurricane I	14 Oct 40	18 Dec 40
Airfield	Shoreham, West Sussex	14 Oct 40	9 Dec 40

Fighter Interception Unit Code ZQ

Aircraft	Blenheim If	Apr 40	
	Hurricane I	Apr 40	
	Beaufighter If	Aug 40	
Based at	Tangmere, West Sussex	18 Apr 40	18 Aug 40
	Shoreham, West Sussex	18 Aug 40	26 Jan 41
C/O	S/Ldr George P Chamberlain	Aug 40	Jul 41

804 Squadron, Fleet Air Arm Code S7

Aircraft	Sea Gladiator	Nov 39	Jan 41
	Buffalo I+	Jul 40	Sep 40
	Martlet I+	Sep 40	Mar 41
Based at*	Hatston, Orkney Islands	23 May 40	
	Skeabrae, Orkney Islands	10 Oct 40	19 Oct 40
	Hatston, Orkney Islands	19 Oct 40	28 Oct 40
	Skeabrae, Orkney Islands	28 Oct 40	7 Jan 41
C/O	L/C John C Cockburn, RN	Dec 39	Nov 40

+ small numbers only * shore bases only; dets on HMS *Furious* 5-8 Sep, 20-23 Sep and 11-19 Oct 40

808 Squadron, Fleet Air Arm Code 7A

Aircraft	Fulmar I	Jul 40	Nov 41
Based at	Worthy Down, Hampshire	1 Jul 40	5 Sep 40
	Castletown, Caithness	9 Sep 40	2 Oct 40
	Donibristle, Lothian	2 Oct 40	*
C/O	Lt H E R Torin, RN	Jul 40	Jul 40
	L/C Rupert C Tillard, RN	Jul 40	May 41

* embarked on HMS *Ark Royal* 31 Oct 40

1 Squadron, Royal Canadian Air Force Code YO

Aircraft	Hurricane I	Jun 40	Feb 41
Based at	Middle Wallop, Hampshire	21 Jun 40	Jul 40
	Croydon, Greater London	Jul 40	Aug 40
	Northolt, Greater London	Aug 40	Oct 40
	Prestwick, South Ayrshire	Oct 40	Oct 40
	Castletown, Caithness	Oct 40	Feb 41
C/O	S/Ldr Ernest A McNab	Jun 40	Nov 40

Pleas to release additional squadrons to stem the German onslaught on the continent were resisted by Air Office Commanding RAF Fighter Command, Air Chief Marshal Hugh C T Dowding. Calls for the deployment of Supermarine Spitfire squadrons to France were declined on the basis that they would be required when the Germans turned their attention to Great Britain. As a result, Fighter Command still possessed a large force of modern fighters by the time France signed the armistice with Germany on June 22, 1940.

The production rate of both the Hawker Hurricane and Spitfire had increased markedly since the start of the war, providing Fighter Command with a large reserve of machines. More important than the actual numbers of aircraft available was the pool of trained pilots. Training fighter pilots became one of the limiting factors to the further expansion of Fighter Command.

DAY FIGHTER

The vast majority of Fighter Command squadrons were equipped with eight-gun monoplane fighters – Hurricanes and Spitfires – by July 1940. Of these two types, the Hurricane was predominant, accounting for 60% of the aircraft operated during the fighting in the summer and autumn of 1940.

Although the Hurricane and Spitfire are the RAF aircraft most closely associated with the Battle of Britain, several other types also served in the front line with Fighter Command during mid-1940. They include the Boulton Paul Defiant turret fighter, flown by two squadrons during the fighting, although it was quickly discovered to be vulnerable to single-seat Luftwaffe fighters once they learned to distinguish it from the Hurricane.

The only biplane to be deployed by Fighter Command during the Battle of Britain was the Gloster Gladiator, although it was considered obsolete for service on the home front by 1940. It found a niche operating from Roborough in Devon, providing air defence for the naval bases in the West Country. Roborough was a small airfield with a grass runway unsuitable for the operation of the more modern monoplane fighters.

Two Fleet Air Arm fighter squadrons are officially credited with having participated in the campaign. They were equipped with Sea Gladiators and Fairey Fulmars and provided protection for naval facilities at Scapa Flow in the Orkneys.

NIGHT FIGHTERS

Considerable effort was expended by the RAF to modernise its day fighter force in the years leading up to World War Two. While night fighter operations had not been ignored, development of a dedicated night fighter was a low priority and the standard aircraft in the role at the start of the Battle of Britain was the Bristol Blenheim. Fighter Command originally wanted to use the Blenheim as a long-range heavy fighter, beefing up its original meagre forward-firing armament by adding a gun pack under the fuselage. Heavy losses within Bomber Command Blenheim squadrons during the Battle of France demonstrated that the aircraft was easy prey for the Luftwaffe's Messerschmitts and the type was instead relegated to the night fighter role until something more suitable entered service. The command's Blenheims saw limited action during the Battle of Britain, although the type played an important role in the development of Airborne Interception (AI) radar during the period.

Airborne radar became a vital component in the definitive night fighter that eventually replaced the Blenheim in the role, the Bristol Beaufighter. Just too late to see extensive use during the summer and autumn of 1940, it went on to play a larger role in the Blitz that followed. Another heavy twin-engined fighter that was beginning to enter service with a Fighter Command squadron during the Battle of Britain, the Westland Whirlwind, did not participate in the fighting.

BELOW:
A Spitfire Ia of 19 Squadron being rearmed at Fowlmere. RAF Fighter Command was primarily equipped with eight-gun monoplanes by the time of the Battle of Britain.
Aeroplane Collection

BRITISH AIRCRAFT
of the Battle of Britain

All of the British aircraft directly involved in the Battle of Britain were fighters, the majority of which were assigned to units of Fighter Command.

Supermarine
SPITFIRE I

The Spitfire was widely regarded as the best fighter available to the RAF in the middle of 1940, gaining a reputation during the Battle of Britain as the aircraft that defeated the Luftwaffe.

ABOVE:
Six Spitfire Ias of 610 'County of Chester' Squadron, one of six Auxiliary Air Force units to fly the type during the Battle of Britain.

TOP RIGHT:
At the outbreak of war, 610 Squadron was based at Wittering, Cambridgeshire. These Spitfire Is are seen at that airfield in October 1939.

The masterpiece of aeronautical designer Reginald J Mitchell, the Supermarine Spitfire, was the predominant British fighter of World War Two. Its potential for growth was exploited to the extent that later marks had little in common with the early aircraft and it was the only British fighter to remain in production throughout the war. While it fought in most of the campaigns undertaken by the RAF during the conflict, it will forever be remembered for the role it played in the Battle of Britain.

The prototype Spitfire (K5054) first flew on March 5, 1936. The Air Ministry order placed on June 3, 1936, was for 310 Spitfire Is. Production had actually started at Supermarine's Eastleigh facility in Hampshire during March 1936, but by the end of the year only six fuselages had been completed. At the time, Supermarine did not have the capacity for such a large order and it took time to organise suppliers and contractors. It was only in mid-May 1938 that test pilot Jeffrey Quill completed the maiden flight of the first production aircraft (K9787) at Eastleigh. On July 27, the aircraft was flown to Martlesham Heath, Suffolk, to begin the service evaluation of the new type.

The first frontline unit to get its hands on the new fighter was 19 Squadron at Duxford, Cambridgeshire, which received K9789 on August 4, 1938, for intensive trials. It became the first unit to fully re-equip with the monoplane, the last of 16 arriving at Duxford by the end of the year. At that point, only 49 had been handed over due to problems encountered ramping up production.

Further orders for batches of 200, 450, 450, 500 and 1,100 were placed with Supermarine, while a contract for another 300 was signed with Westland Aircraft in June 1940, although deliveries from that source only began in the following year. A total of 1,567 Spitfire Is were produced, the others ordered being completed as the later Mk V. By October 15, 1940, a total of 1,426 Spitfires had been delivered to the RAF.

IMPROVING THE BREED

On the day Great Britain declared war on Germany, 19, 41, 54, 65, 66, 72 and 611 Squadrons had re-equipped with the Spitfire I, while 603 and 609 Squadrons of the Auxiliary Air Force (AAF) were converting to the type. Air Chief Marshal Sir Hugh Dowding, commander-in-chief of Fighter Command, refused to allow his Spitfire squadrons to be among those deployed

Supermarine Spitfire Ia

Dimensions: Length 29ft 11in (9.12m); Wing span 36ft 10in (11.23m); Height 12ft 7³/₄in (3.86m); Wing area 242sq ft (22.48m²)

Weights: Empty 4,517lb (2,049kg); Typically loaded 5,844lb (2,651kg)

Powerplant: One Rolls-Royce Merlin II or III 12-cylinder Vee, liquid-cooled piston engine, rated at 1,030hp (768kW) at 16,250ft (4,953m); Fuel capacity 84 imp gal (382 lit)

Armament: Eight 0.303in (7.7mm) Browning Mk II machine guns mounted in the wings

Performance: Max speed 346mph (557km/h) at 15,000ft (4,572m); Cruising speed 304mph (489km/h) at 15,000ft (4,572m); Initial climb rate 1,625ft/min (495m/min); Service ceiling 30,500ft (9,296m); Range at normal cruise 415 miles (668km)

Crew: One pilot

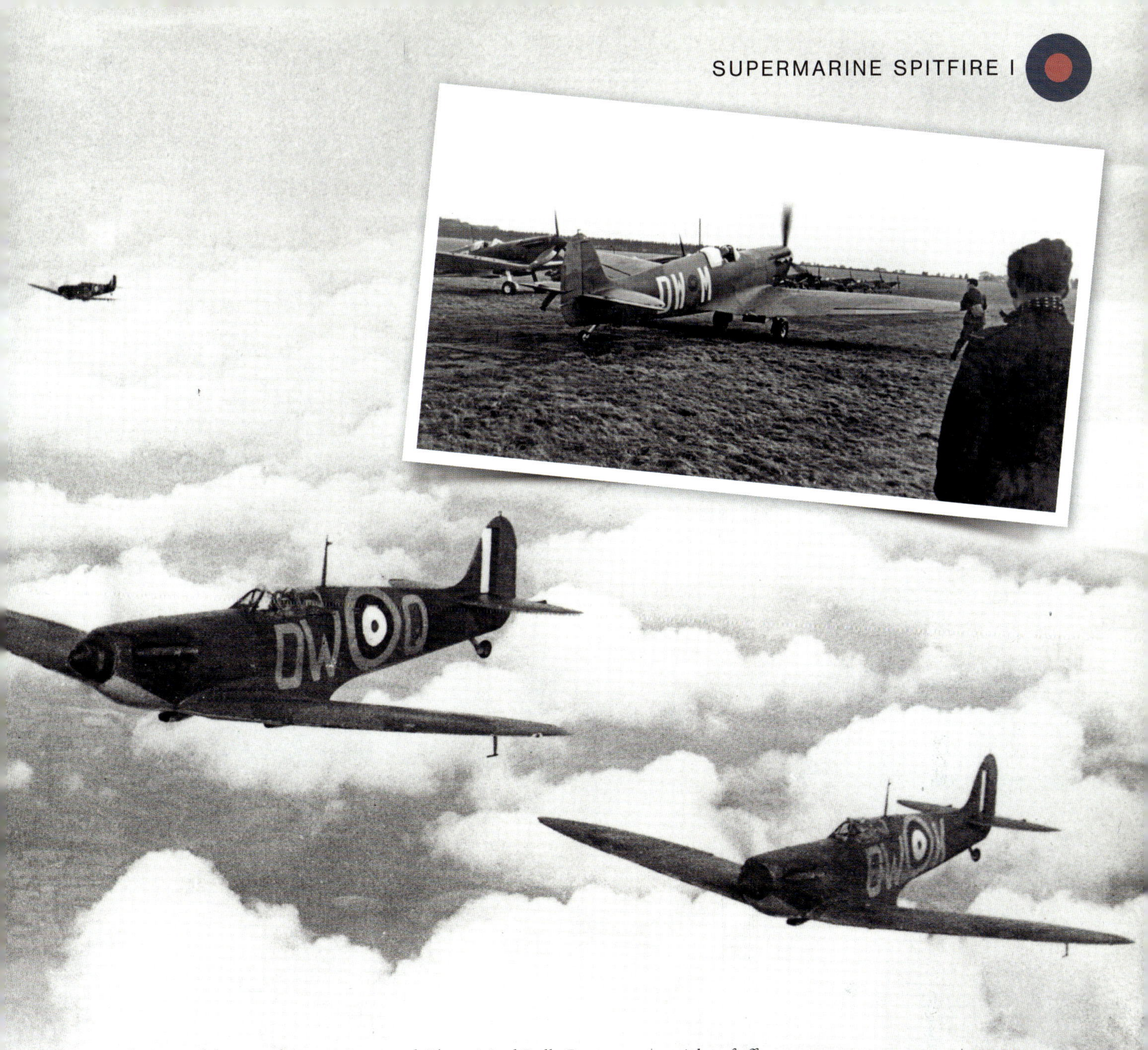

to France at the start of the war, the task falling instead to Hurricane units. Spitfires were reserved for defence of the British Isles, although squadrons flying the fighter were allowed to provide cover for the evacuation of Allied troops from Dunkirk in late May to early June 1940. A total of 72 Spitfires were lost during the fighting over the Channel covering the escape from the continent.

Several changes were incorporated in new-built Spitfires as production increased. The original Rolls-Royce Merlin II was replaced by the Mk III, which used a Coffman cartridge starter instead of an electrical system and had a new mixture of coolant. A simple measure that boosted the aircraft's performance was the use of 100 octane fuel from the spring of 1940. Replacing the standard 87 octane fuel increased the output of the Merlin II to 1,030hp (768kW) at 16,250ft (4,953m) and 1,160hp (865kW) at 9,000ft (2,743m).

A lot of effort was spent investigating different propeller units to get the most power out of the Merlin at different heights. A de Havilland three-blade propeller, with a fine pitch setting for take-off and coarse for high speed, became standard, replacing the original two-bladed wooden Watts unit, which had a fixed pitch.

In June 1940, constant speed units designed by de Havilland and Rotol were tested, with the former »

BELOW: Spitfire Ia N3029 in the colours of 610 'County of Chester' Squadron. The aircraft survived the Battle of Britain, but was lost when the ship on which it was being transported to the Middle East was sunk in January 1943. Pete West

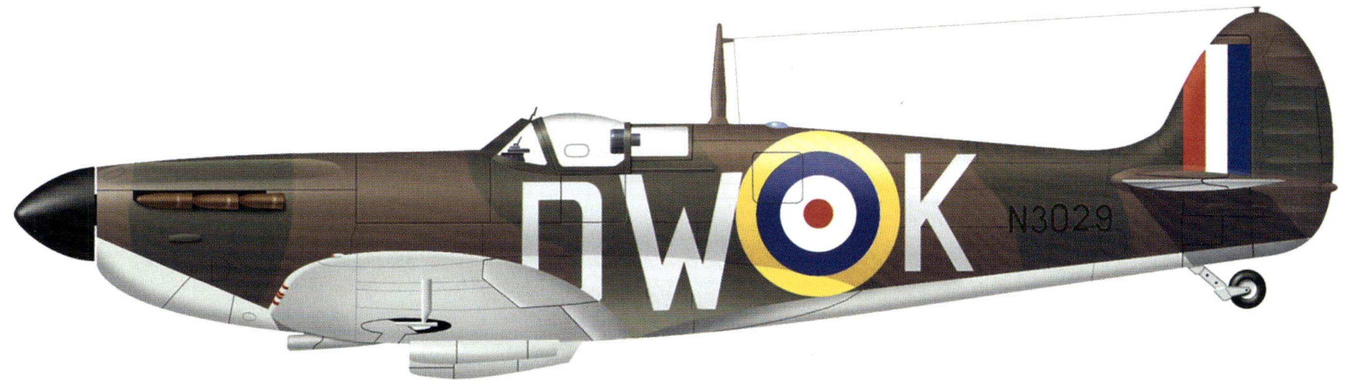

selected for use on Spitfire Is and the latter on the Mk II. This small modification had a terrific effect on performance, adding 7,000ft (2,134m) to the Spitfire's ceiling and making it more manoeuvrable at height. It also reduced the take-off run considerably and increased rate of climb, both vital to position the aircraft above the incoming Luftwaffe raids. Teams were dispatched to Fighter Command airfields where Spitfires were based to retrofit the new unit, which was also installed in new production examples. By August 16, every Spitfire and Hurricane in the RAF had a constant speed unit installed.

Other improvements implemented during the fighting included the

ABOVE: Spitfire I R6801 of 152 Squadron based at Warmwell in Dorset during the Battle of Britain. The aircraft was later converted as a Mk Va. Pete West

BELOW: Spitfire Is of 65 Squadron scramble to get airborne at Hornchurch in Essex on August 13, 1940.

replacement of the original moulded front canopy transparency with a bulletproof windscreen. A quick release mechanism for the canopy was developed by Martin-Baker – later famous for its work on ejector seats – to allow the pilot to get out of the aircraft rapidly in an emergency. Additional armour was added behind the pilot's seat and to the rear of the engine's bulkhead.

A worrying occurrence during the Battle of Britain was the discovery of fatigue cracks on the skins of the wings above the wheels of some Spitfire Is. A temporary fix was developed, adding plates to strengthen the affected area,

while new aircraft used thicker gauge metal from the outset.

CANNONS

The limitations of the rifle-calibre Browning machine gun to inflict critical damage on enemy aircraft during the Battle of Britain prompted renewed interest in fitting cannons to the RAF's frontline fighters. In fact, research into a cannon-armed Spitfire had been ongoing since late 1938. Handling trials of a Spitfire I fitted with the weapons was completed at Martlesham Heath in July 1939, after which it went to Northolt in north London for evaluation by the Air Fighting Development

Unit (AFDU). Tests revealed that the cannons needed to be heated to stop them freezing up at altitude, while the flexibility of the Spitfire's wing could cause distortions in its structure that could jam the weapon's mechanism. In January 1940, the aircraft left the AFDU for Drem in East Lothian, Scotland. On February 22, 1940, Flying Officer George V Proudman of 602 'City of Glasgow' Squadron used the aircraft in combat, sharing in the downing of a Heinkel He 111P-2 with Squadron Leader Alistair D Farquhar.

The first full conversion for the RAF with what had became known as the 'B-wing' went to 19 Squadron

"By October 15, 1940, a total of 1,426 Spitfires had been delivered to the RAF"

in June 1940 and by August 25 five of its Spitfires had been similarly modified. Some of the Brownings were retained just in case the cannons jammed – which they frequently did. To distinguish between the two subvariants of the Spitfire I, the cannon-armed examples became Mk Ibs; those with only machine guns retrospectively became Mk Ias. Only around 30 Spitfire Ibs were produced by converting existing aircraft, but in service the heavier weapon proved exceedingly troublesome and the Spitfire Ib was quickly removed from frontline service.

SPITFIRE II

By late 1938, the political situation in Europe had worsened to the point where it was clear to most people that war was nearly unavoidable. Successive RAF expansion plans had called for increased numbers of fighters, but the slow delivery of Spitfires was a cause for concern. At one point, it was planned to replace the Spitfire with the Bristol Beaufighter on the Supermarine production line. That it did not happen is thanks to the promise of a contract awarded to the Nuffield Organisation (the owners of Morris Motors) for 1,000 Spitfires in April 1938. The contract was provisional on the organisation putting up the money to create a factory to build aircraft under the shadow programme, implemented to increase aircraft production capacity. The money was forthcoming – but only if it could build Spitfires.

This was the genesis of the Castle Bromwich factory in the West Midlands, where the majority of Spitfires were eventually built, starting in June 1940 with the Mk IIa powered by the slightly more powerful Merlin XII. The first Spitfire IIas were delivered to 611 Squadron in August 1940, followed by 19, 74 and 266 Squadrons. A total of 751 Mk IIas were built by July 1941.

CITY OF EDINBURGH

Spitfires shot down 529 Luftwaffe aircraft during the Battle of Britain.

The Auxiliary Air Force's 603 'City of Edinburgh' Squadron, commanded by Squadron Leader Ernest H Stevens, was the top-scoring unit during the campaign, achieving 57.8 victories from a claim of 67.

At the start of the war, the unit was based at Turnhouse outside the city it was named after in Scotland. It became the first RAF unit to be credited with an enemy aircraft destroyed when, along with 602 'City of Glasgow' Squadron, it shot down a Heinkel He 111 over Dalkeith, Midlothian, while the bomber was attempting to photograph naval vessels in the Firth of Forth on October 16, 1939. A second He 111 was downed later that day. On October 28, it was in action again alongside 602 Squadron, bringing down another He 111 that became the first Luftwaffe aircraft to fall on British soil, the earlier pair having come down in the sea.

During the first, relatively quiet eight months of the conflict, dubbed the 'Phoney War', the squadron remained in Scotland tasked with providing air cover for coastal convoys, operating from Montrose and Prestwick in December 1939 and Dyce the following month. It encountered few Luftwaffe aircraft during this period, but activity

increased from June 1940. On July 3, 7, 12, 15 and 17 the squadron was engaged in combat off the east Scottish coast, claiming four He 111s, a Junkers Ju 88 and a Dornier Do 215.

The squadron moved into 11 Group's area of operations on August 27, replacing 65 Squadron in the front line at Hornchurch in Essex. By then, Squadron Leader Stevens had been promoted as a controller at 11 Group headquarters, his role at 603 being taken over by Squadron Leader George L Denholm. The day after arriving at Hornchurch, the squadron fought in a large dogfight with a force of Messerschmitt Bf 109Es, during which four of its Spitfires were shot down and three of their pilots killed. Three Bf 109Es were claimed on September 2, but the following day Hornchurch was bombed, injuring several of the unit's ground crew.

During the Battle of Britain the squadron was in action nearly every day, suffering heavy losses among its pilots during the hectic fighting of September and October 1940. The final claims of the campaign made by the squadron were a pair of Bf 109Es on October 27. No. 603 Squadron stayed at Hornchurch until early December 1940, when it returned to Scotland.

ABOVE:
A 602 'City of Glasgow' Squadron Spitfire 1 (X4382), probably at Westhampnett in West Sussex in September or October 1940.

BELOW:
Spitfire IIa P7531 'L-Z-I' served with 421 (Reconnaissance) Flight based at Gravesend, Kent, just after the Battle of Britain. The flight was formed with Hurricanes with the task of determining the composition of German raids approaching the southeast coast of England. Pete West

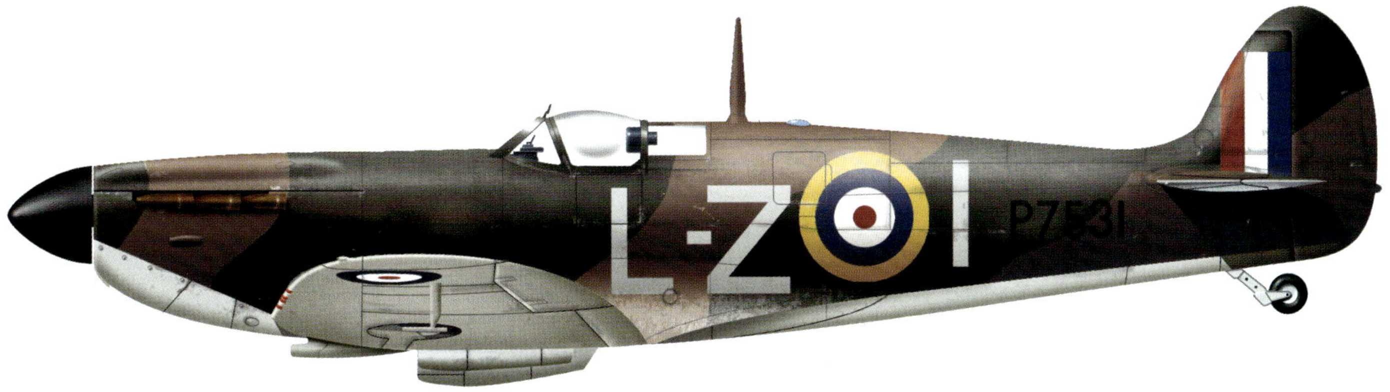

Hawker
HURRICANE

The Hurricane was the aircraft that won the Battle of Britain, its pilots claiming more kills than all the other defences combined.

ABOVE: Brooklands-built Hurricane Mk I P3428 was delivered to 245 Squadron in early 1940. The lack of codes may indicate this image was taken before it was handed over by the factory. Key-Gordon Swanborough Collection

MIDDLE FAR RIGHT: Hurricane Is of 615 'County of Surrey' Squadron landing at their base at Northolt in November 1940. AHB/UK MoD Crown

The Hawker Hurricane brought a step change to RAF Fighter Command when it officially entered service on January 1, 1938. It was the RAF's first monoplane fighter and introduced the retractable landing gear and a fully enclosed cockpit to its pilots, who were more used to flying draughty biplanes. Heavily armed with eight 0.303in (7.7mm) Browning machine guns, it was also the first RAF aircraft with a top speed over 300mph (483km/h). As the probability of war with Germany increased during the late 1930s, considerable effort was expended to get large numbers of the Hurricane to the squadrons to bolster the British defences.

Only a single prototype of the Hurricane was built. Test pilot 'George' P W S Bulman completed the type's maiden flight from the runway at Brooklands, Surrey, on November 6, 1935. In June 1936, Thomas O M Sopwith, chairman of the Hawker Siddeley Group, and his directors authorised the acquisition of tooling to build up to 1,000 Hurricanes.

Production was to take place at Brooklands and Kingston, also in Surrey. This decision was made the month before a formal order was received from the Air Ministry. Although the initial contract was for 'only' 600 aircraft, it was still the largest single production contract for British aircraft placed since the end of World War One.

Production was delayed slightly as Rolls-Royce completed work on the Merlin II engine, so that the first production Hurricane I (L1547) made its maiden flight at Brooklands, with test pilot Philip Lucas at the controls, on October 12, 1937. Early examples of the fighter were fitted with a two-blade, fixed-pitch wooden Watts propeller, and had a top speed of 320mph (515km/h) at 15,600ft (4,755m).

INTO SERVICE

Deliveries commenced on December 24, 1937, to 111 Squadron at Northolt in Greater London, followed by 3 and 56 Squadrons in March and May 1938. Several upgrades were introduced to

improve performance as production ramped up. The 481st Hurricane built (L2027) was the first to have the fabric-covered wings replaced by units with metal skins. A variable-pitch propeller, the de Havilland two-pitch Hydromatic was introduced from late 1938, improving the Hurricane's take-off performance. A new version of the Rolls-Royce Merlin (the Mk III) was required for the new propeller, differing from the original Mk II only in that it had a universal prop-shaft.

Deliveries of Rotol constant-speed units also began in 1938, which also conferred a higher climb rate and an increase in maximum speed. The first aircraft with it flew on January 24, 1939. Fitted with metal clad wings, but without armament, it could reach 344mph (554km/h) at 15,100ft (4,602m). The Rotol unit was a significant factor in the success enjoyed by the Hurricane during the Battle of Britain, the variable pitch getting the most out of the power provided by the Merlin as the aircraft climbed.

Hawker Hurricane I

Dimensions: Length 31ft 5in (9.58m); Wing span 40ft 0in (12.19m); Height 12ft 11½in (3.95m); Wing area 258sq ft (23.97m²)

Weights: Empty 5,085lb (2,308kg); Typically loaded 6,532lb (2,996kg); Max overload take-off weight 6,661lb (3,024kg)

Powerplant: One Rolls-Royce Merlin III 12-cylinder Vee, liquid-cooled piston engine, rated at 1,030hp (768kW) at 16,250ft (4,953m); Fuel capacity 97 imp gal (441 lit). Late production aircraft had provision for a 44 imp gal (200 lit) fixed fuel tank under each wing

Armament: Eight 0.303in (7.7mm) Browning machine guns mounted in the wings

Performance: Max speed 316mph (508km/h) at 17,750ft (5,410m); Cruising speed 272mph (438km/h) at 15,000ft (4,572m); Initial climb rate 2,610ft/min (795m/min); Service ceiling 33,200ft (10,119m); Range 335 miles (539km) with 77.5 imp gal (352 lit) of fuel at typical loaded weight, or 600 miles (965km) with max fuel at overload weight at 175mph (282km/h) at 15,000ft (4,572m)

Crew: One pilot

By April 1939, Fighter Command had 13 squadrons equipped with Hurricanes and the Auxiliary Air Force another two. Five months later, 497 Hurricanes had been built, the majority with the Watts or de Havilland propeller and fabric wings. The two-bladed aircraft remained in frontline service into the early summer of 1940.

A bulletproof windscreen was installed in production aircraft in 1939 and, by the spring of 1940, additional armour had been added aft of the pilot's seat. During the Battle of Britain several pilots added mirrors to the top of the cockpit canopy so they could monitor the vulnerable rear quadrant for enemy aircraft. It was later adopted as a standard feature on new aircraft. Production by both Hawker and Gloster, which built the type at Brockworth in Gloucestershire, had reached five a day by the start of the war.

Four squadrons were deployed to France with the Advanced Air Striking Force and the British Expeditionary Force Air Component (Nos 1, 73, 85 and 87). Between May 19 and June 1, as the German forces rolled across France and the Low Countries, 119 Hurricanes were destroyed.

PROS AND CONS

The Battle of Britain was the Hurricane's finest moment. While the Spitfire caught the imagination of the public, it was the Hurricane that caused the most damage to the Luftwaffe. Hurricane pilots destroyed more enemy aircraft during the Battle of Britain than all other fighters and defences combined, its pilots claiming 1,593 victories. Although the Luftwaffe thought little of the aircraft – German pilots shot down by Hurricanes often insisted it was a Spitfire that had got the better of them – its attributes and sheer numbers made it Fighter Command's greatest airborne asset. A total of 1,715 equipped 36 units of the command during the campaign, making up approximately 60% of its strength during the summer and autumn of 1940.

The Hurricane was widely regarded as 'a pilot's aeroplane'. It had docile handling, yet was highly manoeuvrable, and was less difficult to fly in poor weather than the Spitfire. Up to 18,000ft (5,486m) the performance of the two was comparable, but it fell away above that altitude. To make the most out of the two fighters the Hurricane was usually tasked with intercepting the bombers at medium altitude, while the Spitfire tackled the Messerschmitt Bf 109Es above acting as top cover.

Pilots praised the Hurricane as a steady gun platform. Thanks to its construction materials it was capable of withstanding heavy battle damage, bullets passing through the fabric exterior being easy to repair once back at base. A staggering ›

BELOW: Hurricane I V6799 of 501 Squadron based at Kenley, Surrey, in which Pilot Officer Kenneth W Mackenzie crash-landed on October 6, 1940, after tipping a Bf 109E into the sea with his wingtip. Pete West

ABOVE: A Hurricane I from the second production batch for 300, in the colours of 85 Squadron. Pete West

RIGHT: Gear and flaps down and canopies open, three Hurricanes return to base.

BELOW: A 601 'County of London' Squadron Hurricane I at Tangmere, West Sussex, during the Battle of Britain.

number – approximately 60% – of the Hurricanes brought down on British soil during the Battle of Britain were repaired and returned to service. Key to this figure was the Civilian Repair Organisation, a group of companies dedicated to restoring aircraft so they could be returned to the squadrons. The wings of the Hurricane could be detached outside of the landing gear, meaning that after lowering the wheels the crashed aircraft could be towed by a truck to a repair facility. The wide track landing gear made take-off and landing easy in comparison with most other monoplane fighters, and also permitted operations from rough grass surfaces, allowing its dispersal to poorly-equipped satellite airfields.

One negative aspect of the aircraft was its tendency to catch fire quickly. The wooden structure and fabric covering meant that once alight, the airframe was quickly consumed. The reserve fuel tank situated behind the engine firewall, but ahead of the pilot, lacked armour; it was originally reasoned that it was protected by the Merlin at the front and by the pilot's seat behind. During the Battle of Britain efforts were made to seal the tank with Linatex, which was applied to new production aircraft and retrofitted to those in service. The main wing tanks also had little protection and were more likely to be hit by enemy bullets.

Fire was a factor in the action that resulted in the award of the only Victoria Cross for a Fighter Command pilot. Flight Lieutenant James B Nicolson of 249 Squadron received the gallantry medal at Buckingham Palace on November 25, 1940, for attacking a Messerschmitt Bf 110 while his Hurricane was ablaze during an air battle on August 16. Although he was badly burnt, he survived and after a long convalescence returned to service with the RAF.

BATTLE OF BRITAIN

The top scoring Hurricane operator during the Battle of Britain was 303 'Warsaw-Kościuszko' Squadron, the second Polish fighter unit to form within the RAF, but the first to take part in the struggle over England. It formed at Northolt on August 2, 1940, under the command of Squadron Leader Ronald G Kellett within 11 Group.

Six days after being declared operational on August 24, Pilot Officer Ludwik Paszkiewicz made the squadron's first claim by shooting down a Dornier Do 17. The squadron

"The Battle of Britain was the Hurricane's finest moment"

was heavily involved in the fighting during September, claiming (for example) eight enemy aircraft on the fifth of the month, and going on to become the top scoring squadron within 11 Group. During the fighting, it claimed 121 enemy aircraft destroyed and was credited with 51.5. On October 11, it was withdrawn from southern England and transferred to Leconfield in Yorkshire, its place being taken by the fellow Poles of 302 'Poznański' Squadron.

The second highest unit was 501 'County of Gloucester' Squadron, with 40.25 confirmed kills out of the 101 claimed. Commanded by Squadron Leader Henry A V Hogan, the Auxiliary Air Force unit also suffered the highest losses, losing 41 Hurricanes during the Battle of Britain. It remained in the front line throughout, operating from Middle Wallop in Hampshire, until moving to Gravesend, Kent, on July 25, and finally Kenley in Surrey on September 10 – all airfields heavily involved in the campaign.

Two specialised RAF flights also operated Hurricanes towards the end of the struggle in addition to the frontline squadrons within Fighter Command. Based at Gravesend, 421 (Reconnaissance) Flight was created on September 21, 1940, from a nucleus of 66 Squadron (initially retaining that unit's 'LZ' code as 'L-Z'), equipped with Hurricane IIs. Its mission was to determine what type of raid was heading towards the Kent and Sussex coasts.

It became active on October 1. By then, the German bombers were mainly operating at night against London, but the Luftwaffe continued to conduct daylight fighter sweeps. Radar could not distinguish if the Bf 109s were Jagd ('fighter') or bomb-carrying Jabo ('fighter-bomber') aircraft; Fighter Command could afford to ignore the former but did not want the bombers to reach their targets. The Hurricane pilots would radio in details to 11 Group headquarters at Uxbridge, Middlesex, upon spotting German formations over the Channel.

The unit also provided cover for Ultra, as the intelligence gleaned by the code-breakers at Bletchley Park, Buckinghamshire, was codenamed. Ultra provided an insight into the plans of the German high command, but making use of the information it provided risked exposing the extent to which German codes had been penetrated. The existence of 421 (Reconnaissance) Flight helped provide a plausible reason why the RAF always seemed so well prepared to counter the Luftwaffe operations over England. It re-equipped with Spitfire IIs in November 1940.

The second Hurricane-equipped flight active during the Battle of Britain was 422 (Fighter Interception) Flight based at Shoreham, West Sussex. It was formed on October 14, 1941, with Hurricane Is, tasked with the development of single-seat night fighter tactics. It was expanded and became 96 Squadron on December 18, 1940.

HEAVIER FIREPOWER

Combat operations demonstrated that eight rifle-calibre Browning machine guns in the Hurricane and Spitfire were not always enough to bring down an enemy aircraft. It was found that as originally configured the stream of bullets converged too far ahead of the Hurricane. Experience showed that it was best to close in as near as possible to the target before firing to maximise the chances of a kill, and the weapons were realigned ('harmonised') accordingly.

Trials of heavier weapons in the Hurricane revealed they impacted negatively on the performance of the fighter, so it was decided instead to increase the number of machine guns to an even dozen. To maintain performance, the more powerful Merlin XX engine was installed, with a more streamlined propeller hub. The Air Ministry was reluctant to make any alterations to the production line that would slow Hurricane deliveries during the Battle of Britain, so the first 100 with the new engine were fitted with the eight-gun wing as Hurricane Mk IIA Series 1s. Production examples began leaving the factories in mid-August 1940. The sub-type entered squadron service in September 1940 and proved to be the fastest version of the Hurricane. It was also the last variant to join the RAF before the official end of the Battle of Britain.

Hurricane production continued into July 1944, when the last of the 14,353 built was rolled out. That aircraft, known as 'the Last of the Many', remains airworthy, one of two Hurricanes flown by the Battle of Britain Memorial Flight at Coningsby in Lincolnshire as a fitting tribute to those who have fallen in the service of the country.

ABOVE: A Hurricane I carrying the codes of 501 'County of Gloucester' Squadron.

BELOW: Hurricane I P3179 served only with 43 Squadron. It was shot down near Hove in East Sussex on August 30, 1940. Pete West

Bristol 142M/149
BLENHEIM

Blenheims served with every command of the RAF during World War Two and were operated in all theatres that the British fought in. The aircraft played a major role in the pre-war build-up of Bomber Command, but from the start of the war was found wanting in terms of bomb load and vulnerability to the fighters of the Luftwaffe.

ABOVE:
The antennas mounted on the wings and nose reveal that this Blenheim If is equipped with AI radar. AHB/UK MoD Crown

By the start of the war, the Blenheim I had largely been replaced by the long-nose Mk IV within Bomber Command. A total of 1,089 Blenheims were on strength with the RAF in September 1939, of which 231 were assigned to Bomber Command and 747 with the reserves or based outside the British Isles. Fighter Command operated the other 111.

Fighter Command's initial interest in the Blenheim was as a long-range escort fighter, but it was adopted as an interim night fighter due to delays with the Boulton Paul Defiant. The installed single forward-firing machine gun in the port wing was totally inadequate for the interceptor role. To provide the necessary firepower a pack containing four additional Browning guns, mounted under the bomb bay within which 2,000 rounds of ammunition was accommodated, was designed and built in the workshops of the Southern Railway Company at Ashford, Kent. Blenheim I L1424 was modified with

the pack in 1938 and around 200 similar conversions followed from early 1939 as Blenheim Ifs.

A similar modification was also undertaken to the Bristol 149 Blenheim IV to create the Mk IVf. Most Mk IVfs served with Coastal Command fighter reconnaissance units from May 1940.

The configuration of the Blenheim fighter was subject to much debate within Fighter Command. Air Chief Marshal Sir Hugh Dowding of 11 Group favoured a single-seater,

deleting the upper turret (and gunner) to save weight and reduce drag, but was overruled by the Air Staff. However, from October 1940, in the twilight of the type's operational career, many Mk Ifs had had their turrets replaced by a wooden fairing with retractable twin Browning machine guns.

Unconverted Mk Is began reaching Fighter Command squadrons before Mk Ifs became available from December 1938, re-equipping 23, 29, 64 and 25 Squadrons in that order, followed by 219 Squadron in October 1939. In addition, 600, 601 and 604 Squadrons of the Auxiliary Air Force transitioned to the type. Early in the war, 23, 25, 600 and 604 Squadrons flew patrols over the sea lanes off the English coast, but they were quickly committed to the night fighter role, joining 29, 64 and 601 Squadrons. While 64 Squadron re-equipped with Spitfires in April 1940, the other seven units continued to operate Blenheims and flew them during the Battle of Britain.

MAGIC EYES

The development of Airborne Interception (AI) radar, able to guide individual fighters to enemy aircraft at night, plus ground-based controllers, paved the way for the creation of an effective night fighter force, although many difficulties had to be overcome. The bulk and weight of the original AI equipment (around 600lb; 272kg), plus the need to accommodate a dedicated operator, precluded its use in single-seat fighters. Blenheims thus became the world's first radar-equipped night fighters. Four AI-equipped Mk 1fs were assigned to 25 Squadron on July 31, 1939, followed by three with a special flight of 600 Squadron in November 1939, which in early 1940 formed the nucleus of the Fighter Interception Unit (FIU) at Tangmere, West Sussex.

Early experience with AI was poor. The equipment was difficult to use and interpreting the blips on the screen more of an art than science. Nevertheless, from February 1940 small quantities of AI Mk II radar sets were provided to the Blenheim 1f squadrons. Some of the problems were rectified by the later AI Mk III, which became the standard in the summer of 1940. Development of tactics and training with the new equipment was organised by the FIU.

IN COMBAT

Blenheim crews claimed 30 enemy aircraft killed during the Battle of Britain. Most interceptions were achieved using the 'mark one eyeball' and it was not until the early hours of July 23, 1940, that the first AI-directed interception resulted in the downing of an enemy aircraft. That historic interception was completed in a Blenheim 1f of the FIU, flown by Flying Officer Glyn Ashfield, with observer Pilot Officer Geoffrey Edward Morris and AI operator Sergeant Reginald Harry Leyland, who destroyed a Dornier Do 17 over the Sussex coast. Although the Blenheim was hit by debris from the Do 17 and the crew found they were flying inverted at low altitude, they successfully recovered and made it back to their base at Tangmere.

Fighter Command was not the only operator of Blenheim fighters during the summer and autumn of 1940. Three Coastal Command units equipped with Blenheim If and IVfs, 235, 236 and 248 Squadrons, flew local defence patrols in response to air raids and were included in the official list of units qualifying as having participated in the Battle of Britain when it was published on November 9, 1960.

The only pilot to become an ace flying a Blenheim fighter served with Coastal Command. Flying Officer Reginald John Peacock of 235 Squadron gained his fifth victory on August 18, 1940, leading a flight of three Blenheim IVfs from Thorney Island, West Sussex, against 30 Junkers Ju 88s. He had previously shot down a Messerschmitt Bf 109E on May 12, another on June 27, and shared in the downing of a Heinkel He 115 on August 3 and a Bf 109 on August 11. The victories are all the more remarkable given that the Blenheim was completely outclassed as a fighter by the single-seat German design, being much slower and armed with fewer weapons of smaller calibre and range. For his unique achievement, Flying Officer Peacock was awarded the Distinguished Flying Cross in September 1940.

The Blenheim 1f remained the RAF's principle night fighter until late in 1940, when sufficient Bristol Beaufighters began to be delivered to the squadrons. It was withdrawn from frontline operations the following year. They continued to be flown by Operational Training Units tasked with training night fighter crews until 1943.

Bristol 142M Blenheim If

Dimensions: Length 39ft 9in (12.12m); Wing span 56ft 4in (17.17m); Height 9ft 10in (3m); Wing area 469sq ft (43.57m²)

Weights: Empty 8,840lb (4,100kg); Typically loaded 12,200lb (5,534kg)

Powerplant: Two Bristol Mercury VIII nine-cylinder radial, air-cooled piston engines, each rated at 840hp (627kW); Fuel capacity 278 imp gal (1,264 lit)

Armament: Five 0.303in (7.7mm) Browning machine guns, all firing forward, one in port wing and four in ventral pack, plus one 0.303in (7.7mm) Vickers K gun in a BI Mk I semi-retractable, hydraulically operated dorsal turret

Performance: Max speed 278mph (447km/h) at 15,000ft (4,572m), 237mph (381km/h) at sea level; Cruising speed 215mph (346km/h) at 15,000ft (4,572m); Initial climb rate 1,625ft/min (495m/min); Service ceiling 24,600ft (7,498m); Range 1,050 miles (1,690km)

Crew: Two or three, comprising pilot and radio operator/air gunner, plus radar operator in aircraft equipped with AI

Boulton Paul P.82
DEFIANT

Initially successful operating during the day, the Defiant turret fighter became vulnerable when Luftwaffe pilots changed tactics and learnt to attack it head-on or from below.

The Boulton Paul Defiant is best remembered as a night fighter, but it can be argued that it was as a target-tug, a role for which existing aircraft were modified and new examples built, that it found its niche within the RAF. It was conceived and first entered service as a day fighter before being adopted for nocturnal sorties, and served a limited role in the Battle of Britain.

The distinctive feature of the Defiant fighter was a power-operated Boulton Paul-designed turret mounted at the rear of the cockpit. Advantages envisaged over existing fighters with fixed armament included dividing the tasks of pilot and gunner, freeing the former from tracking and aiming at a target, allowing him to concentrate on flying the aircraft. The traversing turret promised a wider field of fire than fixed weapons, permitting the guns to be used offensively or defensively.

Boulton Paul Aircraft of Wolverhampton in the West Midlands and Hawker were selected to produce prototypes of turret fighters in response to Specification F9/35. The prototype Defiant (K8310) first flew on August 11, 1937, and the type was selected for production. (Plans for Hawker's Hotspur were abandoned after one prototype, as orders for Hurricanes already exceeded the company's capacity to produce them at its factories.) The first production Defiant I (L6950) flew on July 30, 1939 and deliveries to the initial unit, 264 Squadron at Martlesham Heath, Suffolk, started on December 30.

INTO ACTION

Crews of the Defiants received their baptism of fire over the beaches of Dunkirk in France on May 12, 1940, claiming a Heinkel He 111 and Junkers Ju 88 destroyed. Luftwaffe fighters attacking 264 Squadron's aircraft from the rear were met by a burst of fire from the four machine guns, while the turret-equipped fighter also proved effective intercepting bombers. By the end of May, the unit had claimed 65 enemy aircraft destroyed.

The unit's success during the month can partly be attributed to the Luftwaffe's unfamiliarity with the Defiant. In the heat of battle, the aircraft was often misidentified for the Hurricane, for which the traditional rear-echelon attack was the standard tactic. Once German

"Luftwaffe fighters attacking 264 Squadron's aircraft were met by a burst of fire"

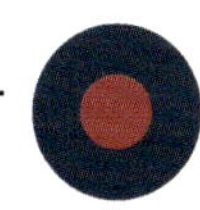

pilots became aware of the turret-fighter, and its vulnerability to attacks from below or head-on, its days were numbered. The weight of the turret also made it slower than the British single-seat fighters and reduced its manoeuvrability.

At the start of the Battle of Britain, the RAF had two frontline units equipped with the type. No.141 Squadron reformed at Turnhouse in Midlothian on October 4, 1939, flying a motley collection of types during its work-up period before receiving Defiants from April 1940. It became operational on the type on June 3, departing Scotland nine days later after being assigned to 11 Group, operating from West Malling, Kent, on patrols over the English Channel.

NOCTURNAL OPERATIONS

On July 19, the squadron engaged nine Messerschmitt Bf 109Es in a fierce dogfight south of Folkestone, Kent, that resulted in it claiming four of the enemy aircraft, but for the loss of six Defiants. Two days after this disastrous encounter, the unit returned to Scotland – initially Prestwick, Ayrshire – primarily to provide protection for convoys offshore. By then, the days of the aircraft as a day fighter were numbered, and in September the squadron began training for operations at night, Squadron Leader William A Richardson being replaced by Flight Lieutenant Edward C Wolfe as the commanding officer.

The squadron's 'B' Flight was deployed south on September 13, flying from Biggin Hill, Kent, for five days before relocating to Gatwick in Surrey. Pilot Officer John Waddington and Sergeant Alfred B Cumbers in N1552 shot down two He 111s on the evening of September 15. The following night, Sergeants George Laurence and William T Chard dispatched a Ju 88.

The entire squadron was reunited in November, when it was transferred to 11 Group, flying nightly patrols and downing additional Luftwaffe aircraft. It began re-equipping with Bristol Beaufighter 1fs in August 1941, relinquishing its last Defiants the following month.

By July 1940, 264 Squadron was based at Duxford, Cambridgeshire, moving to Kirton-in-Lindsey, Lincolnshire, in the last week of the month, with detachments at Coleby Grange in Lincolnshire and Ringway, Cheshire. Although still committed to day operations, the unit also began training for nocturnal combat in April, making one of its aircraft available each night. From June 7 it started night patrols, its daylight operations being limited to a dawn patrol each morning. On August 11 it recorded its first night-time engagement, although without bringing down the enemy and the first confirmed victory in the dark occurred four days later. As the Battle of Britain intensified the unit again returned to day fighting, shooting down a trio of Ju 88s on August 24 and a single He 111 on the 28th. However, these victories were achieved at a high cost, as three and four of the squadron's Defiants, respectively, were shot down during the dogfights, underlining the aircraft's vulnerability during the daylight hours. With the lesson learnt, 264 Squadron was fully committed to night-time operations, although few interceptions were successfully prosecuted during the final months of 1940.

Defiant night fighters went on to be flown by 85, 96, 125, 141, 151, 153, 255, 256, 264, 307, 409, 410 and 456 Squadrons on home defence duties, the last being withdrawn in mid-1942. Production of the aircraft ended in February 1943 after 1,064 had been built, including 713 Mk Is. The type was also flown by squadrons tasked with air/sea rescue, as well as Air Gunnery Schools, while the tugs were widely used by Air Armament Schools and Anti-Aircraft Co-operation Units.

ABOVE: Boulton Paul Defiant I L7026 of 264 Squadron, based at Kirton-in-Lindsey, Lincolnshire, from late July 1940. It was shot down by Messerschmitt Bf 109s off Dover, Kent, on August 28 the same year. Pete West

LEFT: Defiant Is of 264 Squadron, in the standard day fighter camouflage but with several different types of roundel. David Willis Collection

---

Boulton Paul P.82 Defiant I

Dimensions: Length 35ft 4in (10.77m); Wing span 39ft 4in (11.99m); Height 11ft 4in (3.45m); Wing area 250sq ft (23.23m²)

Weights: Empty 6,078lb (2,757kg); Typically loaded 8,318lb (3,774kg); Max take-off weight 8,350lb (3,788kg)

Powerplant: One Rolls-Royce Merlin III 12-cylinder Vee, liquid-cooled piston engine, rated at 1,030hp (768kW); Fuel capacity 104 imp gal (473 lit)

Armament: Four 0.303in (7.7mm) Browning machine guns mounted in a Boulton Paul A Mk IID power-operated dorsal turret

Performance: Max speed 303mph (488km/h) at 16,500ft (5,029m), 250mph (402km/h) at sea level; Initial climb rate 1,900ft/min (579m/min); Service ceiling 30,350ft (9,250m); Range 465 miles (748km) at 259mph (416km/h)

Crew: One pilot and one gunner

Bristol BEAUFIGHTER

Designed as a heavy fighter variant of the Bristol Beaufort torpedo bomber for day and night operations, the Beaufighter played a minor role in the Battle of Britain. Its finest hour came after the Luftwaffe turned to night attacks on British cities.

ABOVE: Radar-equipped Beaufighter If R2101 of 604 'County of Middlesex' Squadron. The aircraft was initially delivered to 25 Squadron before going to 604, but was lost after catching fire on May 7, 1941. Pete West

BELOW: An early production Beaufighter If of 25 Squadron taxiing past the type it replaced, the Blenheim If, at Debden in Essex, probably in late 1940. Key Collection

The first of four prototypes was flown by Captain Cyril F Unwins at Filton in south Gloucestershire, on July 17, 1939, and Specification F17/39 was drawn up by the Air Ministry to cover production of 300 Mk Is. Initial testing revealed that the Beaufighter was around 26mph (42km/h) slower than the Hawker Hurricane, making it unsuitable in the home-based day fighter role. However, its rugged airframe, performance and heavy armament were what was required for a night fighter and when fitted with the Airborne Interception (AI) Mk IV radar it became an outstanding replacement for Fighter Command's Bristol Blenheims. The observer, tasked with interpreting the radar returns, sat under a transparent bubble in the rear fuselage, while the pilot benefited from a bulletproof windscreen free of the distracting reflections that plagued the Blenheim. The Beaufighter's only shortcoming was a tendency to swing on take-off or landing, which took some time and airframe modifications to cure.

Two production Beaufighter Is were built in June 1940, five in July, 23 in August and 15 in September. While many early aircraft lacked AI Mk IV, it became standard in aircraft produced from November.

INTO SERVICE

Instead of concentrating the aircraft within a single squadron, the decision was taken to deliver small numbers to units already operating Blenheim Ifs. This allowed a comprehensive evaluation of the type in operational conditions and permitted the squadrons to develop tactics to make the most of the new aircraft.

The Fighter Interception Unit (FIU) at Tangmere, West Sussex, received the first Beaufighter If on August 12, the week before it moved to Shoreham in the same county, and its initial example fitted with AI Mk IV arrived the next month. Others went to 25, 29, 219, 600 and 604 Squadrons from early September and by October 31, around 28 had been delivered. Limited operational sorties began on September 17, initially during the day so that crews could get used to the new aircraft without the hazards of operating in the dark.

The first confirmed kill using a Beaufighter was achieved by 'B' Flight of 219 Squadron based at Redhill, Surrey, on the night of October 25/26. Pilot Sergeant Arthur J Hodgkinson and his observer Sergeant Gordon W Benn in Mk If R2097 shot down a Dornier Do 17Z to the south of London, without the use of radar.

A total of 911 (excluding four prototype) Beaufighter Is, including both the Mk If night fighter and Ic coastal strike fighter, were built at Bristol's factories at Filton and Weston-super-Mare in Somerset, and by Fairey at Stockport, Cheshire. The Mk If served in the front line with Fighter Command until June 1943, but remained in use with night fighter Operational Training Units (OTU) until the end of the war. Beaufighter Ifs equipped 25, 29, 89, 141, 153, 219, 255, 256, 307, 600 and 604 Squadrons, while the variant was also used for night fighter crew training with 51 and 60 OTUs. Including later marks, Beaufighters were flown by a total of 52 RAF squadrons and the last, operated as target-tugs, remained in service until May 1960.

Bristol 156 Beaufighter If

Dimensions: Length 41ft 4in (12.60m); Wing span 57ft 10in (17.63m); Height 15ft 10in (4.82m); Wing area 503sq ft (46.73m²)

Weights: Empty 14,069lb (6,381kg); Max take-off weight 21,120lb (9,580kg)

Powerplant: Two Bristol Hercules III, X or XI 14-cylinder two row radial, air-cooled piston engine, each rated at 1,560hp (1,164kW) for take-off; Fuel capacity 550 imp gal (2,500 lit)

Armament: Four 0.787in (20mm) Hispano cannons in lower fuselage, plus (from 50th Mk I) six 0.303in (7.7mm) Browning machine guns in wings (four starboard, two port), all firing forward

Performance: Max speed 306mph (492km/h) at sea level, 323mph (520km/h) at 15,000ft (4,572m); Max cruising speed 272mph (437km/h) at 15,000ft (4,572m); Initial climb rate 1,850ft/min (564m/min); Service ceiling 26,500ft (8,077m); Range 1,170 miles (1,883km) at 182mph (292km/h) at 5,000ft (1,524m)

Crew: One pilot and one radio operator/observer

Gloster GLADIATOR

The RAF's last biplane fighter played a small role in the Battle of Britain.

The biplane fighter was considered obsolete by the start of World War Two, but existing stocks were still flown by squadrons awaiting the arrival of more heavily armed monoplane fighters with better performance. Within the RAF, the final generation of biplane fighters was represented by the Gloster Gladiator – delightful to fly, but outclassed by many of the adversaries it would encounter.

By the time Germany had conquered France, the Gladiator had been replaced within Fighter Command's frontline squadrons in Britain, although other units retained the aircraft overseas, primarily in North Africa. At the start of 1940, the only combat unit left flying the type at home was the Fighter Flight, RAF Sumburgh.

move was accompanied by the Flight being transferred to Fighter Command, and on August 1 it was raised in status to become 247 Squadron, being declared operational on the 13th of that month.

The Flight did not engage any enemy aircraft during its time in Scotland, its first combat occurring after its move south, on the night of October 28, when Pilot Officer Richard A Winter intercepted a Heinkel He 111 without result. Nine days later the same pilot damaged another He 111, but a successful kill eluded Fighter Command's Gladiators during the Battle of Britain, primarily as the biplane was too slow to intercept the German bombers. Hawker Hurricanes supplanted Gladiators within 247 Squadron from December 1940.

ABOVE:
The Gladiator I of the Shuttleworth Collection based at Old Warden, Bedfordshire, was painted in 247 Squadron's wartime colours between 1990 and 1996. Key-Duncan Cubitt

LEFT: A 247 Squadron Gladiator II at Roborough, Devon, during the Battle of Britain.
Key Collection

The unit was formed at Turnhouse outside Edinburgh, Scotland, on December 18, 1939, as the Fighter Flight, Shetlands, taking over a detachment of 152 Squadron Gladiator IIs and moving to Sumburgh in the Shetland Islands nine days later. It was renamed the Fighter Flight, RAF Sumburgh, on January 5, 1940 and was tasked with defending the Home Fleet anchored at Scapa Flow in the Orkney Islands, reporting to Coastal Command. When 804 Squadron of the Fleet Air Arm took over the role, the Fighter Flight was reassigned to defend the Plymouth dockyards in Devon. The Gladiators departed Sumburgh in stages from July 21 for Roborough just outside Plymouth, which had a small grass strip that was unsuitable for more modern fighters but adequate for the biplanes. It was used during the day, while a detachment at St Eval, Cornwall, was established for operations at night. The

RAF Gladiators saw considerable action overseas after the Battle of Britain, notably over Malta and in North and East Africa. At home, Coastal Command continued to use the aircraft to fly short-range meteorological reconnaissance sorties into 1944.

SEA GLADIATOR

Of the two Fleet Air Arm squadrons credited by the Air Ministry as participating in the Battle of Britain, one predominately operated the Sea Gladiator. This aircraft differed little from those of the RAF, but had catapult points and a deck-arrester hook, plus a collapsible dinghy mounted in a fairing between the main landing gear. A total of 60 Sea Gladiators were built, while 38 former RAF machines were modified, the first deliveries to HMS *Merlin*, Donibristle in Fife, Scotland, occurring in February 1939.

Air defence for HMS *Glorious* was provided by 804 Squadron while the aircraft carrier ferried RAF Gladiators of 269 Squadron to Norway in late April 1940, in a futile attempt to stop German forces overrunning the country. Transferred to HMS *Furious*, the unit was shore-based at HMS *Sparrowhawk*, Hatston in the Orkney Islands, to cover the Royal Navy's anchorage at Scapa Flow, its operations co-ordinated with the local RAF fighter sector station. During September 1940, the unit provided detachments for two short deployments onboard HMS *Furious*, and the following month moved its Sea Gladiators and the first of its replacement, the Grumman Martlet, to the newly opened airfield at Skeabrae, also in the Orkneys, where it remained until early in the next year. There was little enemy activity over the Orkneys during the Battle of Britain and the Sea Gladiators did not encounter the Luftwaffe when operating from either Hatston or Skeabrae.

Gloster Gladiator II

Dimensions: Length 27ft 5in (8.36m); Wing span 32ft 3in (9.83m); Height 10ft 7in (3.22m); Wing area 323sq ft (30.01m²)

Weights: Empty 3,847lb (1,745kg); Max take-off weight 4,864lb (2,206kg)

Powerplant: One Bristol Mercury VIIIA or VIIIAS nine-cylinder radial, air-cooled piston engine, rated at 725hp (541kW); Fuel capacity 84 imp gal (382 lit)

Armament: Four 0.303in (7.7mm) Browning machine guns, two in fuselage and two under the lower wings all firing forward

Performance: Max speed 215mph (346km/h) at sea level, 224mph (360km/h) at 5,000ft (1,524m); Initial climb rate 2,460ft/min (750m/min); Service ceiling 33,500ft (10,211m); Range 444 miles (714km) at 225mph (362km/h) at 14,600ft (4,450m)

Crew: One pilot

On the PERIPHERY

Many different types of RAF aircraft supported operations during the Battle of Britain but were not directly involved in the fighting, while others were too late to make any impact on the outcome. In addition, a small number of captured Luftwaffe aircraft gave the RAF insight in how to tackle them in the air.

RIGHT: Deliveries of Westland Whirlwinds began during the Battle of Britain, but the fighter took no part in the fighting. Key-Swanborough Collection

Fighter Command bore the brunt of the fighting against the Luftwaffe during the Battle of Britain. One new fighter that entered service with the Command during that period played no role in the campaign. The Westland Whirlwind was the RAF's first twin-engined single-seat fighter, armed with heavy cannons and (as demonstrated by the prototype) capable of high speed.

The sinking of HMS *Glorious* on June 8, 1940, claimed the lives of most of 263 Squadron's aircrew, embarked on the aircraft carrier travelling home from Norway at the end of the disastrous British attempt to stem the German advance into the country. Two days later, the squadron was re-established at Drem in Lothian, Scotland. It was planned to re-equip it with the Whirlwind, but delays to the aircraft meant it received Hawker Hurricane Is instead. It transferred to Grangemouth, Strathclyde, on June 28. Grangemouth was used as a base by units providing air defence for the Clydeside area, although the expected heavy raids failed to materialise. The first Whirlwind arrived on July 6 and two others joined the squadron on the 19th, but problems with the Rolls-Royce Peregrine engine and nose-mounted 0.787in (20mm) cannon armament, plus the slow pace of deliveries, prevented a quick transition to the new aircraft. The last Hurricanes departed the unit in November 1940, by which time it had returned to Drem.

It was only on February 8, 1941 – long after the official end of the Battle of Britain – that a 263 Squadron Whirlwind scored its first confirmed kill, an Arado Ar 196, although Pilot Officer David Stein had been credited with a probable Junkers Ju 88 off the Scillies on January 12. The only other Whirlwind unit was 137 Squadron, which formed in September 1941.

AIR-SEA RESCUE

Until June 24, 1940, when it came directly under the Air Ministry, Fighter Command had administrative control of 22 (Army Co-operation) Group, to which the RAF's Westland Lysander-equipped squadrons were assigned. Experience during the Battle of France confirmed that the Lysander was of marginal military use. Prior to the start of the Battle of Britain they were employed on anti-invasion patrols, but as the fighting commenced they performed a more useful role flying air-sea rescue missions to locate downed aircrew.

Unlike the Germans, the British lacked a dedicated air-sea rescue organisation. While aircraft such as the Fleet Air Arm's Supermarine Walrus could alight to retrieve survivors, the majority of rescues were performed by small surface craft. Unfortunately, the fleet was small and very often they arrived too late or not at all. Between mid-July and October 1940, 215 pilots and aircrew were lost to the seas, prompting the formation of the Air Sea Rescue Service the next year.

It must not be forgotten that the other Commands played their part during the summer and autumn of 1940. Bomber Command launched raids on the continent, striking at targets to blunt the anticipated invasion, such as the barges gathering in the ports and harbours of occupied Europe. Coastal Command patrolled the waters around the British Isles, its aircraft playing a vital if unheralded role against German operations to halt traffic in the English Channel. Three of its Bristol Blenheim squadrons are among the RAF units officially credited as participating in the battle.

CAPTURED EAGLES

Luftwaffe aircraft brought down over the British Isles provided a wealth of technical information about the enemy. A handful of such aircraft were made airworthy again and flown by the Air Ministry, while a Messerschmitt Bf 109E-3 recovered and evaluated by French forces was handed over to the RAF on May 2, 1940. It was test flown at Boscombe Down, Wiltshire, before going to the Royal Aircraft Establishment (RAE) at Farnborough, Hampshire, becoming AE479 in June 1940. On September 20, it went to the Air Fighting Development Unit (AFDU), responsible for refining fighter tactics, returning two months later.

The RAE and AFDU also had a Heinkel He 111H-1 (AW177). The bomber had force-landed with minor damage on February 9, 1940, at North Berwick Law, south of the Firth of Forth, and was recovered and flown again at Turnhouse on August 13 before going to Farnborough. It was operated by the AFDU from mid-September to early October.

A Bf 110C-5 shot down on July 21 by Hurricanes of 238 Squadron near Goodwood, West Sussex, was repaired and reflown by the RAE as AX772 from October 25.

All three aircraft later joined 1426 (Enemy Aircraft) Flight when it was formed at Duxford, Cambridgeshire, on November 21, 1941.

Designed to provide air defence and reconnaissance for the fleet, the Fulmar benefited from a long endurance but was a large and heavy aircraft and, while it lacked the speed vital to a frontline fighter in level flight, its velocity built up rapidly in a dive. By the end of August 1940, approximately 60 Fulmar Is had been built, with production thereafter running at 25 a month, for a total of 159 by the end of the year. The first unit with the type, 806 Squadron, flying Fulmars alongside Blackburn Skuas, embarked on HMS *Illustrious* with the Mediterranean Fleet on June 11, 1940. The squadron recorded the first kill by the fighter on September 2, downing a Cant Z.501 flying boat off Rhodes, Greece.

One Fleet Air Arm (FAA) unit flying Fulmars, 808 Squadron, was assigned to RAF Fighter Command during the Battle of Britain. Formed at Worthy Down on July 1, 1940, the squadron was present when the airfield was attacked by Junkers Ju 88s of Lehrgeschwader 1 on August 15, but did not participate in the fight. It departed HMS *Kestrel* on September 5, arriving four days later at Castletown in Caithness, Scotland, to defend the anchorage at Scapa Flow in the Orkney Islands. The squadron departed for HMS *Merlin*, Donibristle, near Rosyth in Fife, on October 2 and embarked on HMS *Ark Royal* at the end of the month. During its time assigned to the RAF, the squadron claimed no kills and suffered no losses to enemy action.

The Fulmar I was superseded by the Mk II with the Merlin XXX engine, with production ending in December 1942 after a combined total of 600 had been built. Within the FAA, it bridged the gap between pre-war biplane designs and the initial generation of shipborne single-seat fighters that were the equal of their land-based opponents. Fulmars were withdrawn from frontline operations in early 1943.

NAVAL MISCELLANY

At the start of the Battle of Britain, the FAA was poorly equipped with fighters, its most capable type being the Fulmar, although it was not a match for the Messerschmitt Bf 109. Several other types were in service, such as the Blackburn Skua fighter and dive-bomber and the Roc, a development of the former type fitted with a power-operated turret. Both types were obsolete by the start of the Battle of Britain and were not directly involved in the fighting.

The only FAA unit, apart from the Fulmar-equipped 808 Squadron, officially listed as participating in the campaign is 804 Squadron, primarily equipped with Gloster Sea Gladiators. Based at HMS *Sparrowhawk*, Hatston in the Orkney Islands, it was tasked with defending Scapa Flow during the Battle of Britain. It was also involved in evaluating the Brewster Buffalo I for the Royal Navy. From July 1940, 37 Maintenance Unit at Burtonwood, Cheshire, began to receive Buffalos diverted from a Belgian contract, of which 36 had been assembled and test flown by the end of October and 28 handed over to the RAF and Royal Navy. Approximately 15 eventually went to Fleet Air Arm squadrons, including at least two to 804 Squadron. Fitted with armour and carrying a full load of ammunition the portly fighter could only manage around 270mph (435km/h) at 6,000ft (1,929m) and was thus rejected for frontline use by the senior service.

No. 804 Squadron was also the first FAA unit with the Grumman Martlet I single-seat fighter. Martlet was the original name allocated by the Admiralty to the Wildcat, the Mk I being a fixed-wing version ordered by France but delivered to Britain after the German victory on the continent. Deliveries began in August 1940 and they arrived at Hatston the following month, the unit receiving its full complement of 12 in October. The squadron claimed no kills or losses during the Battle of Britain.

Fairey Fulmar I	
Dimensions:	Length 40ft 3in (12.27m); Wing span 46ft 4¹/₂in (14.14m); Height 10ft 8in (3.25m); Wing area 342sq ft (31.77m²)
Weights:	Empty 6,915lb (3,137kg); Typically loaded 9,672lb (4,387kg); Max take-off weight 9,800lb (4,445kg)
Powerplant:	One Rolls-Royce Merlin VIII 12-cylinder Vee, liquid-cooled piston engine, rated at 1,080hp (806kW) for take-off and 1,035kW (772kW) at 7,750ft (2,286m); Fuel capacity 155 imp gal (705 lit), with provision for a 60 imp gal (273 lit) flush-fitting ventral tank
Armament:	Eight 0.303in (7.7mm) Browning machine guns mounted in the wings, plus up to 500lb (227kg) of bombs under the wings. Some aircraft equipped with a single 0.303in (7.7mm) Vickers K gun on a flexible mounting in the rear cockpit
Performance:	Max speed 256mph (412km/h) at 2,400ft (732m), 246mph (396km/h) at sea level; Initial climb rate 1,105ft/min (337m/min); Service ceiling 22,400ft (6,827m); Range 830 miles (1,336km) at 10,000ft (3,048m) at 150mph (241km/h)
Crew:	One pilot and one observer (navigator)

BELOW:
The Fairey Fulmar was designed to defend the fleet from bombers and was not in the same league as land-based single-seat fighters. AHB/UK MoD Crown

Fairey FULMAR

Delivery of the first operational Fairey Fulmar I to HMS *Kestrel*, Worthy Down in Hampshire, during June 1940 began the long overdue re-equipment of the Fleet Air Arm (FAA) with a shipborne fighter with heavy firepower and a reasonable performance.

Battle of Britain
AIRFIELDS

Fighter Command's airfields were in the front line during the Battle of Britain. Work to expand the number available and improve their facilities was under way as the Luftwaffe settled into its new bases in Europe.

ABOVE:
Hurricane Is of 501 'County of Gloucester' Squadron scramble from Gravesend in Kent on August 16, 1940.

Approximately 65 airfields spread across the country housed operational Fighter Command squadrons during the Battle of Britain. The facilities at these sites varied greatly, from stations with the full complement of buildings and personnel required for a wing of aircraft, to those that were barely more than grass strips. The largest concentration was located in the southeast of the country within 11 (Fighter) Group's area, a legacy of the pre-war air defence planning that was primarily concerned with protecting London from aerial attack.

DECLINE AND EXPANSION

At the end of World War One there were around 300 aerodromes or landing fields in Britain, most without any permanent structures. By late 1920, more than 250 had been abandoned and were quickly disappearing back into the landscape, those retained tending to be the ones that already had hangars and domestic buildings erected. By 1924, only 27 were still in use, the majority around London.

When the extent of German rearmament became evident in 1933 it was conceded that London would not be the only target in any future war, and that provision for the aerial defence of other cities and strategic sites across the country was needed. The Air Ministry's Expansion Scheme A extended fighter cover from the south of England to north of the River Tees to protect the industrial heartland in the Midlands and northeast. It meant that airfields would have to be established as bases for fighter aircraft. Other expansion plans quickly followed to increase the number of fighters and bombers for the RAF, the latter types requiring sites in Lincolnshire and Yorkshire so they could reach targets as far as possible into continental Europe.

BUILDING NEW AIRFIELDS

The Air Ministry formed the Works Directorate in the early 1930s to plan and organise the construction of new airfields as part of the general expansion of the RAF. An Aerodromes Board was created within the directorate in May 1934 to find locations for the new airfields, making use of Ordnance Survey charts to identify suitable sites. It sought flat areas that were higher than 50ft

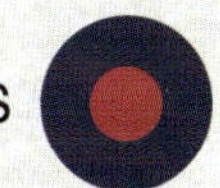

and early 1930s. The shortcomings of grass surfaces were demonstrated during the wet winter of 1936/37, which caused many aircraft to get bogged down in the mud.

In May 1937, the commander of Fighter Command, Air Chief Marshal Sir Hugh Dowding, asked the Air Ministry for paved runways at some of his stations, but was denied on grounds of cost. He continued to push the case but it was not until April 28, 1939, that the Air Ministry decided eight airfields should have runways laid. The sites selected were Debden, Essex; Biggin Hill, Hendon and Northolt in Greater London; Kenley, Surrey; and Tangmere in West Sussex – all of 11 (Fighter) Group; Church Fenton in Yorkshire; and Turnhouse outside Edinburgh in Scotland – both within 13 (Fighter) Group. By the start of the war, only those at Northolt and Turnhouse had been completed, although work was underway at the others (with the »

(15m) below mean sea level to reduce susceptibility to flooding, but less than 600ft (183m) above to avoid low clouds, without any obstructions in the immediate vicinity. The land had to be well drained, as grass runways were the norm.

The ministry's Land Branch oversaw the acquisition of sites for new airfields. The Land Branch's task was greatly eased by the provisions of the Emergency Powers (Defence) Act of 1939, which did away with complicated compulsory purchase orders in favour of the quicker requisitioning process.

Approximately 100 new airfields were created between 1935 and September 1939. Most were roughly circular, with a standard diameter of 3,300ft (1km), the grass surfaces allowing aircraft to take off in any direction into the wind. Hangars were built on the rim of the airfield, with technical buildings behind and airmen's quarters usually located close by. By the start of the war the RAF had 116 airfields.

The first wartime programme to increase the number by 75 aerodromes and satellite sites was outlined in August 1940, but the target quickly increased to 125, of which 104 were completed by the end of the year.

PAVED RUNWAYS

As aircraft speeds increased, the need arose for better surfaces than grass to operate from, but little central planning had been undertaken to improve RAF airfields during the late 1920s

On August 27, 1939, 605 'County of Warwick' Squadron of the Auxiliary Air Force arrived from its peacetime airfield at Castle Bromwich in the West Midlands, with a mix of Hurricanes and Gladiators. It was joined by the Hurricanes of 501 'County of Gloucester' Squadron in late November and, the next month, Bristol Blenheim Ifs of 601 'County of London' Squadron – known as the 'Millionaires' Squadron' because of its wealthy upper-class and titled pilots and officers. The Blenheims were replaced by Hurricanes in March 1940, by which time 605 Squadron had left for Leuchars in Fife.

Tangmere's squadrons were heavily involved in the fighting on the continent following the start of the German invasion of Belgium, the Netherlands and France on May 10. Both 501 Squadron and A Flight of 601 Squadron departed for France to bolster the BEF after the start of the campaign, suffering heavy losses in the fighting. Also involved was 145 Squadron, which moved to Tangmere from Croydon in London on the same day. It was tasked with ferrying Hurricanes across the Channel to reinforce the British Air Forces in France. At the end of the month, 43 Squadron returned to Tangmere and was immediately committed to operations over Dunkirk, providing air cover for the evacuation of the surviving British forces. It claimed seven Messerschmitts Bf 109s

exception of Hendon). At least eight other RAF airfields had paved runways by the start of the war, including the fighter station at North Weald in Essex.

ATTACK TO DEFEND

One of the most famous RAF airfields involved in the Battle of Britain was Tangmere, situated 3 miles (5km) to the east of Chichester in West Sussex. It had been a fighter base since December 1926, initially housing the Gloster Gamecocks of 43 Squadron, which was joined in February 1927 by 1 Squadron flying Armstrong Whitworth Siskin IIIs. Construction of permanent brick barracks blocks, messes and married quarters were completed in 1930 and additional buildings were added in the late 1930s. In 1938, it was enlarged and the maximum length of the runway increased to 5,500ft (1,327m), while a perimeter track was added.

Following the Munich Crisis of September 1938, caused by Hitler's demand to bring the German-speaking areas of Czechoslovakia within the Reich, the hangars were camouflaged and air raid shelters dug. At that point, both 1 and 43 Squadrons were still flying Hawker Fury I biplanes, but both received Hawker Hurricane Is in the following two months. Upon the declaration of the war, 1 Squadron departed to France as part of the Air Component of the British Expeditionary Force (BEF), while in November 1939, 43 Squadron left Tangmere for Acklington in Northumberland.

> *"By the end of the battle, pilots based at Tangmere and Westhampnett claimed more than 300 enemy aircraft"*

and two Bf 110s on June 1, losing two Hurricanes and one pilot. Losses mounted during the next week and 43 Squadron had to be withdrawn from operations to regroup.

FRONTLINE AIRFIELD

No. 1 Squadron returned to Tangmere on June 23, joining 43, 145 and 601 at the airfield. During July, all four were involved in skirmishes over the Channel. At the end of the month, 145 Squadron left for Westhampnett also in West Sussex, which was originally an emergency landing ground for the fighters at Tangmere but had been upgraded as a satellite airfield.

From August 8 to 12, the Tangmere Wing provided air cover for the 'Peewit' convoy travelling from the Isle of Wight to Portland in Dorset, during which its squadrons lost 16 aircraft in combat with the Luftwaffe.

At 1300hrs on August 16, Tangmere was subjected to an attack by a large force of Junkers Ju 87 Stukas. Although some of the raiders were intercepted before they reached Tangmere, considerable damage was done during the few minutes the dive bombers were over the airfield. Two hangars were destroyed and the other three damaged, while the station workshops and fire hydrant pump house received direct hits, along with other buildings on the site. At least ten servicemen and three civilians were killed and more than 20 injured, while 12 aircraft, seven of them Hurricanes, were destroyed or put out of action. However, Tangmere still remained operational.

Despite craters on the aerodrome, all of the Hurricanes of 43 and 601 Squadrons – which had pursued the Stukas and claimed eight – managed to land back at their base. Pilot Officer William 'Billy' M L Fiske III's

Fighter Command Squadrons at Tangmere During the Battle of Britain			
Unit	Aircraft	Arrived (from)	Departed (to)
1 Sqn	Hurricane	23 Jun 40 (Northolt)	1 Aug 40 (Northolt)
17 Sqn	Hurricane	19 Aug 40 (Debden)	2 Sep 40 (Debden)
43 Sqn	Hurricane	31 May 40 (Wick)	8 Sep 40 (Usworth)
145 Sqn	Hurricane	10 May 40 (Croydon)	31 Jul 40 (Westhampnett)
	+	9 Oct 40 (Dyce)	7 May 1941 (Merston)
213 Sqn	Hurricane	7 Sep 40 (Exeter)	29 Nov 40 (Leconfield)
266 Sqn	Spitfire	9 Aug 40 (Wittering)	12 Aug 40 (Eastchurch)
601 Sqn	Hurricane	17 Jun 40 (Middle Wallop)	19 Aug 40 (Debden)
		2 Sep 40 (Debden)	7 Sep 40 (Exeter)
607 Sqn	Hurricane	1 Sep 40 (Usworth)	10 Oct 40 (Turnhouse)
FIU	Blenheim, etc	18 Apr 40*	18 Aug 40 (Shoreham)

+ replaced its Hurricanes with Spitfire Is from January 1941

* Fighter Interception Unit formed at Tangmere.

Hurricane I P3358 caught fire during the combat and he was badly burnt by the time he was extracted from his aircraft. The following day he succumbed to his wounds. An Olympic bobsled champion, Fiske had joined 601 Squadron on July 12, 1940. He was one of 11 American volunteers who flew with the RAF during the Battle of Britain and the second to lose his life.

Tangmere was a Sector Headquarters within 11 (Fighter) Group, responsible for a roughly rectangular slice of airspace from Reading in Berkshire to the southern edges of London in the north, to Southampton in Hampshire and Brighton in East Sussex on the coast in the south. As such, it had a Sector Operations Room into which information on incoming raids was fed, so that it could vector its own

squadrons and those at satellite airfields within the area against them. After the August 16 raid, the Sector Operations Room was moved to St James' School in nearby Chichester.

Tangmere-based squadrons intercepted Stukas again two days after the attack. During the day its units were directed to defend the airfields at Thorney Island and Ford in West Sussex, as well as the radar station at Poling, Sussex. Luftwaffe raids on Fighter Command airfields continued throughout August and the squadrons within the Tangmere sector were heavily involved intercepting them.

A number of different units rotated through Tangmere (*see table*) during the Battle of Britain, nearly all flying the Hurricane. They continued to fight against the Luftwaffe after it changed tactics and began to attack London. By the official end of the battle, pilots based at the airfield and its satellite at Westhampnett claimed to have destroyed more than 300 enemy aircraft.

THE AIR BATTLE
For England

The ultimate objective of the Luftwaffe during the Luftschlacht um England (Air Battle for England) was to force the British to sue for peace, allowing Germany to retain the territory it had occupied in 1939 and the first half of 1940.

Following the armistice with France, the Führer Adolph Hitler hoped that an end to the fighting could be negotiated with Great Britain, but realised that German forces could be required to invade and occupy the country. On July 2, 1940, the armed forces were tasked by the Oberkommando der Wehrmacht (OKW, Supreme Headquarters of the Armed Forces) to begin preliminary planning for an invasion. One of the main preconditions for a successful landing was command of the air, a mission delegated to the Luftwaffe, while the primary obstacle to a seaborne landing was the Royal Navy. It was proposed that U-boats and mines could be used to limit the threat posed by the British senior service.

Hermann Göring, commander of the Luftwaffe, was unenthusiastic about planning for the invasion. He expected air power alone to be decisive in driving Britain to the negotiating table.

THE PLAN

A report prepared by the Luftwaffe presented to the OKW on July 11 stated that it would take 14 to 28 days to achieve air superiority. Aims included eliminating the RAF, and destroying the aircraft manufacturing and supply systems. A secondary objective was to reduce the strength of the Royal Navy. The army's

plan was presented to Hitler on July 13, based upon the assumption that the navy could safely transport it to Britain.

Führer Directive No. 16 issued on July 16 started preparations for the invasion, under the codename Seelöwe (Sealion). Among the four preconditions were for the RAF to be 'beaten down' so that it could not aggressively oppose the German forces crossing the Channel. The others involved sweeping the crossing points clear of mines; closing off the Straits of Dover by laying mines; placing heavy artillery along the coast of France opposite England; and neutralising the Royal Navy as a threat in its home waters, as well as engaging it in the North Sea and Mediterranean, so it could not intervene.

A DIFFERENT CAMPAIGN

On June 30, Göring had issued an operational directive ordering the Luftwaffe to destroy the RAF. Initial estimates predicted it would take four days to cripple Fighter Command in southern England, after which a four-week bombing offence would be launched to destroy all military installations and the aircraft industry. This exceedingly optimistic timescale was later revised, allocating five weeks to establish temporary air superiority over England.

Luftwaffe operations against Great Britain would be significantly different to those undertaken on the European continent. The air arm would have to carry the weight of the offensive alone, no longer working in conjunction with the army. In previous campaigns the army had been able to overrun airfields as it occupied territory, concentrating its opponent's surviving aircraft onto fewer sites that could then be targeted, as well as disrupting the delivery of supplies.

All operations would be conducted from recently captured bases in France, Belgium and the Netherlands and, later in the campaign, Norway. The Luftwaffe would not be able to move closer to its targets, reducing its flight time to hit targets, or increase its reach into England, as it had in other campaigns, by moving to airfields closer to the fighting. Each sortie would involve time flying over the sea, with airmen coming down in the water having to rely on the German air-sea rescue organisation (the Seenotdienst) for recovery.

THE RISE *of the Luftwaffe*

The Luftwaffe was not created overnight. Signs of the revival of German air power were visible during the 1920s, although it was not until 1935 that the Luftwaffe was revealed to the world.

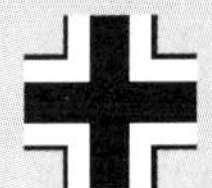

The Treaty of Versailles, signed on June 28, 1919, officially brought World War One to an end. It placed severe limitations on the size of Germany's post-war armed forces and effectively banned the operation of military aircraft.

However, planning for a new air force continued in secret. General Johannes 'Hans' von Seeckt, head of the Reichswehr ('defence of the realm') between 1919 and 1926, envisioned Germany using highly mobile army units supported by air power in any future conflict. He made sure that around 180 officers of the former Imperial Air Service were retained to form the nucleus of a new air force in the future. Many of them went on to enter the Luftwaffe's officer corps in the 1930s.

In 1920, the Luftsportverband ('air sports association') was established to provide basic flight instruction using gliders. With the help of the Reichswehr, its membership gradually increased and by the end of the decade exceeded 50,000. It created a pool of glider pilots who could progress to flying powered aircraft.

SECRET AIR FORCE

Opportunities to train on powered aircraft were minimal, although they increased from the spring of 1926 under the terms of a secret agreement between Germany and the Soviet Union. In return for help with its aircraft industry, the Soviet Union allowed Germany to establish a flying training centre at Lipetsk in the Don basin. It operated between 1926 and 1933, during which time 120 fighter pilots and more than 300 ground crews were trained.

The airline Deutsche Lufthansa was formed in 1926 by amalgamating several unprofitable companies, with Erhard Milch one of its directors. It provided employment and training for pilots and aircrews later destined to join the Luftwaffe, as well as cover for the development of a large number of new designs – including many fast aircraft able to carry 'mail' (if not passengers) that could be adapted for military roles. Lufthansa also had its own pilot training school, the Verkehrsfliegerschule, whose output vastly exceeded the airline's own requirements and increased again after the closure of the Lipetsk facility.

The production of military aircraft within Germany was banned under the terms of the Treaty of Versailles, while the performance of civil designs was severely limited until May 1926, when restrictions were lifted by the Paris Air Agreement. Many German aircraft companies set up operations in neighbouring countries to escape the restrictions, so only 47 aircraft were built in Germany in 1922, rising to 406 three years later, nearly all small civil designs. By 1932, only 3,284 aircraft had been »

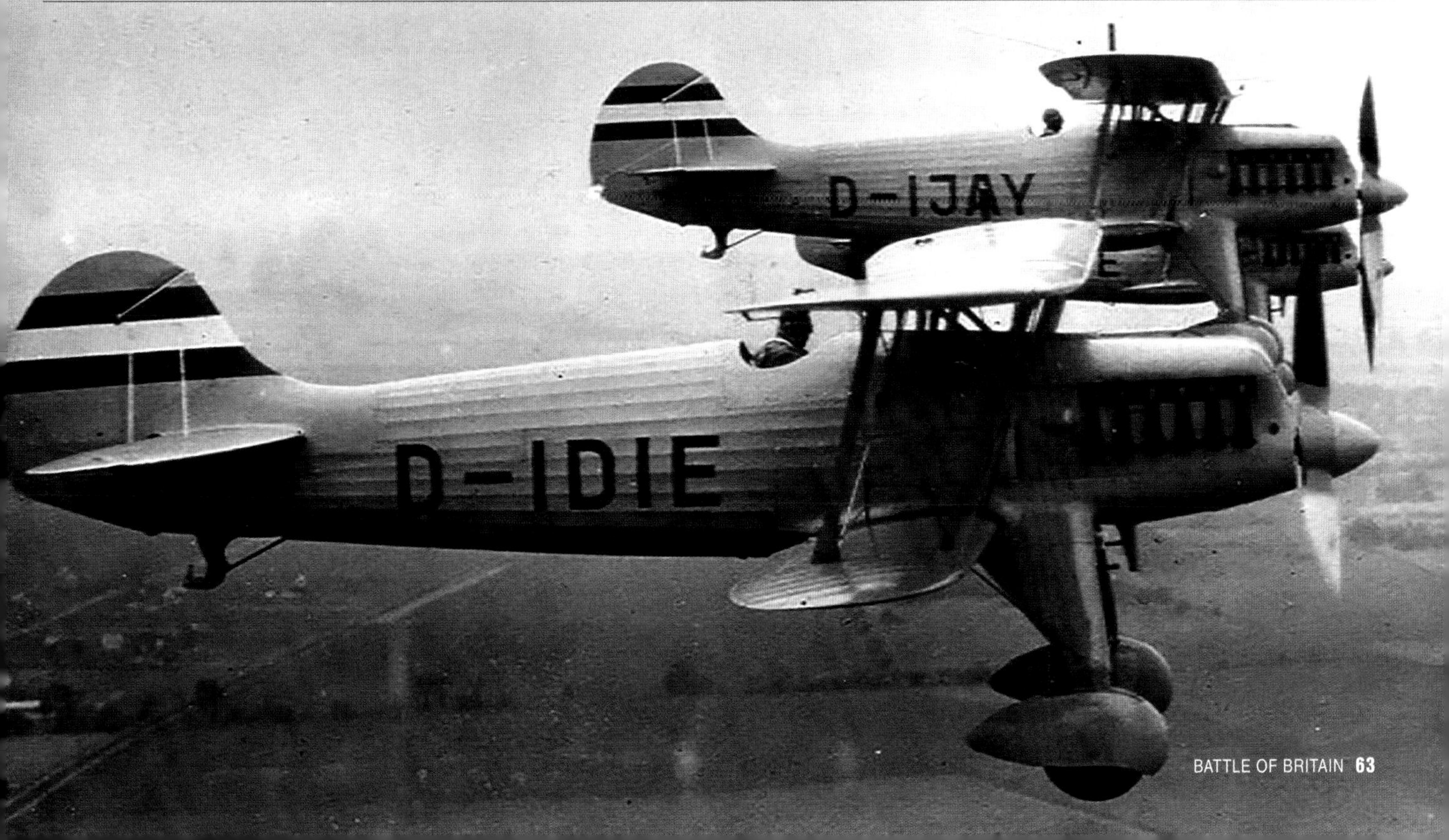

BELOW: The Heinkel He 51 was one of the early fighters developed for the Luftwaffe. These three are part of the pre-production batch of He 51As delivered to the 'Central German Publicity Squadron' in the summer of 1934. All Key Collection unless stated

produced within the country since the end of the war. The total included 365 military types built in secret, most observation or reconnaissance aircraft, although 65 were fighters and 93 bombers or torpedo bombers. It was not until March 16, 1935, that Germany unilaterally lifted all restrictions on the production of all kinds of aircraft imposed by the Treaty of Versailles.

INTO THE OPEN

Soon after Adolph Hitler became Germany's Chancellor in January 1933, Erhard Milch was appointed Secretary of State in the Air Ministry (Reichsluftfahrtministerium, RLM), under Hermann Göring. Along with General Walther Wever, the Chief of the Air Staff, Milch did much to shape the Luftwaffe in its formative years.

Hitler announced the existence of the new force on March 27, 1935, after which it absorbed various flying schools, paramilitary and police units. At the time it was revealed the Luftwaffe had a strength of 20,000 men and 1,888 aircraft. Although Hitler claimed the German air force was equal in strength to the RAF, in reality most of its aircraft

were trainers or interim designs, with few frontline types. Hitler also announced he wanted to achieve parity with France and plans were produced to greatly expand and modernise the Luftwaffe.

Orders for 4,021 (including 116 for Lufthansa) were placed by Milch in the first production programme in 1934, enough to equip six bomber, six reconnaissance and six fighter Geschwader (literally 'squadrons'), each of nine Staffeln ('flying unit') split equally between three Gruppen ('groups'). These units were to act as operational training establishments to turn out instructors, who could then pass on what they had learnt to the next intake.

Production of bombers was given priority, as a deterrent was needed to prevent France or Great Britain interfering in German rearmament and Hitler's plans for expanding the Reich. General Wever was an adherent of the theories on strategic bombing put forward by the Italian General Giulio Douhet and made plans for the Luftwaffe to be equipped with a four-engined heavy bomber. The programme was

known as the 'Ural bomber', as it would have the range to hit targets beyond the Soviet mountain range. Prototypes of the Dornier Do 19 and Junkers Ju 89 were built and flown.

General Wever died on June 3, 1936, when the Heinkel He 70 he was flying crashed. Wever's replacement as Chief of the Air Staff was Albert Kesselring, previously the head of the Luftwaffe's administrative office, an advocate of tactical air power. Kesselring was informed by Göring that Hitler would only ask how many bombers had been produced, not how far they could fly or the weight of bombs they could carry, and as three twin-engine aircraft cost the same as two four-engine aircraft to produce, development of the Do 19 and Ju 89 was abandoned.

This decision left the Luftwaffe without a true heavy bomber. Ironically, on the same day of Wever's accident the RLM issued the specification that would lead to the Heinkel He 177, the only heavy bomber to enter production for the Luftwaffe, although it was not ready by the time of the Battle of Britain.

CONDOR LEGION

During 1935, the Luftwaffe continued to increase in size, while purely military designs were evaluated at its test facility at Rechlin, such as the Junkers Ju 87. In following years the Dornier Do 17, Junkers Ju 88, Heinkel He 111 and Messerschmitt Bf 109 were each sent to the flight test centre in northern Germany, all going on to play a large role with the Luftwaffe during World War Two. At the time they appeared, all four were equal to – if not better than – their counterparts designed in other European nations. Expansion of the manufacturing base allowed production rates to increase to meet the demands of the growing Luftwaffe. The only factor that the new air force appeared to lack was experience of modern air combat techniques.

> *"At the time it was revealed the Luftwaffe had a strength of 20,000 men and 1,888 aircraft"*

An opportunity to rectify this problem presented itself when Spanish right-wing army officers, led by General Francisco Franco, rebelled against the socialist 'Republican' government on July 18, 1936. Within weeks, 20 Junkers Ju 52/3m bomber-transports and six Heinkel He 51 fighters, along with 85 'volunteers', were sent to Spain to support Franco's Nationalist forces. The Ju 52/3ms were initially used to transport troops loyal to Franco to Seville from Tétouan in northern Morocco, one of history's first mass airlifts.

In November 1936, the Legion Condor (Condor Legion) was formed, commanded by Generalmajor ('Brigadier General') Hugo Sperrle. From January 1937, his Chief of Staff was General Wolfram Freiherr von Richthofen, who was responsible for evaluating tactics, doctrine and strategy, especially close air support and dive bomber operations.

The deployment was manned by German 'volunteers', selected from Luftwaffe units, and these were rotated to the Legion to gain combat experience. Many of the pilots who served in Spain went on to become aces and leading bomber crews during World War Two. Fighter pilot Werner Mölders, who eventually achieved a total of 115 victories, scored his first 15 against Republican aircraft. During his time in Spain he also helped developed the Rotte ('pairs') and Schwarm ('finger four') formations, which were better suited to fighter operations than the three aircraft Kette ('chain') previously used. Operations over Spain provided the Luftwaffe with a chance to refine the tactical support techniques vital to the army during the Blitzkreig campaigns across Europe.

GÖRING

Hermann Göring was the Luftwaffe's commander-in-chief from the day the air force was revealed to the world until dismissed from the post by Hitler in April 1945. He had a large impact on the development and use of the service.

An ace in World War One with 22 victories and a leading member of the Nationalist Socialist German Workers' (Nazi) Party, he was immensely proud of 'his' Luftwaffe and used his political influence to strengthen it during the 1930s. He had little understanding of the changes to air power since World War One and no interest in the logistics or technicalities vital to the service. Many of his decisions were based on instinct, rather than the facts, and as a former fighter pilot he favoured that arm of the Luftwaffe above others. As such, many of the decisions he implemented were detrimental to the development or effectiveness of the Luftwaffe, such as his championing of the Zerstörer (destroyer) heavy fighter concept, which saw resources funnelled to the Messerschmitt Bf 110 instead of more manoeuvrable single-engine fighters.

Göring tended to take personal command of high profile operations or those that were important to Hitler. His loyalty to Hitler was rewarded in September 1939, when he was designated as the Führer's successor and deputy in all his offices. Following the fall of France in 1940, Göring was presented with the title Reichsmarschall.

While his boast that the Luftwaffe alone would be able to force the British to surrender failed to become a reality – damaging his authority among many serving Luftwaffe officers – his power and influence reached its zenith in the autumn of 1941, after the initial phase of the invasion of the Soviet Union. His decline began to accelerate when the tide of war turned against Germany the following year.

Luftwaffe EAGLES

In many respects, the quality of Luftwaffe airmen was at its peak at the start of the Battle of Britain. The pilots and aircrew facing the RAF in 1940 were among the best in the world.

ABOVE: Aircrew of 1./ZG 26 in front of a Messerschmitt Bf 110C of I.Gruppe. The best airmen in the Luftwaffe were selected to fly the 'Zerstörer', but most aces flew Bf 109s. David Willis Collection

TOP RIGHT: Well trained ground personnel were crucial to the success of the Luftwaffe in their campaigns across Europe. Key Collection

Many had gained combat experience during the campaigns across Europe, perfecting tactics that they would employ during operations over England. With a string of victorious campaigns behind them, morale was high and they had been well trained by an efficient system.

By the time a bomber pilot joined an operational unit he had amassed between 220 to 270 flying hours, while those assigned to fighter or dive bomber units had 150 to 200 hours. Most began their flying careers at an A/B Schule (elementary flying school) where they received 100 to 150 hours, initially in light aircraft before progressing to more powerful types. Pilots selected for single-engine fighters or dive bombers then went directly to specialised training schools on the types they were destined to fly operationally.

Those streamed for multi-engined aircraft passed on to a C Schule, where they acquired a further 50 flight hours, including instrument training for day and night operations. From there the pilots progressed to a specialist school, where they met the other crew members and learnt to fly as a team. After training, new airmen joined an Ergänzung (a replenishment unit) assigned to the Geschwader (literally, 'squadron'), where they would receive operational training.

OVER ENGLAND

The Luftwaffe lost 2,662 airmen during the Battle of Britain, of which 551 were Messerschmitt Bf 109 or Bf 110 pilots and crew. The period of the heaviest losses occurred during September 1940, when slightly fewer than 1,000 were killed. Such heavy attrition of experienced personnel could not easily be replaced.

Unlike their counterparts in the RAF, Luftwaffe pilots did not fly a specific number of sorties before being released for other duties away from the front line. They were granted short breaks on leave instead. Their 'Air Battle for England' was the longest campaign fought by the Luftwaffe since the start of the war, with the increasing losses and persistence of the RAF defenders adding to the stress of its pilots and aircrews. To survive, a pilot had to be good and lucky.

A total of 40 Luftwaffe pilots claimed ten or more victories during the campaign and, of that number, seven airmen shot down more than 20 RAF aircraft.

HELMUT WICK

The leading ace of 'the Air Battle for England' (die Luftschlacht um England, which includes the Blitz period) was Oberleutnant (equivalent to an RAF Flying Officer) Helmut Wick. He joined the Luftwaffe in 1935 and was transferred to 3. Staffel of Jagdgeschwader (JG) 2 on August 30, 1939. His first confirmed kill was a French Air Force Curtiss 75A Hawk flown by the ace Adjudant Camille Plubeau, shot down near Strasbourg in France on November 22, 1939.

Wick arrived on the western front on May 21, 11 days after the launch of the German offensive in the west, and went on to increase his confirmed score to 14 aircraft during the campaign, including three Bloch 151s and a Morane-Saulnier MS406 on June 5. On August 1, he became the Staffelkapitän of 3./JG 2 and on August 27 was awarded the Ritterkreuz (Knight's Cross of the Iron Cross), by which time he had shot down 22 enemy aircraft.

Wick was promoted to Hauptmann (flight lieutenant) on September 4 and took command of 6./JG 2, downing six more RAF aircraft with this unit. Five days later he became the Gruppenkommandeur (group commander) of I./JG 2, and was promoted again to Major on October 20 as the Geschwaderkommodore (wing commander) of the Jagdgeschwader ('fighter wing'). In less than 15 minutes on November 6 he shot down five RAF fighters near the Isle of Wight, his 48th to 52nd confirmed kills.

He achieved his 55th and 56th victories on November 28 before being shot down by the British ace Flight Lieutenant John Dundas of 609 'West Riding' Squadron. Although Wick baled out of his damaged aircraft, he came down in the sea and his body was never found. During his career Wick flew a total of 168 combat sorties.

Confirmed Kills of the Top Luftwaffe Aces During the Air Battle for England		
Ace	Total	Unit
Oberleutnant Helmut Wick	42	I./JG 2
Major Adolf Galland	35	III./JG 26, Stab/JG 26
Hauptmann Walter Oesau	34	III./JG 51
Major Werner Mölders	28	Stab JG 51
Oberleutnant Hermann-Friedrich Joppien	26	I./JG 51
Oberleutnant Herbert Ihlefeld	24	I./LG 2
Hauptmann Gerhard Schöpfel	23	III./JG 26

The occupation of Belgium, France, the Netherlands and Luxembourg made many airfields available to the Luftwaffe. More than 400 different aerodromes in the Low Countries and northern France were used, many acting as dispersal sites to protect its aircraft against raids by RAF Bomber Command. The Bristol Blenheims of 2 (Bomber) Group began to undertake daylight attacks on airfields in Europe during July, with the number of sorties nearly doubling to 714 the following month. Heavy losses were inflicted on the RAF bomber crews.

The Luftwaffe's dispersal scheme, along with efforts to camouflage its aircraft on the ground using nets and nature cover, was extremely effective. The switch by Bomber Command to night attacks, a change made to reduce the rate of attrition of the Blenheims, made hitting the Luftwaffe's airfields more difficult.

QUANTITY AND QUALITY

The Luftwaffe defined its airfields by role and facilities, ranging from remote dispersals (Aussenliegeplatz) and transit airfields

(Zwischenlandeplatz) with limited or no infrastructure, to Flugplatz (airfield) or Flughafen (airport) equipped with the full range of services. More than 30 different classifications were used.

Work to improve existing airfields in Holland started soon after the start of the occupation, using personnel from the German State Labour Service. New concrete runways were laid, dispersals with aircraft shelters built and equipment installed for navigation and lighting, allowing them to house the bombers of the Kampfgeschwader.

France had initiated its own expansion programme during 1939 to increase the number of airfields in the northeast of the country, with some of the work completed by June 1940. Between June and September 1940 the Germans also built a large number of landing grounds along the Channel coast in preparation for the attack on Britain. By the end of the year, more than 700 airfields and landing strips were available to the Luftwaffe in France.

Each airfield was managed by a Fliegerhorstkommandantur (Fl.H.Kdtr, 'air base command') or a Flugplatzkommando (Fl.Pl.Kdo, 'airfield command'). Two kinds of Fliegerhorstkommandantur existed. The Fl.H.Kdtr A had between 200 to 400 personnel and were based at sites with full services. The Fl.H.Kdtr E were smaller groups with 150 to 224 officers and men. They were designed to be self-contained, mobile units to service the needs of

operational airfields near the front line. Flugplatzkommando usually operated at smaller airfields or landing fields, where fewer personnel (12 to 150) were required.

GROUND SUPPORT

Each Geschwader usually had a Fliegerhorstkompanie ('airfield company') assigned for minor repairs and servicing. Around 150 men were required for a fighter Geschwader and 80 for a bomber unit, the latter relying more heavily on a Luftgau ('air district') to keep it operational. The Luftgau was the Luftwaffe's dedicated support organisation. Luftgaue were stationary commands assigned to fixed geographic areas and each Luftflotte was assigned at least one for operational support. Additional units were established after the occupation of Europe and named after their location, rather than the Roman numerals used to identify those operating in Germany. The organisation responsible for Belgium and northern France was Luftgau Belgien-Nordfrankreich, which had its headquarters in Brussels, Belgium.

Luftgaue freed the flying units from duties such as administration, supply and maintenance, air defence of airfields and communications. Each was typically divided into five Flughafenbericht Kommandanturen ('airfield regional commands'), below which were five or more Einsatzhafen Kommandanturen ('operational airfield commands').

Occupied **AIRFIELDS**

As soon as armed resistance on continental Europe ceased, the Luftwaffe began to move into the airfields of the defeated nations, often hiding its aircraft among the wrecks and damaged buildings it had struck just weeks earlier.

The LUFTWAFFE

German air power was organised along different lines to the RAF. Many of the flying units of the Luftwaffe have no direct equivalent with the British service, although the system behind its organisation was simple and logical.

Overall control of the three German armed forces rested with the Oberkommando der Wehrmacht (OKW, Supreme Headquarters of the Armed Forces), which reported to the Führer, Adolf Hitler. The Luftwaffe was directed from the Reichsluftfahrtministerium (RLM, Reichs Air Ministry). It was split into the Oberkommando der Luftwaffe (OKL, Supreme Headquarters of the Air Force), responsible for the day-to-day running of the Luftwaffe via a number of directorates, and the office of the Reichsminister der Luftfahrt (Reich Minister for Air) that dealt with political, industrial and longer-term planning, as well as civil aviation.

The RLM reported to the Oberbefehlshaber der Luftwaffe (Ob.d.L., Commander-in-Chief of the Air Force), the World War One ace and leading member of the National Socialist German Workers' (Nazi) Party, Reichsmarschall Hermann Göring.

LUFTFLOTTEN

The vast majority of the Luftwaffe's operational units were assigned to regional commands, known as Luftflotten (Air Fleets, the 'n' indicating the plural in the German language), rather than by function as in the RAF. As the title suggests, each Luftflotten was equipped with a full range of combat aircraft including fighters, bombers, reconnaissance and army co-operation types, as well as others assigned to support units for second line functions such as the collection of meteorological data.

They were designed to project air power or provide air defence, as well as provide tactical support to the army. Probably the closest analogy to Luftflotten created by the Allies were the Tactical Air Forces established to support the D-Day landings.

ABOVE: **Dornier Do 17Z 'U5+EA' on a Queen Mary trailer in the centre of Norwich, after being shot down by ground fire on August 23, 1940. Luftwaffe codes represented the unit (first two, 'U5' is KG 2), Staffel or Stab (last letter, 'A' for the Geschwader Stab) and an individual identification (in this case 'E').** Malcolm V Lowe Collection

Four Luftflotten existed at the start of the war, each roughly responsible for a quarter of the territory then incorporated within the Reich. Luftflotte 1 controlled the assets in northeast Germany and the enclave of East Prussia; Luftflotte 2 northwest Germany; Luftflotte 3 southwest Germany, while Luftflotte 4 operated over southeast Germany and the Protectorate of Bohemia and Moravia (Czech Republic) and Austria.

As further countries were subjugated, the area each Luftflotten was responsible for expanded into the contiguous territory. In the west, Luftflotte 2 became responsible for the units based in the Netherlands and the northern half of Belgium. Following the armistice with France on June 22, 1940, a German occupation zone was established in the north and west of the country, including the Atlantic coastline. Luftflotte 3 expanded west to incorporate units based in the newly acquired area.

Operation Weserübung ('Weser exercise'), the invasion of Denmark and Norway, began on April 9, 1940. Denmark was under German control in a mere six hours, while the Norwegian Army was forced to capitulate on June 10. Luftflotte 5 was established on April 12 to control Luftwaffe assets during the invasion. It transferred its headquarters from Hamburg to the Norwegian capital Oslo 12 days later.

Individual units frequently transferred between the Luftflotten as forces were concentrated in a region during a campaign. Three of the five (2, 3 and 5) were directly involved in the Battle of Britain.

Fliegerkorps (Air Corps) controlled a number of units for operational purposes. They were usually subordinated to the Luftflotte with, for example, I. Fliegerkorps under Luftflotte 2 during the summer of 1940. Individual Fliegerkorps were identified by Roman numerals, the full stop after the number performing the same function as the 'st', 'nd', 'rd' or 'th' (as in first, second, third and fourth) in English.

FLYING UNITS

The basic Luftwaffe flying unit for operational and administrative purposes was the Gruppe, which translates as 'group'. In the RAF, a group was an organisation just below the command level, usually comprising a number of squadrons with the same role or based in the same region. There is no direct equivalent to the Gruppe within the RAF. A Gruppe typically had a Stab (literally 'staff', but meaning headquarters) flight, with an authorised strength of three aircraft, and three Staffeln (literally, 'seasons'), each with nine to 12, for a combined total of 30 to 39 aircraft. Three Gruppen were typically assigned to a Geschwader and were numbered I. to III. although some single-seat fighter units sometimes had a fourth or even fifth Gruppe added later in the war. The nine Staffeln within the Geschwader were identified as 1. to 9. Staffel, the first three assigned to I. Gruppe, the second trio to II. Gruppe and 7. to 9. to III. Gruppe.

Although Geschwader translates as 'squadron', coming from the naval use of the word, in the Luftwaffe it was the largest autonomous and mobile flying unit, somewhat equivalent ⟩

Luftwaffe Order of Battle 13 August 1940		
Oberbefehlshaber der Luftwaffe HQ Berlin, Germany		
Aufklärungsgruppe Ob.d.L.		Berlin, Germany
1(F)./AufklGr.OkL	various recce aircraft	
2(F)./AufklGr.OkL	Do 215, He 111H	
Wettererkundungskette Ob.d.L.		
Wekusta 1/Ob.d.L.	Do 17Z, He 111H	Oldenburg, Germany
Wekusta 2/Ob.d.L.	He 111H	Brest/Lanveoc-Poulmic, France
Luftflotte 2 HQ Brussels, Belgium		
Wekusta 26	Do 17, He 111, Bf 110	Brussels-Grimbergen, Belgium
I. Fliegerkorps HQ Beauvais, France		
Kampfgeschwader 1 'Hindenburg'		
Stab KG 1	He 111H	Rosières-en-Santerre, France
I./KG 1	He 111H	Montdidier, France
II./KG 1	He 111H-1/H-27	Montdidier, France
III./KG 1	He 111H-2	Rosières-en-Santerre, France
Kampfgeschwader 76		
Stab KG 76	Do 17Z	Cormeilles-en-Vexin, France
I./KG 76	Do 17Z-1	Beauvais, France
II./KG 76	Ju 88A-1	Creil, France
III./KG 76	Do 17Z-2/3	Cormeilles-en-Vexin, France
5(F)./AufKlGr 122	Do 17P, He 111H, Ju 88A	Haute-Fontaine, France
II. Fliegerkorps HQ Ghent, Belgium		
Kampfgeschwader 2 'Holzhammer'		
Stab KG 2	Do 17Z-2	Arras, France
I./KG 2	Do 17Z-2/Z-3	Épinoy, France
II./KG 2	Do 17Z-2/Z-3	Arras, France
III./KG 2	Do 17Z-2	Cambrai, France
Kampfgeschwader 3 'Blitz'		
Stab KG 3	Do 17Z-2	Le Culot, Belgium
I./KG 3	Do 17Z-2	Le Culot, Belgium
II./KG 3	Do 17Z-2/Z-3	Antwerp/Deurne, Netherlands
III./KG 3	Do 17Z-2	Saint-Truiden, Belgium
Kampfgeschwader 53 'Legion Condor'		
Stab KG 53	He 111H-2	Lille-Nord, France
I./KG 53	He 111H-2	Lille-Nord, France
II./KG 53	He 111H-2/H-3	Lille-Nord, France
III./KG 53	He 111H-2/H-3/H-4	Lille-Nord, France
Sturzkampfgeschwader 1		
II./StG 1	Ju 87B	Pas de Calais, France
IV(St)./StG 1	Ju 87B-2	Tramecourt, France
Erprobungsgruppe 210		
1./ErpGr 210	Bf 110C/D	Calais Marck, France
2./ErpGr 210	Bf 110C/D	Calais Marck, France
3./ErpGr 210	Bf 109E	Calais Marck, France
Lehrgeschwader 2		
I(J)./LG 2	Bf 109E	Leeuwarden, the Netherlands
II(Sch)./LG 2	Bf 109E-7	Böblingen, Germany
7(F)./LG 2	Bf 110	Ghent/Brussels, Belgium
9(H)./LG 2	Bf 110, Hs 126	Belgium
IX. Fliegerkorps HQ Soesterberg, the Netherlands		
Kampfgeschwader 4 'General Wever'		
Stab KG 4	He 111P	Soesterberg, the Netherlands
I./KG 4	He 111H-4	Soesterberg, the Netherlands
II./KG 4	He 111P-2	Eindhoven, the Netherlands
III./KG 4	Ju 88	Schiphol, the Netherlands
Kampfgruppe 100	He 111H-1/H-2/H-3	Vannes-Meucon, France
Kampfgruppe 126	He 111H	Marx, Germany
3(F)./AufKlGr 122	He 111H, Ju 88A	Eindhoven, the Netherlands
Jagdfliegerführer 2 HQ Wissant, France		
Jagdgeschwader 3 'Udet'		
Stab JG 3	Bf 109E	Wierre au Bois, France
I./JG 3	Bf 109E	Colembert, France
II./JG 3	Bf 109E	Samer, France
III./JG 3	Bf 109E	Desvres and Le Touquet, France
Jagdgeschwader 26 'Schlageter'		
Stab JG 26	Bf 109E	Audembert, France
I./JG 26	Bf 109E	Audembert, France
II./JG 26	Bf 109E	Marquise-Ost, France
III./JG 26	Bf 109E	Caffiers, France

Jagdgeschwader 51		
Stab JG 51	Bf 109E	Wissant, France
I./JG 51	Bf 109E	Wissant, France
II./JG 51	Bf 109E	Wissant, France
III./JG 51	Bf 109E	St Omer-Clairmarais, France
Jagdgeschwader 52		
Stab JG 52	Bf 109E	Coquelles, France
I./JG 52	Bf 109E	Coquelles, France
II./JG 52	Bf 109E	Peuplingues, France
Jagdgeschwader 54 'Grünherz'		
Stab JG 54	Bf 109E	Campagne-les-Guines, France
I./JG 54	Bf 109E	Guînes-en-Calaisis, France
II./JG 54	Bf 109E	Hermalinghen, France
III./JG 54	Bf 109E	Guînes-en-Calaisis, France
Zerstörergeschwader 26 'Horst Wessel'		
Stab ZG 26	Bf 110C	Lille, France
I./ZG 26	Bf 110C/D	Yvrench-St Omer, France
II./ZG 26	Bf 110C/D	Crécy-St Omer, France
III./ZG 26	Bf 110C-2/C-4	Barly-Arques, France
Zerstörergeschwader 76		
Stab ZG 76	Bf 110C	Laval, France
II./ZG 76	Bf 110C	Abbeville, France
III./ZG 76	Bf 110C	Laval, France

Luftflotte 3 HQ Paris, France		
Wekusta 51	Do 17, He 111	Versailles-Buc, France

IV. Fliegerkorps HQ Dinard, France		
Lehrgeschwader 1		
Stab LG 1	Ju 88A	Orléans-Bricy, France
I./LG 1	Ju 88A-5	Orléans-Bricy, France
II./LG 1	Ju 88A-1	Orléans-Bricy, France
III./LG 1	Ju 88A-5	Chateaudun, France
Kampfgeschwader 27 'Boelcke'		
Stab KG 27	He 111P	Tours, France
I./KG 27	He 111P	Tours, France
II./KG 27	He 111P/H-3	Dinard, France
III./KG 27	He 111P	Dinard, France
Kampfgeschwader 40		
Stab KG 40	Ju 88A-1	Bordeaux-Mérignac, France
I./KG 40	Fw 200C-1	Bordeaux-Mérignac, France
Sturzkampfgeschwader 3		
Stab/StG 3	Ju 87B, He 111H, Do 17M/Z	Caen, France
Kampfgrüppe 806	Ju 88A	Nantes, France
3(F)./AufKlGr 31	Do 17P, Ju 88, Bf 110	Rennes, France
3(F)./AufKlGr 121	Ju 88	northwest France

V. Fliegerkorps HQ Villacoublay, France		
Kampfgeschwader 51 'Edelweiss'		
Stab KG 51	Ju 88A-1	Orly, France
I./KG 51	Ju 88A-1	Melun, France
II./KG 51	Ju 88A-1	Orly, France
III./KG 51	Ju 88A-1	Orly, France
Kampfgeschwader 54 'Totenkopf'		
Stab KG 54	Ju 88A-1	Évreux, France
I./KG 54	Ju 88A-1	Évreux, France
II./KG 54	Ju 88A-1	St André-de-L'Eure, France
Kampfgeschwader 55 'Greif'		
Stab KG 55	He 111P-2	Villacoublay, France
I./KG 55	He 111H/P	Dreux, France
II./KG 55	He 111H-3/P	Chartres, France
III./KG 55	He 111P-2	Villacoublay, France
4(F)./AufKlGr 14	Do 17M/P, Bf 110	Raum Cherbourg, France
4(F)./AufKlGr 121	Do 17P, Ju 88A	Villacoublay, France

VIII. Fliegerkorps HQ Deauville, France		
Sturzkampfgeschwader 1		
Stab/StG I	Ju 87B	Angers, France
I./StG I	Ju 87R	Angers, France
Sturzkampfgeschwader 2 'Immelmann'		
Stab/StG 2	Ju 87B	St Malo, France
I./StG 2	Ju 87B	St Malo, France
II./StG 2	Ju 87B-2/R-1	Lannion, France

ABOVE: The Adler (eagle) on the nose of this Junkers Ju 88A-1 identifies it as belonging to KG 30. Malcolm V Lowe Collection

to an RAF wing. A typical Geschwader would have around 90 aircraft (at least in theory), although this figure varied widely during the war.

A Geschwader operated aircraft for a single role, which was identified in its title, such as Jagdgeschwader (JG, 'hunting squadron'), Kampfgeschwader (KG, 'struggle', but meaning bomber), Zerstörergeschwader (ZG, 'destroyer', twin-engined fighter) and Sturzkampfgeschwader (StG, dive bomber). Many units were named in honour of a distinguished person, including several after World War One aces.

A Jagdfliegerführer ('fighter air leader') was a functional command responsible for fighter operations, reporting directly to the commander of a Luftflotte. During the Battle of Britain, Jagdfliegerführer 2 was part of Luftflotte 2, and Jagdfliegerführer 3 Luftflotte 3.

ABOVE: Junkers Ju 88A-5 w/n 6129 of 7./KG 4 was shot down on October 27, 1940. The bat and moon emblem reflected the nocturnal operations of the unit. Malcolm V Lowe Collection

INDEPENDENT UNITS

An exception to the general rule was the Lehrgeschwader (LG, literally 'teaching squadron') that undertook operational testing of aircraft and developed new tactics. Each of their Gruppen could operate a different type of aircraft, with the role identified by a letter or letters contained with brackets after the unit number; 'J' for Jagd ('fighter'), 'K' (Kampf, 'bomber'), 'Sch' (Schlacht, 'combat'), 'St' (Stuka) and 'Z' (Zestörer). An example is I(J)./LG 2, which flew Messerschmitt Bf 109Es from Leeuwarden in the Netherlands.

Standard abbreviations were used to identify different components of a Geschwader, made possible by the combination of Arabic and Roman numerals and the logical numbering of the Staffel. For example, II. Gruppe of Kampfgeschwader 2 could be represented as II./KG 2, and 5. Staffel in the same Gruppe as 5./KG 2.

ABOVE: Harry von Bülow-Bothcamp, the Geschwaderkommodore (commanding officer) of JG 2 in front of his Messerschmitt Bf 109E-3. Single-seat fighters did not carry the standard alpha-numeric identification markings. Malcolm V Lowe Collection

ABOVE: Kampfgeschwader 51 had the knickname 'Edelweiss', the mountain flower appearing in the unit's emblem, as carried by the Ju 88A-1 being examined by British technicians in 1940. Malcolm V Lowe Collection

Some Gruppen operated independent of a Geschwader, including the majority tasked with reconnaissance (Aufklärungsgruppen, AufKlGr) and coastal operations (Küstenfliegergruppen, KüFlGr). They could be identified as unassigned units because unlike the majority of Geschwader they used Arabic rather than Roman numerals, and had up to five consecutively numbered Staffeln.

Aufklärungsgruppen were divided into two categories, depending on role, distinguished by either an 'F' or 'H' in brackets after the Staffel number; H for Heer (the abbreviation for Heeresaufklärungsgruppe, 'army reconnaissance group') or F for Fern (Fernaufklärungsgruppe, 'long range reconnaissance group'). As an example, 5(F)./122, based at Haute-Fontaine in France, was the fifth Staffel of long-range reconnaissance group 122.

Another independent unit involved in the Battle of Britain was Erprobungsgruppe (ErpGr) 210, a test unit formed on July 1, 1940, to evaluate the Messerschmitt Bf 109E and Bf 110 in the fighter-bomber and dive bombing roles in operational conditions, while awaiting deliveries of the delayed Bf 210 (from which it derived its numerical designation).

A few independent Staffeln were also assigned to Luftflotten, many of which were concerned with meteorological reconnaissance (Wettererkundungstaffel, abbreviated as Wekusta or Westa).

OTHER SERVICES

Luftflotte 2, 3 and 5 were the main Luftwaffe organisations responsible for prosecuting the campaign against Britain in the second half of 1940. Several other Luftwaffe formations were also involved, in supporting roles. They included the Seenotdienst (sea rescue service), which operated a fleet of small surface craft and water-borne aircraft around the coasts of Germany and the occupied territory.

Naval aviation was divided between two air groups for the east and west, the latter assigned to the Führer der Luft West (commander of air west). It was administrated by the Luftwaffe and operationally controlled by the Kreigsmarine (navy) and was a frequent subject of friction between the commanders of the two, which increased when the Küstenfliegergruppe (coastal air group) began to replace their seaplanes with Dornier Do 17s.

ABOVE: Dornier Do 17Z of Stab/KG 3 based at Le Culot in Belgium in mid-August 1940. Key Collection

Sturzkampfgeschwader 77		
Stab/StG 77	Ju 87B	Caen, France
I./StG 77	Ju 87B	Caen, France
II./StG 77	Ju 87B	Caen, France
III./StG 77	Ju 87B	Caen, France
V(Z)./LG 1	Bf 110C/D	Caen, France
2(F)./AufKlGr 11	Do 17P, Bf 110	Raum Bernay, France
2(F)./AufKlGr 123	Do 17P	Paris, France
Jagdfliegerführer 3 HQ Deauville, France		
Jagdgeschwader 2 'Richthofen'		
Stab JG 2	Bf 109E	Beaumont-le-Roger, France
I./JG 2	Bf 109E	Beaumont-le-Roger, France
II./JG 2	Bf 109E	Beaumont-le-Roger, France
III./JG 2	Bf 109E	Le Havre, France
Jagdgeschwader 27		
Stab JG 27	Bf 109E	Cherbourg-Ouest, France
I./JG 27	Bf 109E	Plumetôt, France
II./JG 27	Bf 109E	Crépon, France
III./JG 27	Bf 109E	Carquebut, France
Jagdgeschwader 53 'Pik As'		
Stab JG 53	Bf 109E	Cherbourg, France
I./JG 53	Bf 109E	Rennes, France
II./JG 53	Bf 109E	Dinan, France
III./JG 53	Bf 109E	Sempy, Brest, France
Zerstörergeschwader 2		
Stab ZG 2	Bf 110C	Toussus-le-Noble, France
I./ZG 2	Bf 110D	Amiens, France
II./ZG 2	Bf 110C-2/C-5/D	Guyancourt, France
Luftflotte 5 HQ Stavanger, Norway		
X. Fliegerkorps HQ Stavanger, Norway		
Wettererkun-dungskette X Fl.Korps	He 111H	Stavanger, Norway
Kampfgeschwader 26 'Löwen'		
Stab KG 26	He 111P	Stavanger, Norway
I./KG 26	He 111H-3/H-4	Stavanger, Norway
III./KG 26	He 111H-3/H-4	Stavanger, Norway
Kampfgeschwader 30 'Adler'		
Stab KG 30	Ju 88A-1	Aalborg, Denmark
I./KG 30	Ju 88C	Aalborg, Denmark
II./KG 30	Ju 88	Aalborg, Denmark
III./KG 30	Ju 88C-2	Aalborg, Denmark
Zerstörergeschwader 76		
I./ZG 76	Bf 110	Stavanger-Forus, Norway
Jagdgeschwader 77 'Herz As'		
II./JG 77	Bf 109E	Stavanger-Trondheim, Norway
Küstenfliegergruppe 506		
Stab/KüFlGr 506	He 115	Stavanger, Norway
1./KüFlGr 506	He 115	Stavanger, Norway
2./KüFlGr 506	He 115	Stavanger, Norway
3./KüFlGr 506	He 115	Stavanger, Norway
2(F)./AufKlGr 22	Do 17P/M	Stavanger, Norway
1(F)./AufKlGr 120	He 111H, Ju 88	Stavanger, Norway
1(F)./AufKlGr 121	He 111H, Ju 88A	Stavanger, Norway
1(F)./Aufkl.Gr.OkL	Do 215, He 111H, Bf 110C	Stavanger, Norway
Seenotdienst	He 59	dets at Sola, Bergen and Trondheim, Norway
Führer der Luft West HQ Jever		
Küstenfliegergruppe 406		
3./KüFlGr 406	Do 18	Hörnum, Germany
2./KüFlGr 106	Do 18	Rantum, Germany
2./KüFlGr 906	Do 18	Hörnum, Germany
Küstenfliegergruppe 706		
1./KüFlGr 406	Do 18	Stavanger, Norway
2./KüFlGr 406	Do 18	Stavanger, Norway
Küstenfliegergruppe 606		
1./KüFlGr 606	Do 17	Brest, France
2./KüFlGr 606	Do 17	Brest, France
3./KüFlGr 606	Do 17	Brest, France
Küstenfliegergruppe 106		
1./KüFlGr 106	He 115	Norderney, Norway

Notes: Excludes support units and those with types not involved in the Battle of Britain, such as the Henschel Hs 126 and communications/liaison aircraft. The Luftwaffe frequently changed bases and dispersed its aircraft among many airfields.

THE AIRCRAFT
of the Luftwaffe

By mid-1940 the Luftwaffe was the largest and most powerful air force in Europe.

Before the Battle of Britain, the Luftwaffe had accomplished all that had been asked of it. Equipped with modern aircraft flown by pilots and crews with recent combat experience, it had gained a fearsome reputation for efficiency. In less than nine months it vanquished the air forces of Poland, Denmark, Norway, Belgium, the Netherlands and France. Only the RAF remained undefeated.

Throughout World War Two the German army was the country's predominant military force. During 1939 and the first half of 1940, the Luftwaffe's main mission was to support the army as it put the theory of Blitzkrieg ('lightning war') into practice. In general, its air force was well equipped for the tactical role it was required to perform in the early phases of the war, gaining air superiority and acting in co-ordination with the ground forces to bring a swift collapse of its opponents.

Blitzkrieg helped shape the composition and equipment of the Luftwaffe during its formative years. Specialised ground attack aircraft, of which the Junkers Ju 87 was the classic example, were designed to provide the army with mobile artillery. Fast medium bombers were able to attack targets behind the battlefield, such as reinforcements moving up to the front.

The main bomber aircraft operated by the Luftwaffe in the first years of the war originally entered service to provide Germany with a deterrent, a counter to any possible consideration by the French or British governments of interfering in the Nazi leadership's plans to annex the territory of surrounding countries. Both the Dornier Do 17 and Heinkel He 111 carried a small bomb load in comparison with later (Allied) designs, but they were fast for their time and adequate for tactical roles in support of the army. The later Junkers Ju 88 repeated the formula.

All three were found wanting when the Luftwaffe was directed to strike London during the Luftschlacht um England (Air Battle for England). By mid-1940, it was clear that raids by unescorted bombers during daylight would result in unsustainable levels of attrition, which reduced significantly when operations were conducted at night. While London suffered heavily during the Battle of Britain and the Blitz, the weight of bombs dropped was small compared with the raids on the German cities later conducted by RAF Bomber Command.

Germany's failure to produce a four-engine heavy bomber has often been cited as one of the reasons why the Luftwaffe was ultimately unsuccessful in its attempt to force Britain to seek an accommodation with Germany in 1940. Large strategic bombers were not considered to be essential to the Luftwaffe's core force in the late 1930s, when Germany's aircraft industry was already stretched to meet the demand for medium bombers and fighters. The emphasis was placed on building the maximum number of bombers, rather than the weight of bombs that could be carried. When it was decided that a heavier bomber was required, the aircraft selected, the Heinkel He 177, had a particularly difficult gestation, primarily because of its over-complex Daimler-Benz DB610 engine (and their tendency to catch fire) and efforts to turn it into a dive bomber.

FIGHTERS

Priority was only given to ramping-up fighter production late in the year before the war started, to bolster defence against potential raids by the RAF or French Air Force. Of the two types selected for mass production, the Messerschmitt Bf 109 was among the best single-seat fighters available in the world at the time. Although originally designed for defence, the Bf 109 was successfully employed offensively, establishing control of the skies ahead of the advancing German army during the campaigns of 1939 and first half of 1940. The only operation in which it did not play a large role was over Denmark and Norway, its limited endurance precluding service against the latter country.

The second fighter, the twin-engined Messerschmitt Bf 110, was conceived out of the flawed Zerstörer (destroyer) concept for a heavily armed aircraft with endurance and long range to sweep ahead of the bombers. It lacked the speed and manoeuvrability to match the latest generation of single-seat fighters and suffered accordingly.

Messerschmitt
Bf 109E

The Messerschmitt Bf 109 was the only single-seat fighter operated by the Luftwaffe over England in 1940. Luftwaffe pilots flew the aircraft from the start of World War Two until the final destruction of the Reich in May 1945. The fighter became the mount of more aces than any other type in the history of air combat.

By the start of the Battle of Britain, the Jagdgruppen ('fighter groups') were equipped with the fourth major variant of the Bf 109, the E series or 'Emil' as it was affectionately known. The first production version, the Bf 109B – known as the 'Bertha' – was powered by the Junkers Jumo 210Da and armed with a pair of 0.31in (7.92mm) MG17 machine guns. Initial aircraft were delivered to the Richthofen Geschwader, JG 132, in February 1937, but soon after converting to the new type, the personnel of II./JG 132 departed for Spain to join the Condor Legion's 2. Staffel der Jagdgruppe ('squadron of fighter group') 88. The

Heinkel He 51 biplanes flown by the German 'volunteers' in support of the Spanish Nationalists were outclassed by the Polikarpov I-16 monoplanes of the Republican forces, but the arrival of the Bf 109B helped level the playing field.

The fighting in Spain played a large role in the development of the Bf 109. Combat experience allowed the Luftwaffe to develop better tactics and gave it a cache of pilots who went on to became leading aces, including Werner Mölders and Adolf Galland. It also highlighted deficiencies in its aircraft, prompting improved versions, and the Bf 109 was no exception. The 'Clara' (Bf 109C) was powered by the

Jumo 210Ga with a deeper radiator bath beneath the nose and added a pair of wing-mounted MG17s to the guns in the nose of the 'Bertha'. Deliveries of Bf 109C-1s began in the early spring of 1938.

DORA TO EMIL

The tenth Bf 109 Versuchs (experimental/developmental) airframe (Bf 109 V10) had its Jumo engine replaced with a Daimler-Benz DB600Aa in June 1937 to serve as the prototype for the combination, effectively becoming the prototype Bf 109D. While it crashed the following month, development continued. Only around 200 production Bf 109D-1s

"'Emil' pilots shot down 272 Hurricanes and 219 Spitfires during the Battle of Britain"

were built, differing little from the 'Clara' aft of the firewall. The 'Dora' was considered a stopgap to allow deliveries of the fighter to continue while Daimler-Benz ironed out the teething problems with the definitive DB601. This version had a Bosch fuel injector instead of a float carburettor, permitting negative g to be pulled without cutting off the supply to the engine (during the transition from level flight to a dive), as well as better economy and greater reliability than its predecessor. It was first installed in Bf 109 V14. Perfecting the DB601 took more time than planned and quantity production only started in 1938, primarily for installation in Heinkel He 111s before priority moved to fighter production later the same year.

Ten pre-series Bf 109E-0s were built by late 1938 for service evaluation, with the armament eventually becoming standardised on four MG17s, two each in the fuselage and wings. Production of engines lagged behind that of airframes, but Bf 109E-1s powered by the DB601A began to roll off the Bayerische Flugzeugwerke AG production line at Regensburg in early 1939. Others were produced by the Erla Maschinenwerk at Leipzig and Gerhard Fieseler Werke at Kassel, and by Wiener-Neustädter Flugzeugbau in Austria.

ABOVE:
The Messerschmitt Bf 109E bore the brunt of the air fighting over England in the summer of 1940. This aircraft is flying off the French coast, which stood in for the white cliffs of Dover in many German propaganda images. Malcolm V Lowe Collection

Messerschmitt Bf 109E-3

Dimensions: Length 28ft 4½in (8.65m); Wing span 32ft 4½in (9.87m); Height 12ft 0½in (3.67m); Wing area 174sq ft (16.17m²)

Weights: Empty 4,189lb (1,900kg): Empty equipped 4,685lb (2,125kg); Typically loaded 5,875lb (2,665kg)

Powerplant: One Daimler-Benz DB601Aa 12-cylinder inverted Vee, liquid-cooled piston engines, rated at 1,175hp (877kW) for take-off and 1,000hp (746kW) at 12,139ft (3,700m); Fuel capacity 106 imp gal (482 lit)

Armament: One 0.787in (20mm) Oerlikon MG FF cannon in each wing and two fuselage mounted 0.31in (7.92mm) Rheinmetall-Borsig MG17 machine guns, plus additional 20mm (0.787in) MG FF/M cannon mounted in the engine of some aircraft

Performance: Max speed fully loaded, 290mph (467km/h) at sea level, 307mph (494km/h) at 3,280ft (1,000m); 336mph (541km/h) at 19,685ft (6,000m); Max continuous cruise 300mph (483km/h) at 13,123ft (4,000m); Climb rate at 5,401lb (2,450kg), 3,280ft/min (1,000m/min); Service ceiling 34,449ft (10,500m); Range 410 miles (660km)

Crew: One pilot

Delivery of Bf 109E-1s to the Luftwaffe began in February. Some early examples were also sent to Spain for the Condor Legion, but only a few had been assembled and reflown before the bloody civil war ended with the Republican surrender on March 28, 1939.

BF 109 AT WAR

A total of 1,091 Bf 109Es had been completed by the start of 1939. On September 1 the Luftwaffe had 1,056 of all four versions on strength with 24 Gruppen (including some awaiting to receive Messerschmitt Bf 110s), plus two night fighter Staffeln. A total of 946 were serviceable.

Relatively few Bf 109-equipped units were committed to the invasion of Poland, but the Luftwaffe quickly gained air superiority, permitting the Jagdgruppen to be used on ground strafing sorties, that accounted for the majority of the 67 that were lost by September 28.

The Bf 109E-3 began to replace the E-1 on the production lines late in 1939, fitted with the slightly more powerful DB601Aa, which had provision for a 0.787in (20mm) MG FF/M canon mounted in the crankcase, firing through the propeller hub. In practice, the weapon was seldom fitted because »

BELOW: Messerschmitt Bf 109E-4 'Yellow 10' of 9. Staffel of Jagdgeschwader 26, part of Luftflotte 2. The aircraft was flown by the ace Adolf Galland during the Battle of Britain. Pete West

ABOVE:
This Messerschmitt Bf 109E-4 was assigned to II. Gruppe of Jagdgeschwader 3 during 1940. Pete West

BELOW:
Crowds gather around the remains of Oblt Karl Fischer's Bf 109E-1, which came down near Queen Anne's Gate in Windsor Great Park after combat on September 30, 1940. Jim Winchester Collection

it had a tendency to overheat and seize, and vibrate the airframe when used. The subvariant gained its 'Kanonenmaschine' ('cannon machine') nicknamed because the machine guns in the wings of the E-1 were substituted for 0.787in (20mm) MG FF cannons. Thus armed, it was widely regarded by Bf 109 pilots as the best of the early versions.

During the period of the 'Sitzkrieg' (as the Germans called the 'Phoney War', the first few relatively quiet months on the western front) the 'Emil' continued to replace Bf 109B, C and Ds, the latter passing to the nascent night fighting force, which was in the process of being expanded. Infrequent encounters with Morane-Saulnier MS406s of the French Air Force or the Hurricanes of the British Expeditionary Force Air Component helped confirm to its pilots that the Bf 109E was generally better than both. While the Hurricane had the edge in manoeuvrability at low altitude and a tighter turning circle, the Bf 109 could always out-climb its opponent.

One 'fault' of the design that remained constant – and of particular concern to its larger pilots – was the narrow and cramped cockpit. Another that was to become of crucial significance was its short range. This was highlighted during the invasion of Denmark and Norway in April, during which the Bf 109 played only a minimal role, partly because of the limited fighter forces possessed by the Scandinavian countries, but primarily because it did not have the reach.

FRANCE

Lack of range was not a problem for Operation Fall Gelb ('Case Yellow'), the assault on France and the Low Countries. When it started on May 10, 1940, the Luftwaffe committed ten Jagdgeschwader equipped with the Bf 109. It achieved air superiority from the outset, allowing the bombers and Stukas free rein to operate in support of the German army. The fighter force moved forward with the army, frequently moving bases as the front line changed, although the speed of the advance caused problems – Luftwaffe units had to wait for its logistical organisation to catch up. Holland capitulated on May 14, the Belgian army surrendered two weeks later and France signed the armistice on June 22.

Losses among the Jagdgruppen during May and June were light. At the time, the Luftwaffe had few reserves available and production of Bf 109Es was below the figure required to make good heavy attrition and expand the force. Following the armistice, the majority of Bf 109 units were withdrawn to re-equip and recuperate, leaving just the three Gruppen of JG 51 in France.

The French campaign highlighted a need for armour protection and from the summer of 1940 new production Bf 109E-3s were fitted with a heavily framed canopy and metal plates to protect the pilot. Installation of improved MF FF/M cannons in the wing, with an increased rate of fire, created the Bf 109E-4. The 0.787in (20mm) cannon was to prove to be a devastating weapon, easily out-gunning the RAF fighters armed with 0.303in (7.7mm) machine guns.

With the failure of Great Britain to sue for peace, plans were drawn up to continue the fight and the Jagdgruppen began to return west. The build up began on July 12 with the return of III./JG 3 and by the end of the month it had been joined by JG 26, 27 and 52. Others soon followed. Most units were concentrated in Luftflotte 2 in Belgium and the Netherlands, comprising JG 3, 26, 51 and 52, plus the Stab and I./JG54, and the fighter-bombers of 3./Erprobungsgruppe (ErpGr, 'tactical development group') 210. Luftflotte 3 in France had JG 2, 27 and 53. By August 13, the start of the all-out attack on the RAF, designated as Adlertag (Eagle Day), the Jagdgeschwader still only had 80% of their strength before Fall Gelb, with 805 serviceable Bf 109Es.

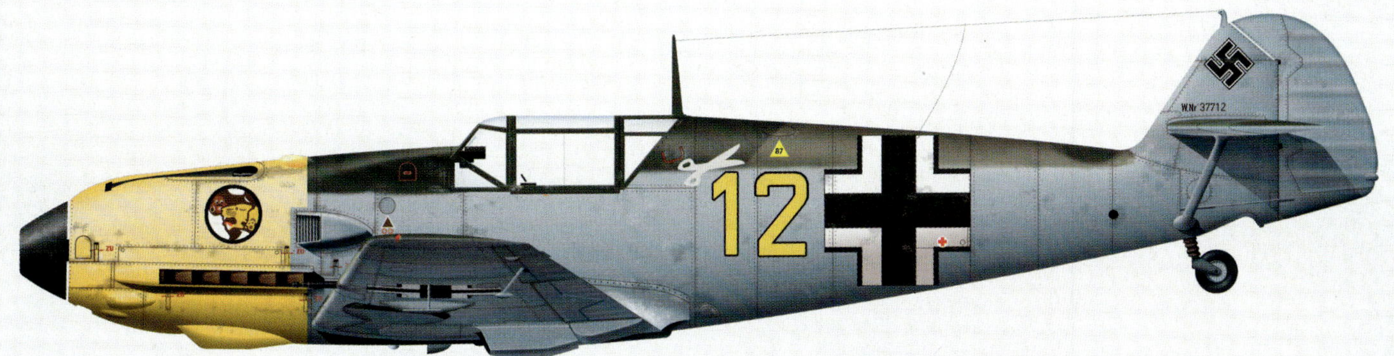

NEW ROLES

Development of the Bf 109 as a Jagdbomber (Jabo, fighter-bomber) and the tactics for its operational use was entrusted to ErpGr. 210, with its 3. Staffel equipped with aircraft fitted with a rack for 110 to 550lb (50 to 250kg) bombs. It started operations against shipping off the British coast in July 1940, attacking targets in a shallow dive. The success of the unit resulted in an order for each Jagdgeschwader to form a Jabo unit, initially with Bf 109E-1s modified as E-1/Bs by adding a bomb rack and later factory-built E-4/Bs, the first version produced without the hollow spinner.

Several other versions were introduced during the Battle of Britain. The Bf 109E-4/N was powered by the DB601N, which had a greater compression rating and burnt higher octane fuel to increase output. Two tactical reconnaissance versions were produced, the Bf 109E-5 and -6, with a different type of camera in the rear fuselage; the E-5 dispensed with the wing-mounted cannons, which were retained in the E-6.

OVER ENGLAND

'Emil' pilots shot down 272 Hurricanes and 219 Spitfires during the Battle of Britain. During the initial weeks operating over England, Bf 109E pilots conducted anti-fighter sweeps, known as freie Jagd ('free hunting') sorties, achieving successes early by employing the aircraft's superiority in the vertical plain – its ability to climb faster than the RAF fighters and 'bunt dive' away – to the full. Many of the Luftwaffe fighter pilots already had combat experience, having served in Spain and on operations over Europe since the beginning of the war. At the start of the campaign they also employed better tactics than their counterparts, such as the loose schwarm ('finger-four'), while the RAF initially stuck to the outdated vic of three before abandoning it and adopting the German formation.

The original division of labour between the Jagdgruppen and Zerstörergruppen was to give the Bf 109s free rein to hunt while the Bf 110s escorted the bombers. It soon became obvious that the twin-engined fighter was not up to the job and from early September the Bf 109 pilots were increasingly ordered to stick close by the bombers, denying them the tactical freedom required to get the best out of their fighters. Limited fuel capacity meant that the 'Emil' could only engage RAF aircraft for around 20 minutes over the southern coast of England, as combat quickly ate into the reserves needed to return to the continent. The Bf 109E had the range to fly only as far west as London. A version that could carry a 66 imp gal (300 lit) jettisonable fuel tank (the Bf 109E-7) was delivered from late August 1940, but the tank was rarely used as it tended to leak and was generally mistrusted by the pilots. The Bf 109's limited range meant that Bf 110 crews had to continue to operate over Britain, with predictable results, while losses also increased among the Jagdgruppen. Luftwaffe records indicate it lost 610 Bf 109s in operations against Britain up to October 31.

ABOVE:
Messerschmitt Bf 109E-3 'Yellow 12' of I. Gruppe of Jagdgeschwader 27, based at Plumetot in France during the Battle of Britain. Pete West

BELOW:
Messerschmitt Bf 109E-4 of Oberleutnant Franz von Werra, the Gruppe Adjutant of II./JG 3, shot down near Marden in Kent on September 5, 1940. Malcolm V Lowe Collection

Messerschmitt
Bf 110

While the Luftwaffe hoped the Bf 110 would prove to be a efficient fighter, it suffered at the hands of more manoeuvrable aircraft. Outclassed by 1940, it went on to become an effective night fighter.

In the 1930s, many countries sought to develop heavily armed fighters with great endurance and long range; the aviation equivalent of the naval destroyer. Germany's military planners were no exception, envisaging that such an aircraft would be well suited to hunting enemy bombers over its territory and pursuing them as they headed back to their bases. The aircraft selected to fulfil the Luftwaffe's Zerstörer (destroyer) requirement was the twin-engined Messerschmitt Bf 110, created by Bayerische Flugzeugwerke AG.

The Zerstörer concept was enthusiastically supported by the Luftwaffe's commander-in chief, Hermann Göring, who dismissed concerns that it would not have the performance or manoeuvrability of lighter, single-engined fighters. Production of the initial Bf 110B, powered by Junkers Jumo 211Ga engines, began at Bayerische Flugzeugwerke's factory at Augsburg-Haunstetten in the summer of 1938. It entered service with Schweren Jagdgruppen ('heavy fighter groups') later the same year.

It was superseded on the assembly line by the C-series, which differed from its predecessor by being powered by the Daimler-Benz DB601A and having repositioned glycol radiators and minor changes to the airframe. On January 1, 1939 the Schweren Jagdgruppen were retitled as Zerstörergruppen, which began to receive Bf 110C-1s later the same month. Continuing development resulted in the C-2, with alternative radio gear and an improved rear gunner's position, while the C-3 was armed with improved versions of the 0.787in (20mm) MG FF cannon. Armour protection for the crew was introduced on the C-4.

TACTICS

During operations over Poland, Bf 110s were used to provide top cover for bombers and conduct sweeps at 19,685ft (6,000m), from which they could dive on their opponents and quickly climb away. The concentrated grouping of the two cannons and four machine guns in the aircraft's nose was devastating; it only took a few seconds worth of fire to achieve a kill. Such tactics allowed Bf 110 crews to avoid prolonged dogfights with the much more manoeuvrable Polish fighters, which could easily out-turn the heavier German aircraft. Using these tactics, Zerstörer crews participating in the Polish campaign gained confidence that the Bf 110 was a capable fighter, but it did not last long. Experience over France and southern England the next year highlighted the vulnerability of the aircraft to faster, single-seat fighters.

Messerschmitt Bf 110C-4

Dimensions: Length 41ft 6in (12.65m); Wing span 53ft 3½in (16.27m); Height 11ft 6in (3.50m); Wing area 413sq ft (38.40m²)

Weights: Empty 11,454lb (5,200kg); Typically loaded 13,289lb (6,028kg); Max take-off weight 14,881lb (6,750kg)

Powerplant: Two Daimler-Benz DB601A-1 12-cylinder inverted Vee, liquid-cooled piston engines, each rated at 1,100hp (821kW); Fuel capacity 240 imp gal (1,091 lit)

Armament: Two 0.787in (20mm) MG151 cannons and four 0.31in (7.92mm) MG17 guns in the nose, and one 7.92mm (0.31in) MG812 twin gun on a pivoted mount in the rear cockpit

Performance: Max speed 349mph (562km/h) at 22,965ft (7,000m); Initial climb rate 2,165ft/min (660m/min); Service ceiling 32,808ft (10,000m); Range 482 miles (775km)

Crew: One pilot and one radio operator/gunner (Bordfunker)

"Crews participating in the Polish campaign gained confidence that the Bf 110 was a capable fighter"

OVER ENGLAND

As of July 20, 1940, the Luftwaffe had 278 serviceable Bf 110s available for operations over the British Isles, the majority of which were assigned to three Zerstörergeschwader (ZG). They were ZG 26 and two Gruppen of ZG 76 assigned to Jagdfliegerführer 2 ('fighter leader') of Luftflotte 2, plus I./ ZG 76 based at Stavanger in Norway as part of Luftflotte 5. The third was ZG 2 under Jagdfliegerführer 3 with Luftflotte 3.

Planning for the campaign envisaged that the Zerstörer would sweep ahead of the bombers to engage the RAF fighters, forcing them to return to their bases to refuel. The bombers would then be able to proceed to their targets unmolested, while the Bf 110s made strafing attacks to destroy Fighter Command's aircraft on the ground.

As Luftwaffe bomber losses mounted, the fighters were increasingly required to provide a close escort. This meant flying at medium altitude with the engines throttled back to maintain formation, robbing the Bf 110s of height and speed – vital to any fighter – and limiting the possibility of employing the successful dive-and-climb tactics.

Combat experience had already demonstrated that the single flexible 7.92mm (0.31in) MG812 machine gun covering the rear quadrant was no deterrent against a determined attack from astern. Lacking the speed or acceleration to escape the attention of hostile fighters, Bf 110 crews circled in groups to cover each other's tails, a tactic first adopted during the French campaign.

Escorting the bombers proved costly to the Zerstörergruppen. During August 1940, the Luftwaffe lost 120 Bf 110s.

FIGHTER-BOMBER

Zerstörers were also employed as fighter-bombers during the Battle of Britain, although only with two Staffeln of a special tactical development unit, Erprobungsgruppe (ErpGr) 210, which was established to develop tactics for the forthcoming Messerschmitt Bf 210 (hence the '210' in its designation). Delays to the Bf 210 programme meant that it was equipped with one Staffel of Messerschmitt Bf 109Es and two of Bf 110Cs and Ds, which were all configured as fighter-bombers. Hauptmann Walter Rubensdörffer was put in command of the Gruppe on July 1, 1940, initially based at Denain in northern France under Luftflotte 2, but later moving to Calais Marck.

Several fighter-bomber variants of the Bf 110 were produced, including the C-4/B and C-7. The C-4/B had a pair of ETC 250 stores racks under the centre fuselage for two 551lb (250kg) bombs, and was normally fitted with the uprated Daimler-Benz DB601N engine, which was standard on the C-7. The Bf 110C-7 could carry a pair of 1,102lb (500kg) weapons and had a strengthened landing gear to cope with the additional weight. Both subvariants were flown by ErpGr 210, which was also the sole operator of the C-6, which had a single 1.18in (30mm) MK101 gun in place of the standard 0.787in (20mm) cannons.

The unit was initially employed against shipping. On August 12, it was sent to destroy the radar stations at Dover and Dunkirk in Kent, and Rye and Pevensey, East Sussex. Although all four targets were hit, their vital importance to the British early warning network meant that repairs started as soon as the dust had settled and all but the station at Dover were back in action within hours.

The forward fighter airfield at RAF Manston in Kent was attacked by nine Bf 110s and 16 Bf 109Es from the Gruppe on August 14. The Bf 110s managed to damage four hangars during diving attacks. Two of the twin-engined attackers from 2. Staffel were brought down, one by anti-aircraft fire from the airfield's gunners, the other crashing after being struck by a third Bf 110 that had been crippled by flak.

The next day, ErpGr 210 put the airfield at Martlesham Heath, Suffolk, out of action for 48 hours. One of the attackers hit a Fairey Battle laden with 1,000lb (454kg) of bombs, which blew up, taking out the watch office. »

TOP: Messerschmitt Bf 110C-3 'M8+GP' of Zerstörergeschwader 76 in August 1940.
Pete West

ABOVE: The heavy armament in the nose was in stark contrast to the poor aft defence, the Bordfunker having to fight off attackers with a single gun mounted in the rear of the long cockpit.

ABOVE LEFT: The Messerschmitt Bf 110C was the main variant operated over England during the summer of 1940.
David Willis Collection

ABOVE:
Messerschmitt Bf 110 crews sat in a long cockpit that could seat up to three, although most operations were undertaken with just a pilot and Bordfunker.

BELOW:
Outclassed as a day fighter by the middle of 1940, production of the Bf 110 continued as a night fighter.

That evening, it was planned to attack Kenley, Surrey, but instead struck Croydon within the Greater London area, counter to Hitler's ban against dropping bombs on the capital. It was a costly mistake. Nine 111 Squadron Hurricanes scrambled from Croydon at 1830hrs, with orders to circle the airfield, and were in position when the Bf 110s arrived half an hour later.

The attack lasted less than ten minutes. Six RAF airmen and 62 civilians were killed and around 190 injured. Many of the bombs fell outside the airfield as they were jettisoned by the Messerschmitts trying to get away from the Hurricanes. Considerable damage was inflicted on Croydon, including the destruction of a hangar full of training aircraft.

However, seven of the Gruppen aircraft were downed, including one Bf 109E-4, and the losses included Hauptmann Rubensdörffer, killed after his Bf 110D was shot down at Bletchinglye Farm near Rotherham, East Sussex. Four days after his death,

he became the first Zerstörer pilot to be awarded the Ritterkreuz des Eisernen Kreuzes (Knight's Cross of the Iron Cross).

EXTENDED RANGE

A requirement for additional range, prompted by the need to provide cover for convoys off the coast of Norway, resulted in the Bf 110D-1/R1, which served with I./ZG 76 in Norway. It had a large blister fuel tank under the fuselage, known as the Dackelbauch ('Dachshund belly'), adding a further 264 imp gal (1,200 lit) to the standard capacity. The Dackelbauch could be jettisoned if the enemy was encountered or when the fuel was exhausted. Loading the airframe with maximum fuel degraded both the performance and handling. After an investigation was launched into several unexplained losses of Bf 110D-1/R1s, it was determined that explosive petrol fumes built up in the tank as fuel was burnt off.

The large numbers of RAF fighters encountered by the Luftwaffe over

southern England misled German intelligence into believing that the north of the country was virtually undefended. To take advantage of the situation, Luftflotte 5 units, including I./ZG 76, were committed to operations from August 15. On that day, despite the problems with the auxiliary fuel tank, the unit was tasked with providing an escort to more than 60 Heinkel He 111H-4s of I. and III./ KG 26 from Stavanger, Norway, as they attacked targets around Newcastle, Tyne and Wear.

The raid was a disaster. Spitfires from 72 Squadron based at Acklington, Northumberland, intercepted the German formations, shooting down the commander of I./ZG 76, Hauptmann Werner Restemeyer. Other RAF units also engaged the intruders and the danger to the Bf 110D-1/R1 crews increased further when several found they could not jettison their Dackelbauch. The Gruppe lost seven aircraft, while eight Heinkels were also destroyed.

The Zerstörergeschwader continued to be committed to the battle for Britain into September, long after it was clear that the Bf 110 was no longer viable in the day fighter role, a fact confirmed by the loss of 83 aircraft during the month. The only alternative, the Bf 109, lacked the fuel capacity to remain over England for long and was not available in sufficient numbers to assume the tasks of the Zerstörergeschwader. The following month, Zerstörer operations had all but ceased. The only Bf 110s regularly flying over the British Isles were the aircraft of the Auflärungsgruppen ('reconnaissance groups'). They flew the specialised Bf 110C-5, which began to enter service early in the summer of 1940. It carried a single camera with an aperture in the floor of the cockpit, the additional weight being offset by deleting the two cannons standard in the fighter versions.

Junkers
Ju 88A

Most historians agree that the Junkers Ju 88 was one of the outstanding and versatile combat aircraft of World War Two. Its airframe proved to be remarkably adaptable and in addition to serving the Luftwaffe as a bomber it was also operated as a night and day fighter, for reconnaissance and as an anti-tank aircraft. By the end of the war, well over 15,000 had been produced.

Unlike the Dornier Do 17 and Heinkel He 111 medium bombers it served alongside early in the war, the Ju 88 was developed from the outset as a military aircraft. It was conceived as a fast bomber (Schnellbomber) able to outpace contemporary fighters while carrying a bomb load of 1,765lb (800kg). The prototype first flew on December 21, 1936, powered by Daimler-Benz DB600Aa engines, but by the third Versuchs (experimental/development) aircraft they had been replaced by the Junkers Jumo 211A mounted in long nacelles on the wing, giving rise to the

nickname 'die dreifinger' (the three-finger). Development was undertaken without any official announcement of the aircraft's existence, and it was only in early 1939 that it was revealed to the world. Details emerged when the fifth prototype set a 1,000km (621 mile) closed circuit speed record of 321mph (517km/h), while carrying a payload of 4,409lb (2,000kg) on March 9.

Later Versuchs aircraft featured refinements to the landing gear as well as slatted dive brakes under the outer wings, the latter added after the specification was amended to allow diving attacks to be undertaken alongside its primary role

as a daytime level bomber.

The weight of bombs carried – already over the stated requirement for the Schnellbomber – was also increased. Up to 28 SC50 bombs (each 110lb, 50kg) could be accommodated in the two bays, while racks added under the wings also permitted external stores to be carried. Each rack was stressed for 1,102lb (500kg), although the typical load was SC100s, each weighing 220lb (100kg). Testing of the pre-series Ju 88A-0s at overload weight demonstrated that the bomber could carry four SC500s (each of 1,102lb, 500kg). »

RIGHT: The Junkers Ju 88A was the last of the Luftwaffe's bombers that saw service in the Battle of Britain to enter service.
Key Collection

However, it was not recommended to overload the Ju 88, as the organisation responsible for testing the new aircraft under operational conditions, Erprobungskommando ('test team') 88, discovered when it began its evaluation in the spring of 1939. Service trials revealed that the aircraft was prone to wing spar failure and the landing gear was not strong enough and could collapse, the likelihood of both increasing at higher weights.

When production standard Ju 88A-1s began to reach Luftwaffe frontline units, satisfactory fixes for all the problems were still outstanding and its pilots were told to refrain from aerobatics in the new type. For many of those transferring from units with Do 17s or He 111s, both of which possessed good handling and few vices, the new bomber was viewed with suspicion.

INTO SERVICE

In August 1939, I. Gruppe of Kampfgeschwader (KG) 25 formed as the first Ju 88A-1 unit, with many of its crews joining it from Erprobungskommando 88. The following month, on September 22, the Gruppe changed its identity to I./KG 30.

The Ju 88A-1 differed little from the pre-series aircraft, its most distinctive feature being the change from four to three propeller blades with a larger chord. Early aircraft were armed with three MG15 machine guns, comprising one to the starboard of the cockpit windscreen, another in the rear of the cockpit and the final weapon in the aft section of the gondola under the nose. Combat experience showed this to be inadequate to deter fighter attacks, resulting in a second rear-firing MG15 being added in the cockpit. Many aircraft were modified in the field with more defensive weapons to cover the lateral quadrants.

Several different production subvariants were operated by the Kampfgeschwader during the Battle of Britain beyond the initial A-1 model. The Ju 88A-2 differed from its predecessor by having Jumo 211G-2 engines in place of the 211B-1, plus attachment points for rockets to assist take-off that could be jettisoned after use.

A major upgrade was planned for the Ju 88A-4, the product of a lengthy process of modifications and improvisation to overcome some of the deficiencies that dogged early versions of the aircraft. The more powerful Jumo 211J was selected for the new version, while the wing area was increased by widening the span from 60ft 3$\frac{1}{4}$in (18.37m) to 65ft 7$\frac{1}{2}$in (20.00m). A stronger landing gear was incorporated to counter the higher gross weights of the Ju 88A-4. Defensive armament was revised and additional armour added to better protect the crew, while the forward bomb bay was deleted, as the new subvariant would carry most of its bombs externally, where the dimensions of the munitions were not a factor.

Delays to the development and production of the Jumo 211J resulted in the decision to mate the new wing and landing gear with the Ju 88A-1 airframe, creating the interim Ju 88A-5, examples of which were delivered to operational units in the later stages of the Battle of Britain. The Ju 88A-6 was equipped with a balloon cable fender and cutter, but as the equipment added 840lb (381kg) to the airframe and had a negative impact on performance, its operational career was brief.

The second Geschwader to convert to the Ju 88A following KG 30 was KG 51, which had two Gruppen equipped with the bomber by mid-May 1940. Next to receive the Ju 88 were Lehrgeschwader (LG) 1 and KG 4.

AT WAR

Little use was made of the Ju 88A during the invasion of France and the Low Countries, although the bomber was used to attack vessels off the coast of Dunkirk on May 29 during the Allied evacuation from mainland Europe. Its real baptism of fire came during the opening stages of the Battle of Britain.

One of the first raids to involve large numbers of Ju 88s occurred on August 12. On that day, almost 100 aircraft from KG 51, with a large fighter escort, crossed

BELOW: Junkers Ju 88A-1 belonging to III. Gruppe Stab of Kampfgeschwader 30, part of Luftflotte 5. The unit was based at Aalborg in Denmark. Pete West

Junkers Ju 88A-1

Dimensions: Length 47ft 1¼in (14.36m); Wing span 60ft 3¼in (18.37m); Height 17ft 5¾in (5.33m); Wing area 565sq ft (52.50m²)

Weights: Empty 16,975lb (7,700kg); Max loaded weight 22,840lb (10,360kg)

Powerplant: Two Junkers Jumo 211B-1 or G-1 12-cylinder Vee, liquid-cooled piston engines, each rated at 1,200hp (895kW) for take-off and 1,210hp (903kW) at 820ft (250m); Fuel capacity 369 imp gal (1,677 lit), plus provision for 268 imp gal (1,218 lit) fuel tank in forward bomb bay and/or 150 imp gal (682 lit) tank in aft bomb bay

Armament: Initially, one fixed or flexible forward-firing 7.92mm (0.31in) MG15 machine gun and two aft-firing MG15s on flexible mounts above and below the fuselage. Later additions included two lateral firing MG15s. Up to 3,968lb (1,800kg) of bombs, typically comprising 28 110lb (50kg) SC50s in two internal bays and four 220lb (100kg) SC100s on underwing racks, or ten SC50s in the aft bay and four 551lb (250kg) SC250s or two SC500 1,102lb (500kg) weapons externally

Performance: Max speed at 19,750lb (8,959kg), 227mph (365km/h) at sea level, 280mph (451km/h) at 18,050ft (5,502m); Cruise speed 217mph (349km/h) at 18,050ft (5,502m); Climb rate 1,312ft/min (400m/min); Service ceiling at 19,750lb (8,959kg), 26,250ft (8,001m); Range without auxiliary tanks, 620 miles (998km) at 217mph (349km/h) and 18,050ft (5,502m), 1,055 miles (1,698km) with 268 imp gal (1,218 lit) fuel tank in forward bomb bay

Crew: Four, comprising a pilot, pilot/bombardier, radio operator/dorsal gunner and ventral gunner

the southeast coast of England. Most of the bombers headed for Portsmouth in Hampshire, but two Staffeln dived on the Chain Home station at Ventnor on the Isle of Wight, causing heavy damage and knocking it out of action for several weeks. The cost to the Kampfgeschwader was heavy as ten Ju 88s were lost, eight of which were shot down by RAF fighters, including the mount of the commander of KG 51, Geschwaderkommodore Johann-Volkmar Fisser.

The Luftwaffe had 252 serviceable Ju 88s available on August 13, which was designated Adlertag (Eagle Day) by the Luftwaffe high command to mark the start of an all-out assault against Fighter Command's airfields. For the Ju 88 units – and also the rest of the Luftwaffe – it did not live up to its name. Around 40 Ju 88s from KG 54 were sent against Odiham and Farnborough in Hampshire, but did not reach the airfields due to a combination of RAF fighters and dense cloud cover. Also in action that day were 80 aircraft of LG 1, dispatched to hit Middle Wallop and the port of Southampton, both also in Hampshire. The docks at Southampton were badly damaged, but the two Staffeln directed to strike Middle Wallop failed to hit it.

Luftwaffe combat reports highlighting encounters with large formations of RAF fighters over south England lead German intelligence to believe that most of the aircraft were concentrated in that region, leaving the north of the country virtually undefended. Hoping to take advantage of

this 'fact', the Luftwaffe decided to launch attacks on the north using the bombers of Luftflotte 5, based at airfields in Norway and Denmark. Among them was the Ju 88 equipped KG 30 at Aalborg-West in Denmark, which had initially trained for the anti-shipping role. On August 15, the Kampfgeschwader sent 50 Ju 88s against the Bomber Command airfield at Driffield in Yorkshire. After the intruders were spotted on radar, RAF fighters from 73 and 616 Squadrons scrambled to intercept the bombers and managed to split up their formation. The main force of approximately 30 Ju 88s pressed home the attack on Driffield, killing 14 military personnel and badly damaging the site, as well as destroying ten Armstrong Whitworth Whitley bombers on the ground. The German bombers paid a heavy price for the damage inflicted, as seven Ju 88s were shot down by RAF fighters, while a further three crash-landed on the continent.

On the evening of the same day, 60 Ju 88s from two Gruppen of LG 1 bombed the airfields at Middle Wallop and nearby Worthy Down, but caused little damage. They also hit Andover, mistaking it for Odiham. The last of 609 Squadron Spitfires that had scrambled after being warned of the raid managed to get airborne from Middle Wallop just as the first Ju 88s arrived over the airfield. They claimed one Ju 88 and four of the Bf 109s escorting them, while other RAF squadrons also engaged LG 1's aircraft over southeast England and the Channel. In total, eight of

the Ju 88s were shot down, while several others suffered damage, including that of the commander of 4. Staffel, Hauptmann Joachim Helbig, which made it home after receiving around 130 hits from fighters.

HITTING THE CAPITAL

The large-scale daylight raids on London in September were undertaken by the units of Luftflotte 2 based in northeast France and the Low Countries. Its forces were bolstered when KG 30 was transferred to it from Denmark, the Geschwader going on to lose five Ju 88s on

September 9 when it raided the London docks. A second Kampfgeschwader, KG 77, was also assigned to Luftflotte 2 soon after replacing its Dornier Do 17Zs with Ju 88s. Nine of its aircraft failed to return from an attack on the port of Tilbury, within the British capital, which was mounted on September 18.

Attrition of Ju 88s reached its zenith on September 27. Out of the 55 bombers of I. and II./KG 77 sent to attack targets in south London, 12 were shot down. The heavy losses were caused by the formation pressing on with the mission after failing to rendezvous with the Messerschmitts expected to defend it. More than 120 Hurricanes and Spitfires descended on the bombers, with predictable results.

Luftwaffe records indicate that more than 300 Ju 88s were lost between July and October 1940. Somewhat surprisingly, given that the Ju 88 was the fastest of the trio, this was higher than either the Do 17 or He 111.

LEFT: An early production Junkers Ju 88A-1, displaying the offset gondola with the bomb sight and aiming window, plus the underwing external bomb racks. Malcolm V Lowe Collection

ABOVE: A crash landed Junkers Ju 88A of KG 51. Although the cowling gave the impression the bomber used a radial engine, the aircraft was powered by the inline Jumo 211. Malcolm V Lowe Collection

BELOW: Junkers Ju 88A-1 w/n 299 of 8./KG 51. Malcolm V Lowe Collection

"Its real baptism of fire came during the opening stages of the Battle of Britain"

Heinkel
He 111

In the minds of the British public, the German bomber most associated with the Battle of Britain is the Heinkel He 111. Fast by the standards of the 1930s, it was larger and carried a heavier bomb load than both the Dornier Do 17 and Junkers Ju 88, but by the start of World War Two it required a heavy fighter escort during daylight to survive in contested airspace.

Siegfried and Walter Günter designed the Heinkel He 111 as a fast airliner and mailplane that could be adapted as a bomber when the existence of the Luftwaffe could be revealed to the world. First bloodied with the Condor Legion during the Spanish Civil War, combat experience showed some of the deficiencies of the early versions of the aircraft and they resulted in Siegfried making major changes to the design to increase speed and enhance the defensive armament.

These features, introduced on the He 111P, became standard on all subsequent versions. They included the extensively glazed, smooth contour nose, which replaced the stepped cockpit of earlier versions and significantly altered the lines of the aircraft. At the front of the nose was a blister in which was mounted a flexible machine gun, offset to starboard so that it did not interrupt the pilot's line of sight forward. The pilot's seat and controls, located over 6ft (1.8m) from the tip of the nose, could be elevated while landing or taxiing, allowing his head to protrude through a sliding panel for better all-round awareness. His face was protected from the slipstream by a small, hinged windscreen at the front of the panel. While the multiple panes in the cockpit provided an excellent view of the forward quadrant, when the sun was directly behind the aircraft reflections could dazzle the pilot. The same problem was encountered if the bomber was caught in the beam of a searchlight.

A streamlined gondola was incorporated under the fuselage for the gunner, replacing the retractable 'dustbin' turret – a feature of many early German bombers – that made the gunner feel rather exposed during fighter attacks. The broad wing remained similar to that designed for the He 111F. All P-series He 111s were powered by two Daimler-Benz DB601A engines.

Production of the initial He 111P-1 subvariant began in late 1938 and the first examples entered service with Kampfgeschwader (KG, 'bomber wing') 157 in April 1939. During that year, production built up rapidly, as the original output from the Heinkel factory at Rostock Marienehe was augmented by Dornier from its site at Wismar. Several subsequent subvariants followed, including the He 111P-2 fitted with improved radio gear. The defensive armament of the P-4 was augmented by adding three more MG15 machine guns and a fifth crew member to help man them, plus

---

Heinkel He 111H-3

Dimensions: Length 53ft 9½in (16.40m); Wing span 74ft 2in (22.60m); Height 13ft 11½in (4.00m); Wing area 943sq ft (87.60m²)

Weights: Empty 15,873lb (7,200kg); Typically loaded 28,924lb (13,120kg); Max take-off weight 14,881lb (6,750kg)

Powerplant: Two Junkers Jumo 211D-1 12-cylinder inverted Vee, liquid-cooled piston engines, each rated at 1,200hp (895kW) for take-off; Fuel capacity 898 imp gal (4,082 lit), plus provision for 183 imp gal (832 lit) tank in port bomb bay

Armament: Five 7.92mm (0.31in) MG15 machine guns on flexible mounts, in the nose; a dorsal gunner's position, firing to rear; in the ventral gondola, firing aft; and port and starboard mid-fuselage gunner's positions. Some aircraft fitted with additional MG15 in right upper nose glazing, or a fixed, rear firing, remotely operated MG15 in the tail cone. Plus one 20mm (0.787in) Oerlikon MG FF cannon, mounted on a pivot, in the ventral gondola, firing forward

Performance: Max speed 273mph (440km/h); Cruise speed 205mph (330km/h); Initial climb rate 886ft/min (270m/min); Service ceiling 26,247ft (8,000m); Range 1,429 miles (2,300km)

Crew: Five, comprising a pilot, radio operator/dorsal gunner, bomb aimer/navigator/nose gunner and two gunners.

more armour plating. The He 111P-6 was powered by DB610N engines.

Large numbers of He 111Ps were built, with 349 in service by the start of World War Two. During the Battle of Britain, He 111Ps were almost completely supplanted by He 111H variants in the Kampfgruppen, although the earlier model remained in service with staff flights, as well as reconnaissance units and those responsible for collecting meteorological data.

PARALLEL PRODUCTION

The H-series became the main production version of the aircraft and was built in many configurations as a bomber, pathfinder, torpedo bomber, transport and glider-tug. The pre-series He 111H-0 and production H-1 differed from the He 111P-2 primarily because it had Junkers Jumo 211A-1 engines.

This change was necessitated by a shortage of available DB601s, as most of the production was allocated to power the increasing numbers of Messerschmitt Bf 109 and Bf 110s on order. Production of the He 111H-1 commenced in May 1939 and to fulfil the large numbers required to re-equip the Luftwaffe's Kampfgeschwader, the new model was assembled not only at Heinkel's factory at Oranienburg but also by Arado at Warnemünde, the Allgemeine Transportgesellschaft in Leipzig and by subsidiaries of the Junkers works.

Externally, the He 111P and H were very similar and improvements developed for one model were also applied to the other. Thus the early He 111H subvariants mirrored those of the P-series in terms of better equipment, armour and defensive armament. The H-2 had Jumo 211A-3s and, from aircraft produced from October 1939, the augmented defensive armament of the P-4. The He 111H-3 bomber retained the upgrades introduced in the H-2 (including the provision for the additional gunner), but was also fitted with a single forward-firing 0.787in (20mm) Oerlikon MG FF cannon in the gondola. The weapon was installed to permit the H-3 to be used on anti-shipping sorties, but proved to be of limited use in the role because the mounting limited its traverse.

A requirement to carry larger bombs than could be accommodated in the He 111's bomb bay resulted in the H-4, which appeared in early 1940. The port side of the bay was covered by a heavy metal plate, to which a single 1,800kg (3,968lb) or two 1,000kg (2,205lb) bombs could be attached. The subvariant was optimised for short-range sorties only, because of the additional drag imposed by carrying weapons externally. Although the He 111H-1 to -4 were the main versions operated during the Battle of Britain, small numbers of other variants were also used, such as the He 111H-8 equipped with a balloon cable-fender and cutter.

EARLY EXPERIENCE

On the day Germany invaded Poland, September 1, 1939, the Luftwaffe had 808 He 111s in its inventory (including 749 Ps and Hs), of which 705 were operational. They were flown by 21 Gruppen and one independent Staffel.

The bomber saw extensive use over Poland, during the period of the so-called 'Phoney War' in the west – the lull before Germany invaded there – and during the occupation of Norway.

ABOVE: RAF gun camera image of 0.303in (7.7mm) strikes on a Heinkel He 111. Many times the small calibre bullets punched holes in the bombers without bringing it down.

Around half of the bombers deployed by Luftflotten 2 and 3 for the invasion of France and the Low Countries were He 111Ps and Hs. In addition to working closely with German ground forces, notably against the French armed forces at Sedan and during the Allied counter-attack at Arras, the He 111 became notorious, bombing towns as well as cities – such as the Rotterdam Blitz on May 14, 1940, when Kampfgeschwader (KG) 54 destroyed large portions of the city in the Netherlands, forcing the country to sue for peace the following day. The bomber was also used over the beaches of Dunkirk as the surviving Allied forces struggled to escape from mainland Europe, as well as targeting the ships off shore.

Losses during the Battle of France among the He 111 Gruppen were relatively light. The bomber proved to have a robust airframe, able to withstand multiple bullet hits, and was considered to be an accurate bombing platform. Maintenance crews found it easy to service. »

BELOW: Heinkel He 111H-3 of Stab III./ KG 53 based at Lille-Nord, France, during the Battle of Britain.
Pete West

BOTTOM: The Heinkel He 111P-2 (such as this example) was externally the same as the earlier P-1.
Pete West

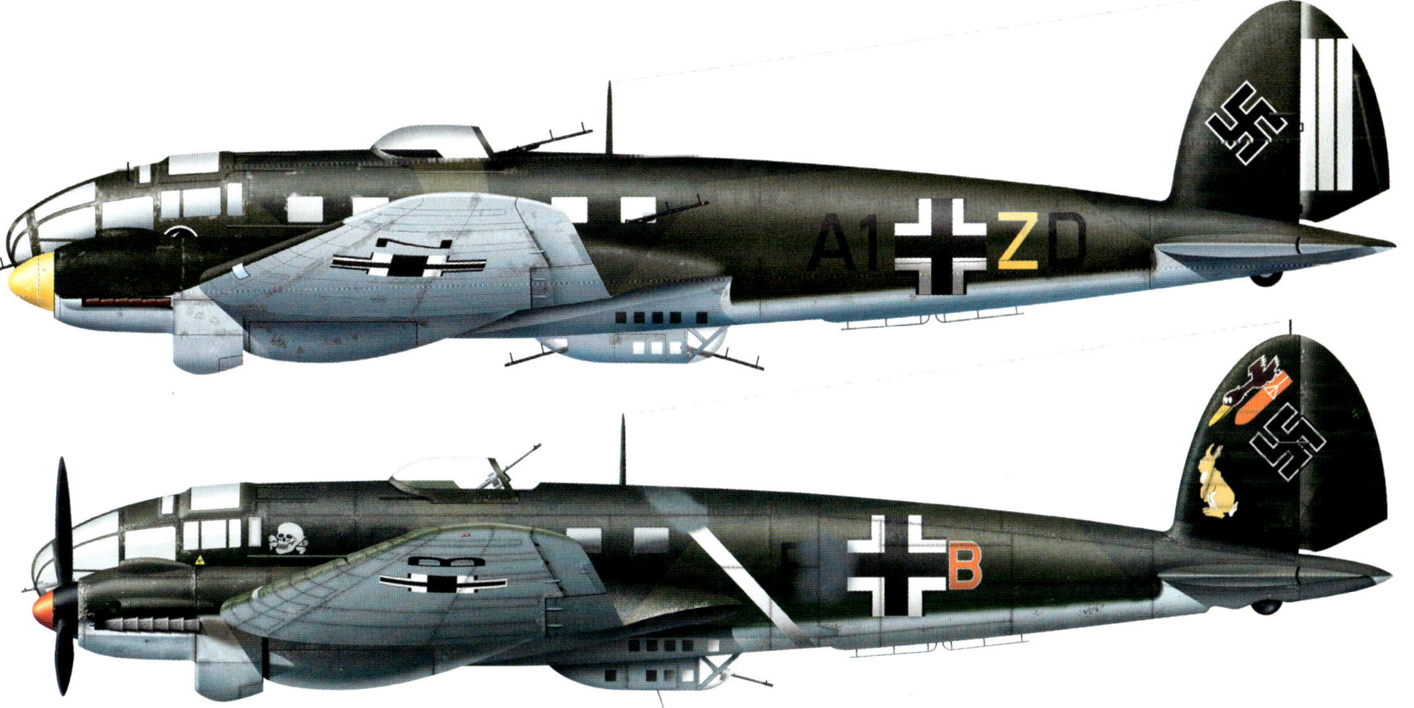

RIGHT: **While operations by day proved costly for the Heinkel He 111 Kampfgeschwaders, the change to night attacks almost eliminated the threat from the British defences early in the Blitz against London.**

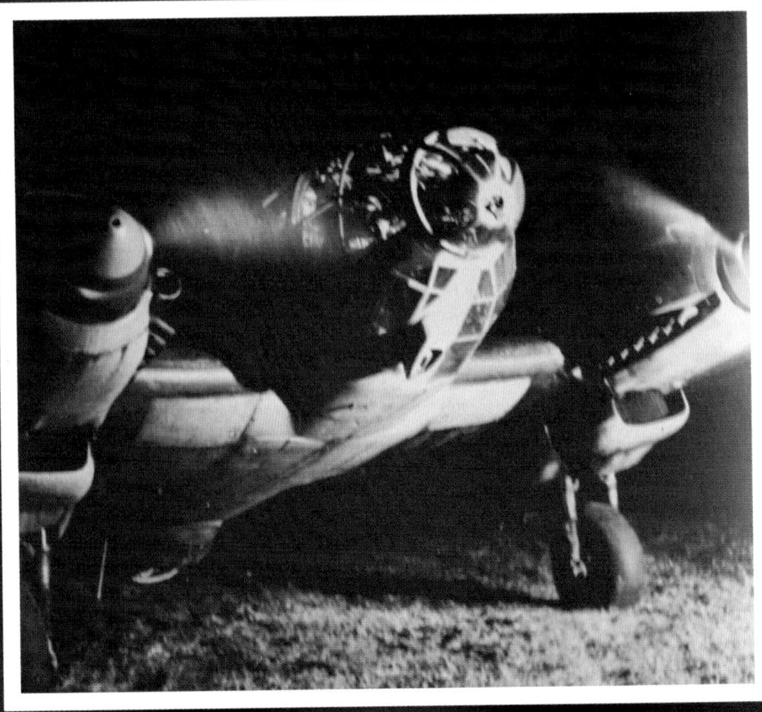

OVER BRITAIN

Heinkel He 111-equipped Kampfgeschwader fought throughout all phases of the Battle of Britain and the night-time Blitz that continued into 1941. A total of 34 Gruppen assigned to Luftflotte 2, 3 and 5 operated the bomber, although only KG 26, 27, 53 and 55 were exclusively equipped with the type.

Early in the battle, it became obvious to the crews that the aircraft was incapable of defending itself against the RAF's eight-gun fighters and required a close escort of Messerschmitts if losses were going to be kept at sustainable levels. While the airframe maintained its reputation of being able to absorb punishment, the concentration of most of the crew in the nose section made the bomber vulnerable to head-on attacks. The nose glazing, with its excellent view of the outside world, could also feel rather exposed when the crews had to face attacks by fighters. Field modifications to increase the number of defensive guns and add additional armour were common. Luftwaffe records state a total of 242 He 111s were destroyed between July and October 1940, significantly lower than the faster Ju 88.

Initial operations supported the campaign against shipping. Attacks in strength started on July 10, 1940, and eight days later the bomber appeared over the British coast for the first time, attacking harbour installations. Heinkels also sowed mines at various locations with, for example, the He 111P-4s of KG 4 dropping magnetic mines in the Thames and Humber estuaries, and at the entrances to the ports of Penzance and Falmouth in Cornwall; Plymouth, Devon; Liverpool, Merseyside; Southampton, Hampshire; and Belfast, Northern Ireland, between August 8 and 12.

Large formations of He 111s began to be engaged by the RAF once the emphasis switched to attacking airfields. At the start of that phase of the Battle of Britain, on August 13, the Luftwaffe had 434 He 111s available. The first large scale raid involving the bomber took place two days later, when 60 aircraft based at Stavanger in Norway of KG 26 attacked targets around Newcastle, Tyne and Wear, in an operation co-ordinated with Junkers Ju 88s of KG 30, which bombed the airfield at Driffield in Yorkshire. The bombers were escorted by Bf 110s of I./ZG 76, but RAF aircraft fought through to the bombers, shooting down eight He 111s and forcing others to jettison their bombs into the sea.

Other notable raids include KG 55's attack on the Bristol aero engine works at Filton outside Bristol, on September 25. As a result of the damage inflicted, production at the factory was curtailed for several weeks. More than 250 people were killed or injured in the raid, while three of the 58 He 111s were brought down by fighters and anti-aircraft guns. The same unit also participated in the attack on Southampton the next day, during which the Supermarine Spitfire factory at Woolston was hit several times.

"The bomber proved to have a robust airframe, able to withstand multiple bullet hits"

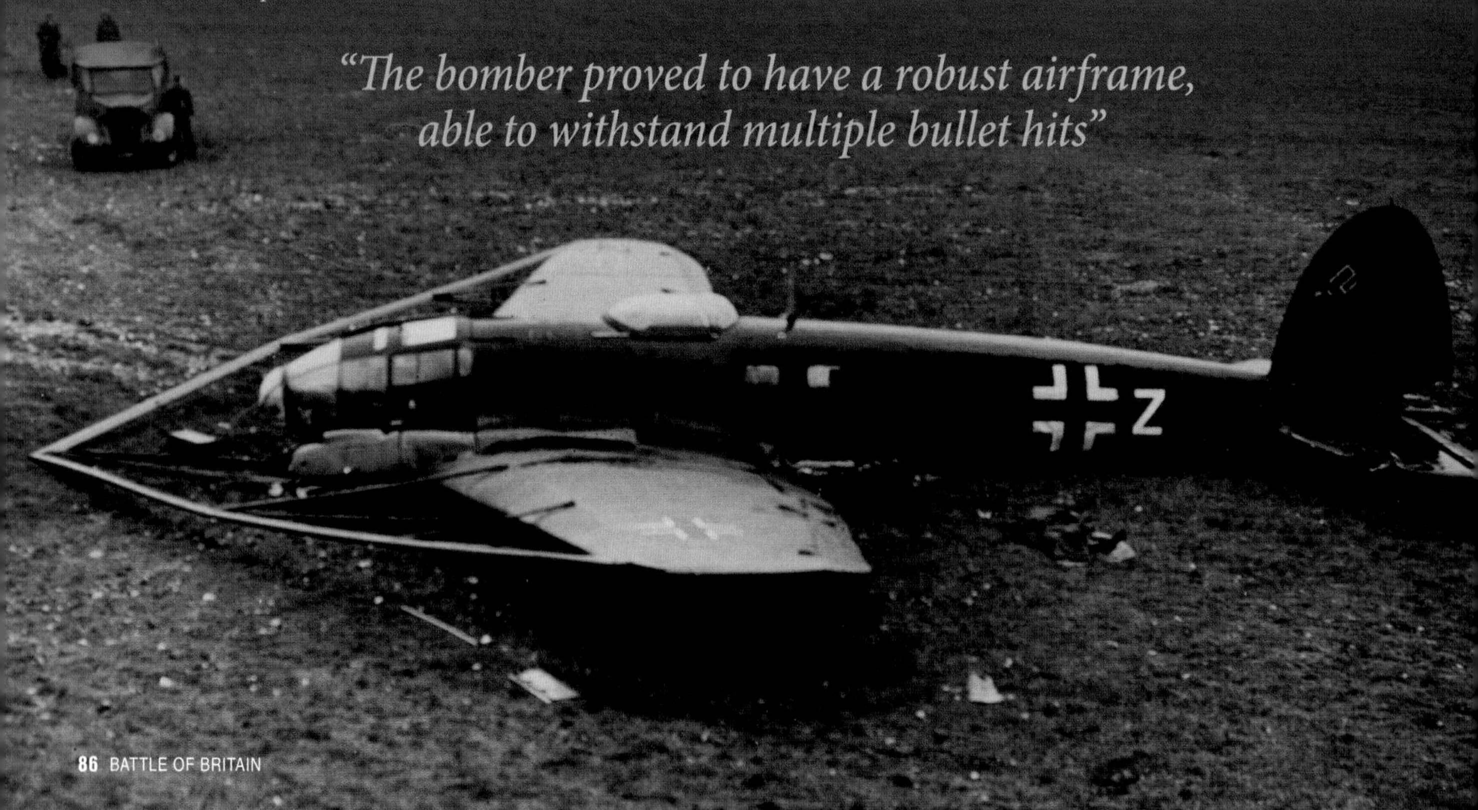

BELOW: **A downed Heinkel He 111H-8 of KG 54. The version was fitted with a balloon fender, which proved cumbersome in operation.** David Willis Collection

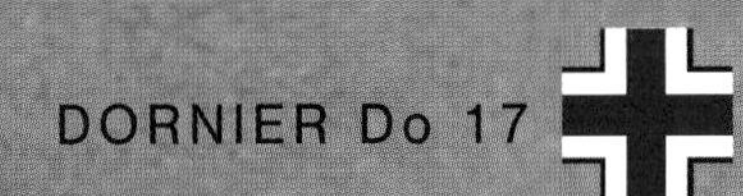

Dornier **Do 17**

Designed as a bomber fast enough to evade fighters (a so-called Schnellbomber), the Dornier Do 17 entered service with the Luftwaffe during 1937 in the guise of the Do 17E-1 bomber and F-1 reconnaissance aircraft. Its slender fuselage gave rise to the nickname Fliegender Bleistift ('flying pencil') and its good handling, especially at low altitude, made the aircraft popular with its crews.

From late 1937, production switched to the Do 17M-1 bomber and P-1 reconnaissance variants, developed in parallel. Both had more powerful BMW engines installed: the Do 17M-1 the 900hp (675kW) Bramo 323A-1, and the Do 17P-1 the smaller, lighter and more economical 865hp (648kW) BMW 132N, selected to give the reconnaissance version the desired range. The bomb bay of both was lengthened in comparison with earlier models to accommodate up to 1,000kg (2,205lb) of munitions, or in the case of the Do 17P-1, cameras. Defensive armament comprised four machine guns, one more than the Do 17E/F, the addition being a forward-firing 7.92mm (0.5in) MG15 that could be manually aimed by the navigator/ bombardier or clamped into position and fired by the pilot.

The definitive production variant was the Do 17Z. Combat experience gained while in service with the Condor Legion during the Spanish Civil War highlighted the need for better protection for the undersides of the aircraft and more room for the crew than the cramped space available in the M and P models. A redesigned forward fuselage thus became the distinguishing feature of the Do 17Z, raising the roof of the cockpit so that the pilot sat surrounded by heavily framed glass panels. The bombardier's position in the nose was also glazed with small flat panels, while a ventral gondola under the nose extended back to the leading-edge of the wing. Defensive armament was further increased to six MG15 machine guns, while the greater internal space allowed an additional, fourth, crew member to be accommodated to man them. While the new forward fuselage improved the crew's operational efficiency, it came at the cost of additional weight and aerodynamic drag.

DEFINITIVE VERSION

Prior to the Do 17Z, the new cockpit section was used by three Do 17S-0 prototypes and the initial production version with it was the Do 17U, designed as a specialised pathfinder variant powered by Daimler-Benz DB600A engines. Only a dozen production Do 17Us were built. Plans to power the Do 17Z with the DB600 had to be revised when the engine was reserved for new fighters – the alternative found for the initial production Do 17Z-1 was the BMW-Bramo 323A-1 Fafnir radial. While the new Do 17 variant retained the handling and manoeuvrability of the earlier versions, it was under-powered, resulting in a decrease in the bomb load from 1,000kg (2,205lb) to just 500kg (1,102lb).

Re-engining with Bramo 323Ps with two-stage superchargers restored the bomber's ability to carry the original weight of bombs, but required

ABOVE: Nicknamed the Fliegender Bleistift ('flying pencil') because of its slim fuselage, the Dornier Do 17 was popular with its crews. The original contours were altered significantly when the raised cockpit – as on this Do 17Z of 7./ZG 3 – was introduced.

Dornier Do 17Z-2

Dimensions: Length 51ft 9⅔in (15.79m); Wing span 59ft 0½in (18.00m); Height 14ft 11½in (4.56m); Wing area 592sq ft (55.00m²)

Weights: Empty 11,484lb (5,209kg); Max overload weight 19,481lb (8,837kg)

Powerplant: Two BMW-Bramo 323P Fafnir nine-cylinder radial, air-cooled piston engines, each rated at 1,000hp (746kW) for take-off and 940hp (701kW) at 13,123ft (4,000m); Fuel capacity 341 imp gal (1,550 lit), plus 197 imp gal (896 lit) auxiliary fuselage tank

Armament: Two fixed or flexible forward-firing 0.31in (7.92mm) MG15 machine guns, two MG15s in side windows, one MG15 firing aft in rear of canopy, and one MG15 in the ventral position covering the rear quadrant. Up to 2,205lb (1,000kg) of bombs carried internally, typically 20 110lb (50kg) SD50s or four 551lb (250kg) SD250s

Performance: Max speed fully loaded, 186mph (299km/h) at sea level, 255mph (410km/h) at 13,120ft (3,999m); Max cruise speed fully loaded 168mph (270km/h) at sea level, 186mph (299km/h) at 13,120ft (3,999m); Climb rate 1,188ft/min (362m/min); Service ceiling 22,966ft (7,000m) at 18,832lb (8,542kg); Range with auxiliary fuel tank and 1,102lb (500kg) of bombs, 720 miles (1,160km)

Crew: Four, comprising pilot, navigator/bombardier, radio operator/gunner and gunner

a reduction in the fuel capacity, decreasing the radius of action at maximum weight to only 205 miles (330km). This version was produced as the Do 17Z-2.

Another subvariant produced was the Do 17Z-3 reconnaissance bomber, with automatic cameras mounted in the crew entry hatch. Some aircraft became Do 17Z-5s after inflatable flotation bags and other survival equipment were installed, for use as long-range maritime reconnaissance aircraft. Several night fighter versions were also created, although they did not participate in the Battle of Britain. Production of the Do 17 ceased early in the summer of 1940, after 500 Z-1/2s and 22 Z-3s had been delivered.

AT WAR

The day after Germany invaded Poland, September 2, 1939, the Luftwaffe had nine Kampfgruppen ('bomber groups') equipped with Do 17s within four Kampfgeschwader (KG). They had 370 Do 17s assigned, of which 319 were operational. The total included 212 Do 17Zs (188 serviceable), with Do 17M-1s making up the majority of the others. In addition, long-range reconnaissance Aufklärungsstaffeln (reconnaissance Staffeln) had 235 serviceable Do 17s out a total of 262 on strength, primarily comprising Do 17P-1s, although one unit had the older Do

17F-1. Each of the headquarters' flights (Stab) of the nine Stuka-equipped Gruppen were also assigned three Do 17M-1s, primarily to guide the dive bombers towards their targets.

Several Kampfgeschwader began to convert to the Junkers Ju 88 soon after the Battle of France. By mid-August 1940, Do 17Zs equipped three Kampfgeschwader assigned to Luftflotte 2, with KG 2 and 3 of II. Fliegerkorps both having three Gruppen each, while KG 76 assigned to I. Fliegerkorps had two, the third having converted to the Ju 88.

During the Battle of Britain, Dorniers specialised in low-altitude raids, where its radial engines performed best. It was well suited to such tactics, as the airframe was strong and exceptionally manoeuvrable, while its ability to reach speeds of up to 370mph (595km/h) in a shallow dive helped it evade RAF fighters. However, combat experience highlighted that the aircraft's defensive armament was inadequate to fend off a determined attack, resulting in additional MG15s being fitted to many aircraft by units in the field.

OPERATIONS OVER ENGLAND

Dorniers were at the centre of one of the first large-scale dogfights to take place during the Battle of Britain. About 26 bombers of I./KG 2 were ordered to attack the large 'Bread' convoy as it passed off Dover in Kent on the afternoon of July 10. Fighter cover for the formation was provided by Messerschmitt Bf 110s from I./ZG 26 and Bf 109Es of I./JG 3. The Luftwaffe formations were intercepted by RAF fighters from at least five squadrons and a fierce air battle ensued, with both sides making multiple claims. Only two Dorniers were destroyed, including one flown by Hauptmann Walter Krieger, the Staffelkapitän of 3./KG 2 – brought down after colliding head-on with a Hurricane flown by Pilot Officer Thomas Higgs of 111 Squadron. Although I./KG 2 dropped more than 150 bombs on the convoy, 'Bread' suffered only one hit.

The bomber was also involved in the initial raids on RAF airfields on August 12, KG 2 attacking Hawkinge and Manston in Kent in conjunction with the fighter bombers of EprGr

"By mid-August 1940 Do 17Zs equipped three Kampfgeschwader assigned to Luftflotte 2"

210. The following day, 74 Do 17s from the same wing bombed the naval base at Sheerness and the airfield at Eastchurch, also both in Kent. Eastchurch was a Coastal Command airfield, but just happened to have two Spitfire squadrons in residence when KG 2 struck. However, only one British fighter was destroyed on the ground, but five Dorniers were lost and a similar number damaged.

Eastchurch was struck again on August 15 by KG 3, during a raid that also targeted Rochester, badly damaging the Short Brothers aircraft factory, delaying deliveries of Stirling bombers to the RAF, and the Pobjoy engine works. A strong fighter escort limited losses to two Dorniers shot down and six damaged.

On August 18, KG 76 was ordered to attack Kenley in Surrey, with 27 Do 17s of I. Gruppe and (most of) II. Gruppe bombing from high altitude, while the wing's other Gruppe of Ju 88s were to dive bomb the airfield's buildings. Once the main force was clear, the Do 17s of 9. Staffel (part of II. Gruppe) would sneak in at low level to hit anything left standing.

Things went badly from the start, when the main force was delayed heading west after the rendezvous with the escorting fighters was hampered by cloud. Unaware of the delay, 9. Staffel headed for Kenley ahead of the main force. Its progress was tracked by the Observer Corps and the defences were alert and ready when the nine Do 17s attacked the airfield. Only two of the bombers made it back to France, including one flown by Beobachter (observer, in command of the aircraft) Wilhelm-Friedrich Illg who flew his aircraft after his pilot was mortally wounded.

The main force of Do 17s arrived over Kenley with RAF fighters airborne and waiting, spoiling their bomb runs, while the Ju 88s attacked West Malling in Kent, their alternative target.

LONDON

In early September, when the Luftwaffe began medium-altitude daylight attacks on London, Do 17 losses began to increase. Although the Dornier Do 17 suffered the lowest loss rate of the three German bombers during the Battle of Britain, enemy action and accidents had reduced the existing fleet to the extent that most of the sorties during the Blitz had to be undertaken by Heinkel He 111 and Ju 88s.

Nevertheless, the aircraft participated in some notable raids on the capital, including the initial assault on London on September 7, which was lead by Do 17s of KG 2, the unit bombing the docks and inflicting heavy damage.

On September 15, two large operations were undertaken with the intention of destroying Fighter Command in the air. The first was to use 27 Do 17s of I. and III./KG 76 as bait to lure RAF fighters into a decisive dogfight with three Gruppen of Bf 109s (about 120 aircraft). The bombers formed up into nine ketten (vees of three aircraft) over Amiens in France, but entered thick cloud that forced two aircraft to lose contact with the formation and return to base, before meeting the Messerschmitts over Pas-de-Calais. Approximately 40 additional Bf 109s from Lehrgeschwader (literally 'training unit') 1, half carrying bombs, also joined the raid.

British fighters soon rose to meet the formation, the Dorniers escaping unscathed after being fired on by two squadrons of Hurricanes, which were quickly engaged by the Bf 109s. Low on fuel after fighting off the initial waves of British aircraft, many of the Bf 109s were forced to turn back for home before the bombers reached the London suburbs. With elements of three RAF units already harassing the German formation, the odds were tipped in favour of the British when the five squadrons of the Duxford Wing joined the fight. As was standard practice, the RAF fighters tried to evade the escort and aim for the bombers. Six Do 17s were shot down and most of the survivors damaged, four dropping out of formation on the way home, but managing to limp back to the continent. The target of both the Do 17s and fighter bomber Bf 109s, a railway junction south of Battersea power station, received multiple hits.

The second raid launched on September 15 targeted various London docks and involved 25 Do 17s of III./KG 2 and 18 of II./KG 2, plus ten Do 17s of II./KG 3, and Heinkel He 111s from other Kampfgeschwader. A total of 361 fighters were assigned to protect the bombers. Clouds obscured the aiming points resulting in the majority of bombs hitting sites of no military value. RAF fighters harried the German aircraft all the way back to the coast, scoring several victories.

BELOW: Small numbers of Dornier Do 17M/Ps were operated by Junkers Ju 87 Stuka Geschwader to guide the dive bombers to their units. This Do 17P served with Stürzkampf-geschwader 2 in 1940.

Ever since the aeroplane became a weapon of war, finding a solution to the problem of accurately hitting a target on the ground has been high on the list of air force requirements. One of the methods devised was to aim the whole aircraft at the target before releasing the weapon. Thus was born the dive bomber, which was adopted by the Luftwaffe during its formative years in the early 1930s as a method of providing close support to the army. The aircraft that became synonymous with the method of attack was the Junkers Ju 87, commonly known as the Stuka, an abbreviation of Stürzkampffflugzeug – dive bomber aircraft.

The Stuka's ability to place bombs on targets with precision provided the army with 'flying artillery' in support of its Blitzkrieg campaigns in Poland and western Europe. It gained a fearsome reputation during those operations, terrorising troops and civilians alike with a loud scream as it dived, generated by a siren attached to a landing gear leg. In addition to flying over the battlefields, the Ju 87 also sank more ships than any other aircraft. Escorted by the Luftwaffe fighters, the Stuka was an effective tactical weapon, but operations during the Britain of Britain revealed the aircraft to be slow, with weak defensive armament, and it was particularly vulnerable pulling out of its dive. While it remained in service until the end of the war, going on to destroy huge numbers of Soviet tanks on the Eastern Front, its reputation never recovered.

BS AND RS

Eleven dive bomber Gruppen ('groups') were assembled for the assault on Britain, with approximately 400 Stukas, deployed along the coastal areas of France in Normandy and Brittany. At the time of the Battle of Britain, the Stürzkampfgeschwader (StG, 'dive bomber wing') were primarily equipped with Ju 87B-1/2s and Ju 87Rs. The Ju 87B-1 had a Junkers Jumo 211A, which had more power than the A model's Jumo 210C, an automatic control that pulled the aircraft out of its dive, and neat spats over the main wheels. Changes to the weapon racks were introduced on the Ju 87B-2, which could carry heavier bombs of up to 2,205lb (1,000kg), permitting a single SC1000 to be slung under the fuselage. The landing gear was strengthened to accommodate a higher gross weight, while the Jumo 211D engine fitted provided more power. Standard B-models lacked armour for the crew of two, a deficiency later rectified by adding optional equipment as the Ju 87B-1/U3 or -2/U3.

The short range of the early Stukas was addressed in the R series, which had additional fuel in the outer wings

Junkers
JU 87

The Junkers Ju 87 'Stuka' dive bomber was an integral part of the Blitzkrieg campaigns that rolled across Europe in the nine months from September 1939, but its weaknesses were exposed during operations over England.

and provision for under wing drop tanks, increasing capacity to 237 imp gals (1,080 lit). The Ju 87R-1 entered service with I./StG 1 after the Norwegian campaign, and was the only Gruppe with the type at the start of the Battle of Britain, the others flying Ju 87Bs.

KANALKAMPF

Stukas were initially involved in the Kanalkampf offensive against Channel convoys and coastal ports that lasted for much of July, sinking six warships and 14 merchantmen. The 'Jumbo' convoy approaching Plymouth in Devon was attacked without damage on July 1. Three days later, 33 Stukas of III./StG 51 targeted Portland, Dorset, hitting the auxiliary anti-aircraft ship HMS *Foylebank* in the harbour, killing 176 of its crew for the loss of one dive bomber that was hit by fire from the warship.

On July 9, a total of 28 Stukas from I./StG 77 attacked a convoy off Portland. Three Spitfire Is of 609 Squadron based at Warmwell, Dorset, intercepted the formation and Flying Officer David M Crook shot down the Stuka flown by the commander of I./StG 77, Hauptmann Friedrich-Karl von Dalwigk zu Lichtenfels. Further losses to the Stürzkampfgruppe were prevented by the intervention of escorting Bf 110Cs. Portland was attacked twice again two days later. Sorties against convoys and ports continued throughout the month. Most of the raids were 'hit and runs' and benefited from heavy fighter cover. Even so, by the end of July, 15 Stukas had been shot down.

The last major operation against a convoy was launched on August 8, targeting 'Peewit', which had sailed from Medway in Kent the previous evening. An initial wave of Stukas from StG 1 was prevented from attacking by RAF fighters, but in the afternoon approximately 60 aircraft from StG 2 and 3, plus escorting Bf 109Es, found the convoy off the Isle of Wight, sinking four ships and damaging seven for the loss of three of its own aircraft. After a third wave from StG 77 attacked 'Peewit' that

evening, only four of the 20 vessels that set sail remained undamaged when the convoy arrived at Swanage, Dorset.

PHASE TWO

Stukas were sent against several RAF airfields on Adlertag (Eagle Day, August 13), the start of the wider Adlerangriff (Eagle Attack) plan to destroy the RAF. They only managed to hit Detling near Maidstone in Kent, badly damaging it and destroying 22 aircraft on the ground. Five of the 27 Ju 87Rs of II./StG 2, which failed to find Middle Wallop in Hampshire, were shot down during a one-sided duel over the Dorset coast by Spitfires of 609 Squadron. The promised fighter escort for the Stukas had not materialised, because of a last minute postponement to operations on Adlertag due to bad weather conditions. Not every unit received the message, including the Stukas.

The next day, two Stukagruppen from Luftflotte 2 were caught up in a dogfight involving more than 200 aircraft over Kent between Dover and Folkestone and were forced to withdraw without hitting their targets. They were more successful the next day, attacking the airfields Hawkinge and Lympne in Kent, although no aircraft were there when the Germans struck. Gruppen I and II of StG 1 raided Portland the same day, suffering four losses.

Raids on August 16 and 18 highlighted the vulnerability of the Stuka during operations where the Luftwaffe lacked air superiority. The Chain Home radar station at Ventnor on the Isle of Wight, and the airfields

at Lee-on-Solent, Hampshire, and Tangmere, West Sussex, were targets on August 16. While Tangmere was badly damaged, with nearly all its buildings hit, the attacking force paid a heavy cost. The Messerschmitts assigned to protect the Stukas were engaged by Spitfires, leaving Hurricanes to hound the dive bombers all the way back to the Normandy coast, downing nine and damaging many more.

On August 18, a total of 109 Stukas from the three Gruppen of StG 77 and I./StG 3, escorted by 102 Messerschmitt Bf 109Es, attacked the airfields at Gosport in Hampshire, and Thorney Island and Ford in West Sussex, plus the nearby Poling Chain Home radar station. It was largest raid over Britain ever undertaken by the Stuka Gruppen. The dive bombers struck three of the targets without interference from the RAF fighters scrambled against the armada, but over Thorney Island I./StG 77 was intercepted by two squadrons of Hurricanes, which downed ten of the dive bombers. Two more Stukas from II./StG 77, heading home after devastating Ford, were shot down by 602 Squadron Spitfires over the sea, while the same RAF unit also claimed a third aircraft belonging to III./StG 77. The total cost of the raids to StG 77 was 17 aircraft shot down or written-off, and a further seven damaged. Such heavy losses could not be sustained and the Stuka was withdrawn from operations over England.

Junkers Ju 87B-1

Dimensions: Length 36ft 5in (11.10m); Wing span 45ft 3⅓in (13.80m); Height 13ft 2in (4.01m); Wing area 343sq ft (31.90m²)

Weights: Empty 5,980lb (2,713kg); Max loaded weight 9,560lb (4,336kg)

Powerplant: One Junkers Jumo 211Da 12-cylinder, liquid-cooled piston engine, rated at 1,200hp (895kW) for take-off and 1,100hp (821kW) at 4,920ft (1,500m); Fuel capacity 106 imp gal (480 lit)

Armament: Two fixed forward-firing 7.92mm (0.31in) MG17 guns and one 7.92mm (0.31in) MG15 gun on a flexible mount in the rear cockpit firing aft; up to 2,205lb (1,000kg) of bombs carried externally, typically one 1,102lb (500kg) SC500 or one 551lb (250kg) SC250 and four 110lb (50kg) SC50 bombs

Performance: Max speed 211mph (340km/h) at sea level, 238mph (383km/h) at 13,410ft (4,087m); Max cruise speed 209mph (336km/h) at 12,140ft (3,700m), economical cruise speed 175mph (282km/h) at 15,090ft (4,599m); Climb rate 1,406ft/min (429m/min); Service ceiling 26,250ft (8,001m); Range without external load 490 miles (789km), 370 miles (595km) with one 1,102lb (500kg) SC500 bomb

Crew: Two, comprising a pilot and radio operator/gunner

Focke-Wulf
Fw 200 CONDOR

The small Fw 200 fleet had a major impact on shipping around Britain.

The impact of the Focke-Wulf Fw 200 Condor on Allied shipping during the Battles of Britain and Atlantic was out of proportion with the small number of aircraft involved. During May 1940, the Fw 200C-0s of Kampfgeschwader (KG, 'bomber wing') 40, based at Oldenburg in Germany, were tasked with dropping magnetic mines at the entrance of harbours on the east coast of Britain.

Adapted from an airliner as a maritime patrol aircraft, the Condor was unstable during take-off, unwieldy to fly at heavy weights and had a tendency to break its back while taxiing on the ground. At the end of the Battle of France, KG 40's Staffel was reduced to two aircraft (from the standard inventory of nine), although the delivery of new-built Fw 200C-1s with ventral gondolas and additional armament, along with the conversion of KG 40's staff flight (Stab) to Junkers Ju 88A-1s, helped increase its strength for the assault on Great Britain. However,

Focke-Wulf Fw 200C-1 Condor

Dimensions: Length 76ft 11½in (32.85m); Wing span 107ft 9½in (32.85m); Height 20ft 8in (6.30m); Wing area 1,290sq ft (119.85m²)

Weights (Fw 200C-3): Empty 34,489lb (17,005kg); Max take-off weight 54,056lb (24,520kg)

Powerplant: Four BMW 132H nine-cylinder radial, air-cooled engines, each rated at 830hp (619kW); Fuel capacity 1,773 imp gal (8,060 lit), plus optional 198 imp gal (900 lit) auxiliary tank in gondola; two or three 66 imp gal (300 lit) drums could be stowed in fuselage to refill tanks in flight

Armament: Forward firing MG FF 20mm (0.787in) cannon at front of under-fuselage gondola and MG15 7.9mm (0.3in) machine gun at rear; forward firing 7.9mm (0.3in) MG15 in fixed cupola on upper forward fuselage. Up to 4,630lb (2,100kg) of bombs on racks on the nacelles of the outboard engines and wings, plus a fifth rack on the under-fuselage gondola; typical load four 551lb (250kg) SC250JA bombs, with fifth rack usually occupied by 551lb (250kg) cement-filled marker bomb

Performance: Max speed 224mph (360km/h); Max cruise 208mph (335km/h); Climb rate 590ft/min (180m/min); Service ceiling 19,685ft (6,000m); Range 2,212 miles (3,560km)

Crew: Five, comprising pilot, co-pilot, navigator/bombardier, radio operator and gunner

production rates for the four-engined aircraft remained low, with only 26 Fw 200C-1s rolling off the production line in Bremen during 1940.

THE SCOURGE

After being ordered to support attacks on the British Isles, KG 40 moved to Bordeaux-Mérignac on the Bay of Biscay in June 1940, falling under IV. Fliegerkorps of Luftflotte 3. Mine-laying operations became secondary as more aggressive anti-shipping and long-range maritime patrols were undertaken around the British Isles. Between August 1, 1940 and February 9, 1941, Fw 200s sank 85 Allied vessels totalling 363,000 tons, resulting in the British Prime Minister Winston Churchill describing the aircraft as "the scourge of the Atlantic". Condors also helped other assets (such as U-boats) find targets by locating and reporting the position of convoys and other allied shipping.

One of KG 40's first victims after the move to France was the 255-ton trawler *Volante*, sunk on July 12 by bombs dropped by a Condor. The most notable attack occurred on October 26, when Fw 200C 'F8+BK' flown by Oberleutnant Bernhard Jope crippled the 42,348-ton troopship *Empress of Britain* – at the time the tenth largest merchant ship in the world – approximately 87 miles (140km) west of the Isle of Arran. Two 551lb (250kg) SC250 bombs hit the troopship, killing at least 25 seamen and setting it ablaze. Tugs took the *Empress* in tow, but its fate was sealed two days later by torpedoes fired from the U-boat U-32.

BOMBING RAIDS

Only very occasionally did KG 40's Condors attack targets on land – they were too few in number and more productively employed against shipping. Losses and the low production rate of the Fw 200 had reduced the Kampfgeschwader's inventory by September 7 to just seven aircraft, of which four were unserviceable.

A solitary Condor made a dawn raid on Belfast Lough, County Down in Northern Ireland, on September 13, initially bombing and machine-gunning motor vessels (including HMT *Arctic Pioneer*) and trawlers. After attacking ships anchored in Bangor Bay, it dropped incendiaries on the coastal town, starting fires but causing no casualties. Three 245 Squadron Hawker Hurricanes scrambled from Aldergrove outside Belfast failed to locate the intruder.

At 0716 hrs on October 14, a Condor flown by Oberleutnant Hans Buchholz dropped five 551lb (250kg) bombs on the Rolls-Royce factory at Hillington near Glasgow, in Scotland. Buchholz again tried to hit the same site one week later, but was prevented from doing so by dense clouds over the target.

A further raid on Glasgow by three Condors was mounted on November 29, which is understood to have resulted in bombs dropping on a northwest suburb of the city and to the south of it, as well as on Falkirk. More problematic for the German authorities was the three bombs that landed on Dublin in the neutral Irish Republic on the morning of December 20, injuring four people. The navigator was significantly off in his calculations; the intended target was Liverpool.

The Seenotdienst (sea rescue service) operated a variety of flying boats and floatplanes, as well as small surface craft, providing a valuable contribution to the effort by recovering aircrew (from both sides) that came down in the sea. Established to operate over the North and Baltic Seas, it moved into bases along the coastlines of territory occupied by Germany in 1939 and 1940 to expand its reach. By the start of the Battle of Britain the Seenotdienst had a presence in both France and the Netherlands, from which it could operate over the English Channel. The Seenotdienst was officially absorbed into the Luftwaffe in July 1940.

In addition to the air-sea rescue assets, maritime operations were undertaken by Küstenfliegergruppe (KüFlGr, 'coastal flying group') of the German coastal air service. A number of different types were operated, including the Dornier Do 18 and Heinkel He 115, which were occasionally encountered by the RAF during the period of the Battle of Britain.

VINTAGE FLOATPLANE

First flown in September 1931, the Heinkel He 59 coastal reconnaissance floatplane was the stalwart of the Luftwaffe's air-sea rescue effort during the Battle of Britain. During the early phases of the campaign, the fleet was painted all-white with large red crosses and carried civil registrations. The British alleged that the aircraft were also used to sow mines in the Thames estuary and land spies along the coast, making them 'fair game'. After several of the vintage biplanes were shot down, the white scheme gave way to camouflage and the aircraft were armed.

Luftwaffe records indicate that 21 He 59s were lost to enemy action from the start of July to the end of October 1940. Among them were two destroyed on October 8 off the coast of Cherbourg by Blenheim IVfs of 235 Squadron, one of the three Coastal Command units officially credited with participating in the Battle of Britain. One of the pair was shot down, while the second crashed. Another He 59 was downed by Sergeant Rupert J Ommanney of 229 Squadron on October 26. He was flying one of three Hurricanes that engaged the German aircraft over the English Channel off Boulogne, France. ➤

ABOVE:
A Heinkel He 59C-2 of Seenotflugkommando 1, which was forced down by a Spitfire pilot of 54 Squadron on July 1, 1940, and beached at Deal, Kent.
Pete West

BELOW: Armed and camouflaged Heinkel He 59 of the Seenotdienst air-sea rescue organisation.
Adrian Mills Collection

Supporting CAST

Many aircraft types not directly involved in the fighting over Britain during 1940 supported Luftwaffe operations.

COASTAL FLOATPLANE

The twin-engine Heinkel He 115 floatplane played a peripheral role in the Battle of Britain, sowing mines and undertaking air-sea rescue missions. Seven Küstenfliegergruppe equipped with He 115B/Cs were operational during the campaign, comprising 3./KüFlGr. 106 and 3./KüFlGr. 906 based at Schellingwoude in the Netherlands under IX. Fliegerkorps ('air corps'); 1./KüFlGr. 106 of Marinegruppe Nord (Northern Naval Group) based at Norderney, Germany; 1./KüFlGr. 906 of Fliegerführer Ost ('flight leader east') at Aalborg-See, Denmark; and 1. to 3. Staffel of KüFlGr. 506 based at Stavanger in Norway with X. Fliegerkorps.

RIGHT: The Dornier Do 18D Wal flying boat remained in service due to delays to its replacement.

From the early stages of the battle, the floatplane was active in the coastal waters around Britain, with several downed by anti-aircraft artillery or RAF fighters. A Spitfire flown by Flying Officer Alistair J O Jeffrey of 64 Squadron was used to shoot down a He 115 he caught laying mines in the Thames estuary on July 19. Another from 3./KüFlGr. 506 was destroyed over the North Sea on August 13 by Flying Officer John H Laughlin of 235 Squadron, in a Blenheim If. A third He 115 was forced down by a combination of anti-aircraft fire and Hurricanes from 145 Squadron on October 2.

BELOW: A Heinkel He 115B, typical of those based in Norway during 1940.

THE WHALE

Delays to the Blohm & Voss Bv 138 flying boat meant that the ageing Dornier Do 18 Wal (Whale) remained in service with five Staffeln of Küstenfliegergruppe during the Battle of Britain. Its poor performance and inadequate defensive armament rendered it obsolete by then, but with no replacement available, the outdated flying boat remained in service. Its main claim to fame in World War Two is the dubious distinction of being the first type of aircraft shot down by a British aircraft, when one of three intercepted by Blackburn Skuas of 803 Squadron of the Fleet Air Arm was downed over the North Sea on September 26, 1939. At least two others suffered similar fates during the Battle of Britain, on September 2 and 28, the latter example at the hands of a Blenheim pilot.

ARADO AR 196

Originally designed to operate from German warships, the Arado Ar 196 floatplane also served with a number of shore-based units. They were used for maritime reconnaissance and helping to locate downed airmen, although its ability to land on the open sea and rescue survivors was poor and in most cases the actual pick-up had to be performed by other types.

During the Battle of Britain, the floatplane was occasionally encountered by RAF aircraft operating over the English Channel and North Sea. On October 12, 1940, an Ar 196 from Bordfliegerstaffel ('embarked air squadron') 1./196 was shot down south of St Catherine's Point on the Isle of Wight by 145 Squadron Hurricanes flown by Flight Lieutenant Adrian H Boyd and Flying Officer Dudley S G Honor.

PHOTO-RECONNAISSANCE DORNIER

Another land-based aircraft operated by the Luftwaffe during the Battle of Britain was the Dornier Do 215, which was originally conceived as an export variant of the Do 17Z bomber. Sweden placed an order for 18 Do 215A-1s in the autumn of 1939. They differed from the Do 17Z primarily by having Daimler-Benz DB601A engines instead of BMW-Bramo 323 Fafnirs. The order was embargoed before the start of the war and the airframes adapted for long-range reconnaissance as Do 215B-0s and -1s. They entered service in early 1940 with a Staffel (3. Aufkl.St/Ob.d.L.) of the Aufklärungsgruppe (Aufkl.Gr, 'reconnaissance group') of the Luftwaffe high command, based at Stavanger in Norway from April 1940.

Further development of the type was authorised, resulting in the Do 215B-4, with a revised camera payload. It was also able to carry up to five 50kg (110lb) bombs. By May 1940, three Staffel of the Aufkl.Gr/Ob.d.L. had Do 215s on strength, and the type was also issued to other independent reconnaissance units.

At least three were intercepted by RAF fighters during photographic missions over the British Isles, on September 18 (over Kent); September 21 (attacked during a mission over Liverpool, crashing in North Wales) and October 24 (caught photographing Coventry and Birmingham in the West Midlands). Just over 100 Do 215s were built, some of which were converted for the nocturnal intruder role from late 1940.

> *"The floatplane played a peripheral role, sowing mines and undertaking air-sea rescue missions"*

ITALIAN

Falcons, Arrows and Storks over England

Italy's dictator, Benito Mussolini, declared war on Great Britain and France on June 10, 1940. The Regia Aeronautica (Italian Air Force, literally Royal Air Force) was soon involved in the fighting over France, but was initially reluctant to operate over Britain.

The commanders of the Regia Aeronautica were aware that its aircraft were poorly equipped for an assault across the English Channel, and were happy to leave that burden to the Luftwaffe alone. However, the Italian foreign ministry within the Palazzo Chigi in Rome was keen for the country's armed forces to take part in the Battle of Britain in some small measure, primarily as a gesture of support. This desire increased as, by the autumn of 1940, it appeared that the German forces would prevail.

In mid-1940, the Regia Aeronautica still lacked a modern single-seat fighter in the class of the British Spitfire or German Messerschmitt Bf 109. Its bombers were also deficient in terms of range, performance and armour. Of particular concern was the equipment (or rather lack of it) in Italian aircraft, as many of the Regia Aeronautica's fighters did not have radio gear installed. The idea of flying and fighting in an open cockpit aircraft

at altitude in the frigid autumn air over Britain was not appealing to pilots used to operations in the more temperate climate of southern Europe and North Africa. Many Italian pilots also lacked the instrument and blind flying skills required for nocturnal bombing raids.

The Luftwaffe was not keen on fighting alongside its Italian counterparts either, partly for nationalistic reasons – not wishing to have to share the glory of subduing England – but also the difficulty of integrating its Axis partner into operations and providing them with the logistical support they would require.

But the foreign ministry got its wish and an independent air corps, the Corpo Aereo Italiano, was mustered under the command of General Rino Corso Fougier and formally established on September 10, 1940. It included approximately 200 aircraft of three main combat types – the Fiat CR.42 Falco (Falcon) and G.50 Frecce (Arrow) fighters and Fiat BR.20M

Cicogna (Stork) medium bomber. In addition, a squadron of CANT Z.1007bis Alcione (Kingfisher) bomber and reconnaissance aircraft was attached to the corps. Small numbers of Caproni Ca.133s and other support types were assigned to the corps to ferry supplies, personnel and spare parts around.

The Corpo Aereo Italiano began its transfer to airfields in Belgium on September 22 when the G.50s departed Italy. Bad weather delayed >

Fiat CR.42 Falco Serie I

Dimensions: Length 27ft 2¾in (8.30m); Wing span (upper) 31ft 9¾in (9.70m); Height 10ft 9⅝in (3.30m); Wing area 241sq ft (22.35m²)

Weights: Empty 3,763lb (1,707kg); Typically loaded 5,042lb (2,287kg); Max take-off weight 5,302lb (2,405kg)

Powerplant: One Fiat A.74 RC.38 14-cylinder radial, air-cooled piston engine, rated at 840hp (627kW); Fuel capacity 77 imp gal (350 lit), plus optional 22 imp gal (100 lit) auxiliary tank

Armament: Two fixed 0.5in (12.7mm) Breda-SAFAT machine guns firing forward

Performance: Max speed 266mph (428km/h) at 13,120ft (3,999m), 256mph (412km/h) at 9,840ft (3,000m); Initial climb rate 2,320ft/min (707m/min); Service ceiling 33,300ft (10,150m); Range 488 miles (785km) at 214mph (344km/h) at 19,685ft (6,000m), 630 miles (1,014km) with auxiliary tank

Crew: One pilot

NEAR RIGHT: German officers examine an 85ª Squadriglia, 18° Gruppo Fiat CR.42 at Maldeghem.

BELOW: Fiat BR.20M MM22267 of 242ª Squadriglia, 99° Gruppo, 43° Stormo Bombardamento Terrestre, at Chièvres in Belgium. The bomber was shot down on November 11, 1940, during a raid on Harwich, Essex. Italian State Archive

their arrival at Ursel until October 17. Of the 77 BR.20Ms that attempted to fly direct to Belgium over the Alps on September 27, only 60 arrived as planned, as two were destroyed and the other 15 had to land en route with mechanical problems. It was only by October 19 that all aircraft were in position. Once in Belgium, the corps was placed under the operational control of the Luftwaffe's II. Fliegerkorps, part of Luftflotte 2.

Fiat BR.20M Cicogna

Dimensions: Length 54ft 8⅔in (16.68m); Wing span 70ft 8¾in (21.56m); Height 14ft 1¼in (4.30m); Wing area 797sq ft (74.00m²)

Weights: Empty 13,889lb (6,300kg); Typically loaded 21,825lb (9,900kg); Max take-off weight 22,267lb (10,100kg)

Powerplant: One Fiat A.80 RC.41 18-cylinder two-row radial, air-cooled piston engine, rated at 1,000hp (746kW) for take-off; Fuel capacity 797 imp gal (3,622 lit)

Armament: Defensive armament of two 7.7mm (0.303in) Breda-SAFAT MC.7,7 machine guns mounted in nose in Fiat H turret and ventral positions, and one 0.5in (12.7mm) Breda-SAFAT MC.12,7 machine gun in a retractable Fiat M.1 turret in dorsal position. Up to 3,527lb (1,600kg) of bombs, typical loads including 12 110lb (50kg), 12 220lb (100kg), four 551lb (250kg), two 1,102lb (500kg) or two 1,764lb (800kg) GP bombs

Performance: Max speed 251mph (404km/h) at 13,451ft (4,100m); Initial climb rate 902ft/min (275m/min); Service ceiling 26,247ft (8,000m); Range 1,709 miles (2,750km)

Crew: Four or five, latter comprising pilot, co-pilot, navigator/bombardier, radio operator/gunner and gunner

---

The Belgian airfields allocated to the Corpo Aereo Italiano were not ideal for operations against Britain, as the short range of its fighters meant they could only spend a brief period – around 10 minutes – over the southern counties of England before being forced to head back to base.

FIGHTERS

The Fiat CR.42 Falco had the distinction of being the last single-seat biplane fighter to be manufactured by the combatants in World War Two. Production began in 1939 and continued until 1943 by which time more than 1,780 had been built for Italy and export customers Belgium, Hungary and Sweden. Early production aircraft were armed with one 0.303in (7.7mm) and one 0.5in (12.7mm) machine gun, but most built had two 0.5in weapons. Around 300 were in service with the Regia Aeronautica when Italy entered the war, and despite its light armament and outdated configuration, the Falco

proved to be effective against French fighters in June 1940.

The Corpo Aereo Italiano had three squadrons of CR.42s assigned, around 50 aircraft, which were based at Maldeghem in East Flanders. They were used to escort Fiat BR.20M bombers on daylight raids over England, but were outclassed by the RAF monoplane fighters they encountered. However, in the hands of a good pilot, the CR.42 proved difficult to hit as the biplane could usually outmanoeuvre the RAF fighters, especially in a turn. The CR.42s left Belgium in February 1941.

In addition to the CR.42, the Corpo Aereo Italiano had approximately 48 Fiat G.50 Freccias of 20° Gruppo Caccia Terrestre assigned. The Freccia was an open cockpit monoplane fighter, armed with a pair of 0.5in (12.7mm) Breda-SAFAT machine guns, but while slightly faster than the CR.42 it was less agile. At the time it was deployed to Belgium, the G.50 lacked armour protection for the pilot's seat or fuel

"Corpo Aereo Italiano bombers participated in 17 raids over Britain, four of which had to be cancelled due to bad weather"

tanks. Its radius of action was limited to only 275 miles (443km).

The G.50-equipped Gruppo arrived at Ursel in Belgium in October 1940. There is no record of the fighter being encountered by the RAF over the British Isles. Instead, it was used on defensive patrols along the coast of Brittany and at night.

BOMBERS

The twin-engined BR.20 Cicogna was the first Italian all-metal bomber to enter service in September 1936. It was the air force's standard bomber when Italy entered the war, but was already obsolete. By then, the improved BR.20M had entered service, with a different nose configuration for the bombardier and slightly longer fuselage, although it was heavier than its predecessor resulting in a decrease in maximum speed. The BR.20M could still only carry up to 3,527lb (1,600kg) of bombs and the reduction in speed increased its vulnerability to fighters. It was also not equipped for the cold climate of northern Europe, as it was originally designed to operate around the Mediterranean. It lacked anti-icing equipment and the crew of at least one BR.20M of the Corpo Aereo Italiano was forced to abandon their attack and return to base due to the build up of ice on the wings.

Corpo Aereo Italiano bombers participated in 17 raids over Britain, four of which had to be cancelled due to bad weather. The first was a night attack on Harwich, Essex, and Felixstowe, Suffolk, on October 24, but three of the 18 BR.20Ms involved were destroyed in accidents, including a crash soon after take-off that killed the six-man crew. Ramsgate in Kent was struck day five days later by 15 BR.20Ms escorted by 39 CR.42s and 34 G.50s, with no response from RAF Fighter Command. Later targets hit included Ipswich in Suffolk (four raids in November, and the last on January 2); Norwich, Norfolk (November 20); and Great Yarmouth, Norfolk, and Lowestoft, Suffolk (both on November 28 and 29, although none reached their targets during the first attack).

Harwich, with its important port, was the most frequently visited target, with six attacks launched in November and three more in December. A raid against the town mounted on November 11 – involving a feint against London – became the most costly for the Italians. A large force of escorting G.50s and Luftwaffe Messerschmitt Bf 109s turned back when they encountered bad weather, leaving 42 CR.42s to defend the scattered bombers. Of the ten BR.20Ms that departed Chièvres in Belgium, three were shot down by RAF Hurricanes, two into the sea. Another three (possibly four) bombers crash-landed on the return flight.

Two of the CR.42s were shot down protecting the bombers. An oil pipe on a third CR.42 broke before the dogfight and the pilot had to force-land on the shingle beach at Orford Ness in Suffolk. The Falco was repaired by the British and in late November 1940 flown to Farnborough, Hampshire, where (as BT474) it was examined by the Royal Aircraft Establishment. From April 1941 it was with the Air Fighting Development Unit at Duxford, Cambridgeshire. The aircraft was preserved and between 1979 and 2016 resided in the Battle of Britain Hall of the RAF Museum at Hendon, north London.

RETURN TO ITALY

The final operational sorties flown by the Corpo Aereo Italiano took place on January 2, 1941, during a night raid on Ipswich, and involved four (or possibly five) BR.20Ms of 13° Stormo. Technical problems prevented two of the bombers carrying out the attack.

By then the general staff of the Regia Aeronautica had decided to withdraw the corps to Italy, mainly to prop up its forces attacking Greece, which had already repulsed an Italian offensive, and as a counter to British forces in Cyrenaica in North Africa. Aircraft and aircrew began to depart Belgium on January 10, 1941, although two squadrons of G.50s of 20° Gruppo remained in western Europe flying defensive sorties. The opportunity was taken to train some of the G.50 pilots on the Bf 109E at Cazaux in France, although the squadrons did not re-equip with the German fighter when they finally left for home in mid-April 1941.

Italy's impact in the campaign against Britain was minimal. In comparison with the Luftwaffe, its bombers inflicted little damage on their intended targets, due to the limited number (ranging from four to 16) sent on each raid. Its fighter pilots failed to shoot down any RAF aircraft. The cost to Italy of operations over Britain included the lives of around 43 aircrew and approximately 36 aircraft, most of which were destroyed in accidents. Its major achievement was helping to cement the relationship with Germany, which was forced to come to the aid of Italian forces struggling in North Africa and Greece in early 1941.

MIDDLE LEFT: Fiat BR.20M MM22621 of 241ª Squadriglia force-landed at Tangham Forest, near Woodbridge, Suffolk, on November 11, 1940, after an engine was put out of action by RAF Hurricanes of 257 Squadron. The hamper was one of two found on the aircraft.

LEFT: Corpo Aereo Italiano personnel working on a pair of Fiat G.50s of 20° Gruppo of the 56° Stormo Caccia Terrestre, late in 1940. Italian State Archive

Order of battle of the Italian Air Corps, October 1940		
Corpo Aereo Italiano		
13° Stormo Bombardamento Terrestre		
11° Gruppo		
4ª Squadriglia	Fiat BR.20M	Melsbroek
11ª Squadriglia	Fiat BR.20M	Melsbroek
43° Gruppo		
3ª Squadriglia	Fiat BR.20M	Melsbroek
5ª Squadriglia	Fiat BR.20M	Melsbroek
43° Stormo Bombardamento Terrestre		
172ª Squadriglia RST	CANT Z.1007bis	Chièvres
98° Gruppo		
240ª Squadriglia	Fiat BR.20M	Chièvres
241ª Squadriglia	Fiat BR.20M	Chièvres
99° Gruppo		
242ª Squadriglia	Fiat BR.20M	Chièvres
243ª Squadriglia	Fiat BR.20M	Chièvres
56° Stormo Caccia Terrestre		
18° Gruppo		
83ª Squadriglia	Fiat CR.42	Maldeghem
85ª Squadriglia	Fiat CR.42	Maldeghem
89ª Squadriglia	Fiat CR.42	Maldeghem
20° Gruppo		
351ª Squadriglia	Fiat G.50	Ursel
352ª Squadriglia	Fiat G.50	Ursel
353ª Squadriglia	Fiat G.50	Ursel

Stormo (Wing); Gruppo (Group); Squadriglia (Squadron); Stormo Bombardamento Terrestre (Land-based Bomber Wing); Stormo Caccia Terrestre (Land-based Fighter Wing); RST – Ricognizione Strategica Terrestre (Land-based Strategic Reconnaissance)

Nap of the Earth ATTACK

The efforts of the Luftwaffe resulted in August 18, 1940, being described as the hardest day of the Battle of Britain for both sides. For the Germans it was the low-level raid on RAF Kenley that proved the most spectacular and costly, as **Chris Goss** relates.

RIGHT: Hptm Joachim Roth.

By the start of the Battle of Britain, Germany had bolstered its defences with modern aircraft. Some targets, however, required low-level work and the Dornier Do 17, which was being replaced by the Junkers Ju 88, was still considered capable enough for the planned attack on RAF Kenley. One unit that specialised in low-altitude missions was 9 Staffel/Kampfgeschwader 76 (9./KG 76), a component of KG 76's third Gruppe led by Hptm Alois Lindmayr. The crews of 9 Staffel had been active in the Battle of France, losing a number of aircraft and crew, including its Staffelkapitän Oblt Rudolf Strasser during a low-level sortie against Valenciennes on May 19, 1940. The Staffel was then led by Hptm Joachim Roth and based with the rest of the Gruppe at Cormeilles-en-Vexin, northern France. The plan for the August 18, 1940 raid on RAF Kenley on the Kent/Surrey border, was that Ju 88s of Hptm Friedrich Möricke's II./KG 76 would deliver the initial blow from medium altitude, after which 9./KG 76 would carry out a low-level attack. The

BELOW: Leading Kette passing Beachy Head.

remaining Do 17s of III./KG 76 and Maj Theodore Schweitzer's I./KG 76 would mount the final wave, but not at low level.

TARGET KENLEY

Roth briefed his crews that morning as to the target and their approach

method. Nine aircraft were slated for participation, several carrying either war reporters or additional officers so they could gain operational experience. Flying in three formations of three aircraft (a formation known as a Kette), the lead Do 17 was flown by Oblt Rudolf Lamberty with Roth as observer. In addition to two other crew was Hptm Gustav Peters who was also along for familiarisation. To their left in the formation was Uffz Mathias Maassen, and to the right Fw Wilhelm Raab. The second Kette to the left had Fw Johannes Petersen flying the lead, with Uffz Günther Unger to the left and Fw Adolf Reichel to the right. Leading the final Kette was Oblt Hermann Magin, with Uffz Bernhard Schumacher and Fw Otto Stephani on his flanks. War reporters Rolf von Pebal and Georg Hinze accompanied Reichel and Magin respectively, while staff officer Oberst Dr Otto Sommer was flying with Petersen.

However, weather over the target delayed take-off and the 9 Staffel crews were forced to hang around the dispersal sunbathing, as Günther Unger wrote afterwards:

LEFT: Aircrew of 9./KG 76 seen relaxing some time before the attack on Kenley, August 18, 1940.

"Gradually we became impatient. Were we going to be sent home to our billets today without flying [the] mission as had happened so often in the past?"

TIME TO FLY

Just before midday, the order to take off finally came, with 9./KG 76 formating over Cormeilles and heading for the French shore. In an attempt to confuse Allied defences, 9./KG 76 would cross the British coast to the west with the remainder of KG 76, with He 111s of KG 1 (targeting RAF Biggin Hill) further east. To make matters more difficult for the RAF, Messerschmitt Bf 110s of Zerstörergeschwader 26 (ZG 26) and Bf 109s of Jagdgeschwader (JG) 3, JG 26, JG 51 and JG 54 were over Kent either on fighter sweeps or close escort for all but 9./KG 76. This would be unfortunate for Roth and his crews as due to a delay in gathering over France, 9./KG 76 would end up over Kenley five minutes before II./KG 76

LEFT: Cyprus Road, Burgess Hill, 1309hrs, as taken by a photographer aboard one of the Do 17s.

was briefed to be overhead – and the RAF was waiting.

The route taken just clipped Beachy Head over the cliffs to the east of Seaford, between Lewes and Southease and then turned north over Burgess Hill to approach Kenley from the south in line abreast, as low as possible. Amazingly, war reporter Rolf von Pebal was able to take a series of photographs of the approach, as did Georg Hinze, but for reasons which would later become obvious, the latter was not able to secure imagery after the attack.

The approach was uneventful but as Kenley came into sight, 111 Squadron intercepted the Dorniers. Twelve Hurricanes led by Flt Lt Stanley Connors spotted the Do 17s at 50ft and chased

RIGHT: A 9./KG 76 Do 17 practising low-level flying off the French coast.

BELOW: Dornier Do 17 F1+AB of Stab I./KG 76 over England, summer 1940. It is thought this is the aircraft of either Maj Theodore Schweitzer or Hptm Robert von Sichart.

them. Connors managed to latch on to the lead Kette, joined by Plt Off Peter Simpson, only to be shot at by almost all the German gunners. Connors broke away, his aircraft damaged either by return fire or shots from the ground and, with his Hurricane on fire, he crashed near Leaves Green. His body was thrown from the wreck. Simpson was luckier, just being wounded in the foot, and he managed to force-land on Woodcote Park Golf Club at Epsom. Ground defences, which included parachute cable (PAC) equipment that fired steel wires then held aloft by parachute, were quickly in action. The first German aircraft to be irreparably damaged was flown by Fw Johannes Petersen leading the left-hand Kette. Flying slightly higher than the others, it was singled out by ground fire and was soon ablaze. The bomber then ran into one of the parachute cables and plunged into a garden in Kenley's Golf Road on the edge of the airfield, killing all of the crew. At the same time a burst of gunfire hit the port engine of Uffz Günther Unger's bomber and at low-level he struggled to keep control. The same fate had befallen Uffz Bernhard Schumacher's aircraft, its port engine belching brown smoke. Meanwhile, the lead Do 17 had been forced to pull up due to PACs, which allowed a Bofors gunner to strike the bomber's port wing, rupturing a fuel tank and setting it alight. As Rudolf

Lamberty struggled to escape from Kenley and banked right, the flames got stronger and he saw the 111 Squadron Hurricanes of Sgts Bill Dymond and Ron Brown (which were joined by the Spitfire of Sqn Ldr Aeneas MacDonell of 64 Squadron) about to swoop. The first pass further damaged the Dornier, forcing Lamberty to immediately crash-land his burning mount near Biggin Hill, where he and his four crew were quickly captured; all were wounded or injured.

Despite what had happened to the bombers, three hangars and numerous other buildings were destroyed at Kenley, the telephone system was cut and several 615 Squadron Hurricanes and a Blenheim were destroyed. Nine airmen, mainly from 64 and 615 Squadrons, were killed and another seven wounded.

RUNNING FOR HOME

The German survivors had to get home after the assault, but casualties grew. Oblt Hermann Magin was mortally wounded when a bullet hit him in the chest. His observer, Obfw Wilhelm-Friedrich Illg, leant over him, grabbed the control

column and forced the bomber into a climb before levelling the machine so they could bale out. Illg found that he could not turn the aircraft as Magin's legs were jammed against the rudder pedals and they were flying towards central London. Fw Willi Henke and war

LEFT: **Oblt Rudolf Lamberty.**

LEFT: **East Grinstead as photographed by Georg Hinze who was with Oblt Hermann Magin's crew.**

BELOW: **The engine cowling of Uffz Günther Unger's Do 17 with Seaford in the background.**

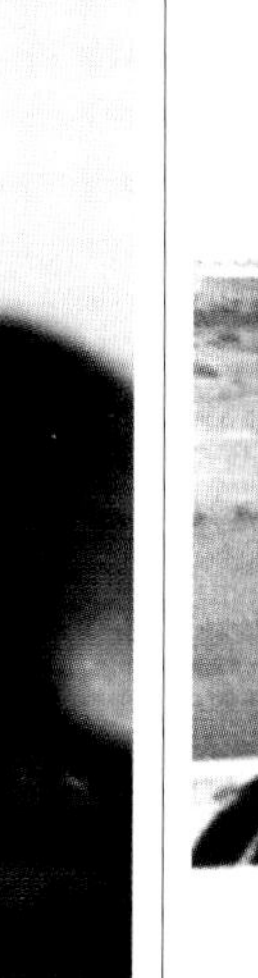

reporter Georg Hinze lifted out Magin's body and Illg got into the pilot's seat, managing to turn south but still having to avoid being hit by anti-aircraft fire. The crew took stock and it became clear Magin was very seriously wounded, the bullet having smashed his left arm and entered the left of the chest; his flying suit was soaked with blood. They crossed the Channel without incident and aimed to make a wheels-down landing at Saint-Omer. It took four attempts but Illg eventually succeeded in setting down further south at Rely-Norrent-Fontes. Magin never regained consciousness and died before he could be taken to hospital. For his actions that day, Illg, who had never flown a Do 17 before, was recommended for the Ritterkreuz (Knight's Cross) and promotion to officer, but before he could receive these, he too was shot down and taken prisoner on the first day of the following month.

Back at Kenley, Fw Otto Stephani was flying for his life, trying to evade three Hurricanes. With his port engine smoking badly, one crew member dead and another badly injured (and who would die of his wounds three days later), he was lucky to make it as far as the Channel. Meanwhile, Günther Unger struggled to reach the Channel, only to be intercepted by Sgt Harry Newton of 111 Squadron. As Newton came in for the kill, Unger's gunner Uffz Franz Bergmann managed to hit the Hurricane, which immediately burst into flames. The RAF pilot pulled for altitude and baled out, his Hurricane crashing at Woldingham in Surrey, but the Dornier struggled onwards.

The surviving German aircraft, all of them sustaining varying degrees of

damage and with wounded or dead crew, made it to the Channel but two of their number did not reach France. The first to ditch $15^1/_2$ miles (25km) off the French coast was Uffz Bernhard Schumacher; he and two of his crew managed to clamber into a dinghy but Fw Fritz Gaiser could not inflate his life jacket and drowned. Next to ditch was Günther Unger. All his crew got out and were rescued that evening off Boulogne, but the entire group suffered from shock and exposure. Meanwhile Uffz Mathias Maassen managed to land near Boulogne, while Otto Stephani had jettisoned all he could, including the body of Uffz Peter Fretz, and force-landed just behind the beach at Calais. Fw Adolf Reichel could go on no longer so crash-landed in a corn field near Abbeville. Last to alight was the aircraft flown by Wilhelm-Friedrich Illg at Rely-Norrent-Fontes.

FAR LEFT: Fw Günther Unger of 9./KG 76 was forced to ditch in the Channel on the return flight.

LEFT: A Do 17 of KG 76 showing the results of an attack by an RAF fighter.

and carrying war reporter Hans Theyer, crash-landed near Calais with serious combat damage.

The human cost to 9./KG 76 in the attack was five aircrew captured, eight killed and six wounded. Of those who survived that day, three would be taken prisoner later in the Battle of Britain and one more killed in 1940, while another three men would be captured in 1941 before KG 76 moved to the Russian Front. However, thanks to two fortunate war reporters who survived the fateful day, dramatic evidence of the attack still exists 85 years after the event.

LEFT: This damaged bomber is the Do 17 of I./KG 76 that crashed at Hurst Green on August 18, 1940, after being shot down by 32 Squadron's Plt Off Alan Eckford.

If 9 Staffel's fortunes were not bad enough, 1./KG 76 lost a Do 17 flown by Oblt Walter Stoldt, which crashed at Hurst Green in Surrey, killing him and one of his crew as well as war reporter Walter Surk; another two Do 17s each from 2 and 3 Staffels returned damaged with a wounded crewman. A Ju 88 of 5./KG 76, flown by Ofw Karlo Geier, crashed near Hurst Green killing all four crew and another from 6./KG 76, and the same fate befell Ofw Karl Krebs whose aircraft came down near Aylesford. War reporter Willi Perchemeier wrote later: "The target was Kenley aerodrome… it was intended our Ju 88 Gruppe would lure away British fighters and flak attention from another Do 17 Staffel, which would attack at low-level. In addition, we would then dive bomb the target. We flew at 4,000m and a short time after the flak stopped, the fighters appeared. One of them hit our port engine which immediately burst into flames."

Another Ju 88 from 5./KG 76 returned damaged with one wounded crewman, while the Dornier flown by Lt Ernst Leder of 8 Staffel crashed off Dungeness, killing all five crew. Yet another from 8./KG 76, flown by Uffz Werner Windschild

LEFT: Adolf Reichel's Do 17 after it belly landed near Abbeville, France, on the return flight.

Confirmed Luftwaffe aircrew in the Kenley attack

Kette 1
F1+DT: Pilot Oblt Rudolf Lamberty, Hptm Joachim Roth, Fw Hugo Eberhardt, Obfw Valentin Geier, Hptm Gustav Peters. All POW
F1+?T: Uffz Mathias Maassen, Fw Max Schümann (w)
F1+LT: Pilot Fw Wilhelm Raab, Lt Erwin Wittmann (w), Uffz Erich Malter, Gefr Werner Seuffert

Kette 2
F1+HT: Pilot Fw Johannes Petersen, Oblt Hans-Siegfried Ahrends, Uffz Karl Greulich, Fw Hans Dietz, Obstlt Dr Otto Sommer. All (†)
F1+?T: Pilot Uffz Günther Unger, Fw August Meier, Uffz Karl Mortiz, Uffz Franz Bergmann
F1+CT: Pilot Fw Adolf Reichel, Uffz Albert Haas, war reporter Rolf von Pebal

Kette 3
F1+JT: Pilot Oblt Hermann Magin (†), Obfw Wilhelm-Friedrich Illg, Uffz Hans Strahlendorf, Fw Willi Henke, war reporter Georg Hinze
F1+?T: Pilot Uffz Bernhard Schumacher, Fw Fritz Gaiser (†)
F1+?T: Pilot Fw Otto Stephani, Uffz Rudolf Grömmer, Uffz Nikolaus Schwab (†), Uffz Peter Fretz (†).

(†) killed   (w) wounded

After the BATTLE

The Battle of Britain was a turning point in the war. It secured the British Isles for offensive operations over Europe.

Brit
ish authorities officially date the Battle of Britain as taking place between 10 July and October 31, 1940. In Germany it is seen as part of the wider Luftschlacht um England (Air Battle for England), which effectively continued until most of the Luftwaffe units were withdrawn from western Europe to prepare for the attack on the Soviet Union in June 1941.

At no point did the Luftwaffe gain air supremacy over Britain and although Fighter Command came close to collapse, it remained operational throughout. The Royal Navy also remained intact and capable of intercepting any attempted crossing of the English Channel by an invasion fleet. The Luftwaffe failed to achieve its primary objectives.

Adolph Hitler postponed Operation Seelöwe (Sealion), the planned invasion of Britain, indefinitely on September 17, 1940. For the British, this removed the immediate threat. As the months progressed the chances of an invasion in 1940 diminished; the approach of winter and the bad weather associated with it would make any attempted sea invasion difficult, pushing back the prospect of an invasion to the summer of 1941, when conditions would again be favourable. By then, the war had progressed in a different direction.

Those on the distribution list within the British government and at the higher military levels were aware that the threat of invasion had been

lifted via Ultra, the product of the code breakers at Bletchley Park in Buckinghamshire. Around September 7, Ultra revealed that the Luftwaffe was reaching the limit of its resources and that German intelligence had greatly underestimated the RAF's strength; it also put a date on the invasion, September 15. That date saw some of the fiercest fighting in the skies over England, when the head of Fighter Command, Air Chief Marshal Sir Hugh Dowding, decisively committed his forces in southern England against the Luftwaffe, resulting in the largest losses for the Germans of the campaign. It was a turning point.

LOOKING TO THE EAST

The German campaign against Britain was expected to be a repeat of the quick victories achieved against the countries of continental Europe. It aimed to force a negotiated or military solution so that Germany could turn its forces to the east, against the Soviet Union. Planning by the German high command for the assault had started in July 1940. Revised plans for what became Operation Barbarossa were ordered by Hitler on December 18, 1940, with the date for the start of operations set for May 15, 1941. The plan depended on the German army being able to achieve its aims before the Russian winter set in, which would greatly limit its mobility. Delays caused by having to intervene in Yugoslavia in April 1941 and the need for additional

time to marshal the forces required in the east meant that German forces actually crossed the Soviet border on June 22, 1941.

LEGACY OF THE BATTLE OF BRITAIN

The Battle of Britain was the first time that German forces were prevented from achieving their aims. It was the first large campaign in which air power was the major and deciding factor. Only a small number of people were involved in the fighting in comparison to the land battles of the war, and casualties were relatively light, but it was a major victory for the British.

Much of the ground work for the successful defence during the summer of 1940 was laid in the pre-war years, when fighter production increased and the infrastructure and equipment of Fighter Command improved. The battle demonstrated the importance of technology in air warfare, including the 'Dowding System' of air defence connecting radar, tracking and communications, to make the most efficient use of the limited number of RAF fighters.

The defeat of the Luftwaffe in the Battle of Britain and the invasion of the Soviet Union committed Germany to a long war of attrition on two fronts that it was ill prepared to fight. Britain remained as a base of resistance to German control of Europe, growing in strength and gaining new Allies until the day came in June 1944 to begin the liberation of occupied Europe.

The COST

Both sides suffered heavy losses of men and machines during the Battle of Britain.

A total of 537 RAF airmen were killed, while the equivalent figure for the Luftwaffe was 2,662. The higher number of German casualties was a factor of the different types of aircraft they flew during the campaign; the bombers carrying a crew of four or five, while the Messerschmitt Bf 110 usually flying with two on board. As the vast majority of RAF aircraft engaged in the battle were single-seat fighters, fewer of its flying personnel went into harm's way each time they scrambled to meet the intruders.

The total number of RAF aircraft shot down during the fighting was 1,023. The Luftwaffe lost 1,887. Several factors contributed to the higher German number, including the different types of aircraft the Luftwaffe operated during the campaign. Generally, when fighters intercept bombers, the latter almost always come off worse. Messerschmitt Bf 109 pilots had to keep a close eye on fuel levels while operating over enemy territory, as the aircraft's limited supply could quickly be consumed during dogfights, making it difficult to return home.

In addition to the chances of falling victim to Fighter Command's fighters, German aircraft operating over England faced other defences, including land-based anti-aircraft artillery and guns mounted on ships around the coast. The guns of the British Army's Anti-Aircraft Command claimed around 300 aircraft during the battle. Luftwaffe crews nursing damaged aircraft had the option of coming down on British soil, but those who survived a crash landing would have to sit out the rest of the conflict as prisoners of war. Some would risk the flight home to their bases over the Channel; many did not make it.

OVER-CLAIMING

Much research over the years has gone into confirming and identifying the victories claimed by both sides during the campaign. Confirming that an opponent last seen trailing smoke and heading for the ground had in fact been destroyed, while trying to avoid a similar fate, was difficult.

Over-claiming of enemy aircraft destroyed has occurred throughout the history of air warfare. Germany claimed the Luftwaffe destroyed 147 RAF aircraft on August 18. The real figure was 33. At the height of the battle, on September 15, RAF pilots stated they shot down 185 Luftwaffe aircraft, three times the actual figure. While the exaggerated figures were widely distributed – to boost morale or as propaganda – each side obviously knew what its own casualties were. Late in September, the head of Fighter Command, Air Chief Marshal Hugh C T Dowding, conceded to Sir Archibald Sinclair, Secretary of State for Air, that he believed the claims were at least 25% higher than the actual figure.

Military personnel were not the only ones caught up in the conflict. British civilian deaths during the Battle of Britain were approximately 12,300, with more than 20,000 injured. A further 32,000 would die during the Blitz.

Aircraft Losses During the Battle of Britain					
Date	RAF	Luftwaffe	Date	RAF	Luftwaffe
July 10	2	11	September 5	20	27
July 11	6	17	September 6	20	33
July 12	5	9	September 7	25	41
July 13	6	6	September 8	5	16
July 14	1	3	September 9	17	30
July 15	2	5	September 10	3	13
July 16	1	4	September 11	29	29
July 17	1	4	September 12	1	7
July 18	5	6	September 13	3	7
July 19	10	5	September 14	13	13
July 20	9	12	September 15	31	61
July 21	2	12	September 16	1	10
July 22	2	4	September 17	6	8
July 23	2	5	September 18	12	20
July 24	5	15	September 19	0	10
July 25	9	19	September 20	8	8
July 26	1	5	September 21	1	11
July 27	2	5	September 22	1	6
July 28	6	11	September 23	11	17
July 29	6	11	September 24	6	11
July 30	1	9	September 25	6	16
July 31	7	7	September 26	8	9
August 1	4	13	September 27	28	57
August 2	3	7	September 28	17	12
August 3	0	6	September 29	6	9
August 4	1	2	September 30	21	47
August 5	2	8	October 1	7	9
August 6	6	6	October 2	2	18
August 7	4	3	October 3	1	9
August 8	21	24	October 4	1	15
August 9	3	6	October 5	7	14
August 10	0	1	October 6	2	9
August 11	28	38	October 7	17	19
August 12	18	32	October 8	8	17
August 13	15	39	October 9	3	9
August 14	9	20	October 10	8	12
August 15	35	76	October 11	9	10
August 16	24	44	October 12	11	13
August 17	2	5	October 13	4	6
August 18	33	67	October 14	1	4
August 19	5	11	October 15	15	16
August 20	2	8	October 16	3	15
August 21	4	14	October 17	5	16
August 22	4	4	October 18	6	14
August 23	1	8	October 19	1	6
August 24	20	41	October 20	5	11
August 25	18	23	October 21	2	7
August 26	29	42	October 22	6	12
August 27	7	11	October 23	1	4
August 28	15	32	October 24	3	12
August 29	10	24	October 25	14	24
August 30	25	40	October 26	8	10
August 31	41	39	October 27	14	16
September 1	13	16	October 28	0	14
September 2	14	37	October 29	12	28
September 3	15	20	October 30	9	8
September 4	17	28	October 31	0	2

BELOW: One that did not make it back. A Messerschmitt Bf 109E with bullet holes on the rear fuselage is examined by curious British service personnel. Key Collection

SURVIVING
Battle of Britain Aircraft

Very few aircraft that fought in the Battle of Britain remain today in comparison with the huge numbers flown by both sides during the summer and autumn of 1940. The nature of conflict and accidents during the war meant that aircraft were written-off at a high rate.

ABOVE: The number of airworthy Hurricanes – including several Battle of Britain veterans – has increased greatly over the last two decades. Hawker Restorations worked on nearly all of the projects, including R4118.

Those that survived service were withdrawn when they became obsolete and most were scrapped. Towards the end of the conflict, a small number deemed worthy of preservation were allocated to the Air Historical Branch, responsible for the archive and records service of the RAF, and many of the aircraft from the Battle of Britain owe their existence to this policy.

Several aircraft that were operated in the Battle of Britain have been 'resurrected' from remains recovered from crash sites or even components. The work of warbird restorers, notably Hawker Restorations in the UK, has increased the population of survivors considerably in the last couple of decades. Hawker Restorations is responsible for most of the Hurricanes currently flying. The end of the Cold War meant that wreck sites in the territory of the former Soviet Union could be investigated by western warbird collectors and the remains of many aircraft were exported for restoration, some back to airworthy condition.

Defining what constitutes a surviving Battle of Britain aircraft is subjective. Aircraft shot down during the campaign obviously did not – but what if the wreck was recovered and rebuilt 70 years later? Several of the aircraft described below were reconstructed using the parts of many different aircraft, or incorporating new components. How much of the original airframe has to survive to make it a genuine veteran of 1940?

In addition to the aircraft detailed below, large components of several others exist in museum collections. Examples include the conserved, but unrestored, remains of Hurricane I P1375 of the RAF Museum stored at Stafford, Staffordshire. Pilot Officer Gerald H Maffett was shot down in the aircraft during combat with Messerschmitt Bf 110s on August 17, 1940, crashing at Walton-on-the-Naze, Essex. He baled out at low level but was killed when his parachute failed to open in time. Another example is the cockpit section and Rolls-Royce Merlin engine of Hurricane I P3179, displayed at the Tangmere Military

Aviation Museum on the former RAF airfield in West Sussex from at least 2003. Sergeant Dennis Noble of 43 Squadron, based at the airfield, was fatally wounded in the aircraft during a dogfight with Heinkel He 111s and Messerschmitt Bf 109s on August 30.

The notable exception detailed below is the RAF Museum's Dornier Do 17, currently far from a complete airframe, but as it is a unique example of a Luftwaffe bomber from the campaign it is included.

HURRICANE I L1592

The 47th Hurricane off the Brooklands production line in Surrey, Hurricane I L1592 has been displayed within the Science Museum at South Kensington in London since May 1961 as 'KW-Z', the code it wore while with 615 'County of Surrey' Squadron during the Battle of Britain. It is the only survivor with the Hurricane's original fabric-covered wings.

Taken on RAF charge on May 19, 1938, it was issued to 56 Squadron at North Weald, Essex, on June 3, transferring to 17 Squadron the

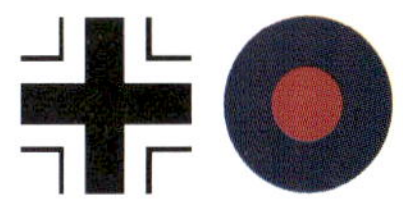

following month. In October 1939, it was with 43 Squadron at Tangmere, returning to Debden in north Essex with 17 Squadron that November. The Hurricane returned to 43 Squadron in February 1940, initially based at Acklington, Northumberland, and remained with the unit when it moved to Wick in the county of Highland in Scotland at the end of the month.

On April 10, while being flown by Flying Officer J D 'Eddie' Edmonds, it shared in the destruction of a He 111. The squadron moved to Tangmere on May 31. The next day Pilot Officer Anthony Woods-Scawen damaged two Messerschmitt Bf 109s during a sortie over Dunkirk in France, but damage to the Hurricane resulted in a wheels-up landing at Tangmere. On July 23, the Hurricane joined 615 Squadron at Kenley, Surrey, and was crash-landed

by Pilot Officer David J Looker at Croyden in Greater London on August 18, after he was injured during combat with Bf 109s over Sevenoaks, Kent.

After repair at Henlow, Bedfordshire, the fighter was delivered to Christchurch, Dorset, for the use of the Station Defence Flight, with the code 'ZQ-U'. The flight was an 'ad hoc' unit formed to defend the airfield; L1592 was used to intercept a Dornier bomber on November 10, without result. It left Christchurch on August 25, 1941.

After a brief period of storage at 15 Maintenance Unit (MU) at Wroughton, Wiltshire, the Hurricane was employed by several second line organisations, starting with 9 Air Observer School (until late April 1942), then 5 and 9 (Pilots) Advanced Flying Units. It was finally retired to 22 MU at Silloth, Cumbria, on October 8, 1943, moving to Sealand in Flintshire, Wales, in 1945. From then until December 1954, when it was passed to the Science Museum, it served as an exhibition airframe with the Air Historical Branch. Initially stored at Sydenham in south London by the museum, L1592 was restored by

Hawker at Dunsfold, Surrey, prior to being placed in the aviation gallery on the top floor of its South Kensington building.

HURRICANE I P2617

Gloster-built Hurricane I P2617 was delivered from Brockworth in Gloucestershire, to 20 MU at Ashton Down in the same county in mid-January 1940, before going to 6 MU at Brize Norton, Oxfordshire, on February

24. It was first issued to 615 'County of Sussex' Squadron at Abbeville in France, where the unit was part of the British Expeditionary Force, before being transferred to 607 'County of Durham' Squadron at the same French airfield. The aircraft flew during the Battle of France before leaving that country for Croydon on May 20.

Between June and September, 607 Squadron was based at Usworth, Tyne and Wear, repelling a large raid by He 111s and Do 17s on August 15. The squadron, including P2617, moved south to Tangmere and became operational within 11 Group on September 8. It moved north again, to Turnhouse outside Edinburgh, on October 10, but 16 days later P2617 was transferred to 1 (RCAF) Squadron at Prestwick in South Ayrshire and later Castledown, Caithness, making a wheels-up landing on November 20, 1940. It was repaired by Gloster at Brockworth and, after a period of storage at Wroughton and Kemble, Gloucestershire, it was issued to 9 Service Flying Training School (SFTS) at Hullavington in Wiltshire on July 31, 1941. The Hurricane was with 8 SFTS at Montrose, Forfarshire, from January ›

ABOVE:
The remains of Sergeant Dennis Noble's Hurricane I P3179, displayed at the Tangmere Military Aviation Museum in West Sussex.

LEFT: For many years, the wreckage of Hurricane I P1375 was displayed within the Battle of Britain Hall at Hendon in north London.

LEFT: Hurricane I L1592 'flies' in the aviation galley of the Science Museum in South Kensington, where it has remained for over 60 years.

TOP: Hurricane I P2617 within the 'E-Pen' in the Battle of Britain Hall at Hendon in 2004.

ABOVE: Former Soviet Air Force Hurricane IIa DR348 was restored in its 253 Squadron markings with its first identity, P3717. It is seen at Turweston in Buckinghamshire in April 2017, soon after making its post-restoration flight.

BELOW: During July 1951, Hurricane I P2617 appeared in the film *Angels One Five* wearing the false identity 'P2619' and 56 Squadron markings as 'US-B'.

1942, and then 9 (Pilots) Advanced Flying Unit at Hullavington between March 1942 and August 1943, after which it was placed in storage with 22 MU at Silloth.

As a Battle of Britain veteran it was selected for preservation by the Air Historical Branch in April 1944. It was stored at various maintenance units and is thought to be have been at Stanmore Park in north London from the late 1940s – it was also displayed numerous times at Horse Guards Parade during Battle of Britain week, as well as appearing in the films *Angels One Five* in 1951 and *Reach for the Sky* four years later. In 1958, the aircraft was with 71 MU at Bicester, Oxfordshire, which used it as a travelling exhibit, a role it continued until 1972. In the middle of that year it was put on display at the newly-opened RAF

Museum at Hendon, moving over to the Battle of Britain Hall at the same site when that was opened in 1978, wearing 607 Squadron markings as 'AF-F'. It was moved back into the main RAF Museum building after the retitled Battle of Britain Experience was refurbished to celebrate the RAF's centenary in 2018.

HURRICANE I P3351

Hurricane P3351 was built at Brooklands in early 1940 and issued on June 1 direct to 73 Squadron at Le Mans in France, returning to England 18 days later, as the German army advanced. By July 7, the fighter was with 72 Squadron at Church Fenton in Yorkshire, before following A Flight to Prestwick 12 days later for night fighter training. It was damaged while landing at night at Prestwick on July 21. After being repaired the Hurricane was transferred in September to 32 Squadron based at Acklington and later Middle Wallop in Hampshire.

In December 1940, it was at Martlesham Heath, Suffolk, with 71 'Eagle' Squadron manned by American volunteers, but after another crash landing and repairs in May 1941 it was issued to 55 Operational Training Unit (OTU) at Usworth, where it was damaged again on September 9.

P3551 was dismantled and rebuilt as a Hurricane IIa Series 2 with the new military markings DR393. It was crated at Glasgow Docks in late January 1942 and embarked on the transport SS *Ocean Voice* on May 3 for delivery to the Soviet Union. The fighter crashed near Murmansk in the winter of 1943.

In 1991, the remains of the aircraft were recovered from the crash site. The hulk was returned to England and was with Jim Pearce's Sussex Spraying Services at Lancing in West Sussex from September 1992. The next year it was sold to Sir Tim Wallis for the Alpine Fighter Collection (AFC) at

Wanaka in New Zealand, with work to return it to the air beginning in April 1994 at AJD Engineering/Hawker Restorations at Sudbury, Suffolk. On August 25, 1995, with restoration at the halfway point, the Hurricane was handed over for shipping to New Zealand, where AFC and Air New Zealand Engineering at Christchurch continued the work. Returned to its former RAF identity as P3351, with the codes 'TP-K' and registered as ZK-TPL, it first flew again on January 12, 2000.

In early 2013, it was sold to Jan Frisco Roozen, arriving in France for its new owner on February 10. Registered as F-AZXR, it was reassembled by Aero Restorations at Dijon and test flown on May 14. It was sold in 2002 and in late 2024 was at Elmsett, Suffolk, with AJD Engineering/Hawker Restorations, having been acquired by the Letecké Muzeum Tocná of the Czech Republic. The Hurricane was being restored as 'P3143' 'NN-D' of 310 (Czechoslovak) Squadron.

HURRICANE I P3717

Built as part of the third production batch, Hurricane I P3717 was initially issued to 238 Squadron in mid-1940. It passed to 253 Squadron at Kirton-in-Lindsey in Lincolnshire on July 13, 1940, and was still with the unit when it moved to Kenley, Surrey, on August 29. The following day it was flown by Pilot Officer Wlodzimierz M C Samolinski in action over Surrey against the Messerschmitt Bf 110s of Zestörergeschwader (ZG, 'destroyer wing') 2, the Polish pilot claiming one of the twin-engined fighters during the dogfight. The Hurricane was badly damaged in the fight and returned to Hawker for repairs.

It later served with 257 and 43 Squadrons, before going to 55 OTU and 8 Flying Training School (FTS), after

"As a Battle of Britain veteran it was selected for preservation"

which it became one of a batch of 40 Mk Is selected for upgrade as Mk IIas for delivery to the Soviet Union, gaining the new identity DR348. It officially left for Russia on October 11, 1941.

The wreck of the aircraft was recovered by Jim Pearce from Russia and shipped to his facility in West Sussex in September 1990, with the intention of using it as the basis of a static restoration. By early 1994, the remains were with Steve Milnthorpe's Hurricane and Aircrew Collection at Hinckley, Leicestershire, forming part of a complex Hurricane restoration that included parts of many other aircraft. In 2002, it moved to Sudbury for work by Hawker Restorations and was for sale by the end of the year, being destined for new owner Hugh Taylor of Hawker Hurricane Ltd as G-HITT. It was transported by road to Turweston, Buckinghamshire, on February 10, 2015, making its first post-restoration flight as P3717 'SW-P' on March 21, 2017, and was based at Old Warden, Bedfordshire, soon after.

HURRICANE I R4118

One of a batch of 100 Hurricane Is built by Gloster and delivered in July and August 1940, R4118 was initially delivered to 605 Squadron at Croydon on August 17. The fighter flew 49 sorties and was involved in the shooting down or damaging of five enemy aircraft before suffering battle damage on October 22, requiring repairs away from base.

On January 18, 1941, it joined 111 Squadron at Dyce in Aberdeenshire, later being relegated to training duties with 59 and 56 OTUs. In late 1943,

it was crated for transport to India, arriving in Bombay, but is understood not to have been re-erected. It was relegated to an instructional airframe on October 4, 1944, and donated to the Banaras Hindu University during 1947.

The derelict remains of the Hurricane were rediscovered by Peter Vacher in March 1982 and negotiations to bring it back to the UK started in 1996. This took until June 2001 to be concluded, allowing the aircraft to be crated and shipped back to the UK. It was registered as G-HUPW in August 2001.

Return to the air was entrusted to Hawker Restorations and the Hurricane flew initially again from Cambridge Airport on December 23, 2004, wearing its former 605 Squadron colours as 'UP-W'. Peter sold the fighter to Hurricane Heritage in September 2015 and it moved to Old Warden the following month. It currently operates from White Waltham, Berkshire, and Duxford, Cambridgeshire.

HURRICANE I V7497

Hurricane I V7497 was built by Hawker at Langley in Berkshire and delivered to the RAF in August 1940, going to 20 MU at Aston Down, Gloucestershire, on September 17 for outfitting. It was issued to 501 Squadron at Kenley two days later. On September 28, during its eighth sortie with the squadron, the fighter was damaged by Bf 109s during a dogfight over Deal on the coast of Kent, Pilot Officer Everett B Rogers taking to his parachute and surviving the encounter. The Hurricane came down on Chartway Street in East Sutton, Kent.

The remains were excavated and stored in a barn before going to Sudbury for repairs by Hawker Restorations, which registered it as G-HRLI on April 25, 2002. Work to return the aircraft to the air concluded with its first flight since 1940 on August 30, 2018, from Hawker Restorations' 'flight test facility' at Elmsett in Suffolk. During September 2018 it arrived at Duxford for Hurricane 501 Operations.

SPITFIRE IIa P7350

One of the first Spitfires built at the Castle Bromwich factory outside Birmingham in the West Midlands, Spitfire IIa P7350, was brought on charge with the RAF on August 13, 1940. It joined 266 Squadron at Wittering in Cambridgeshire on September 6 as 'UO-T', the unit later moving to Hornchurch, Essex, where it was transferred to 603 'City of Edinburgh' Squadron on October »

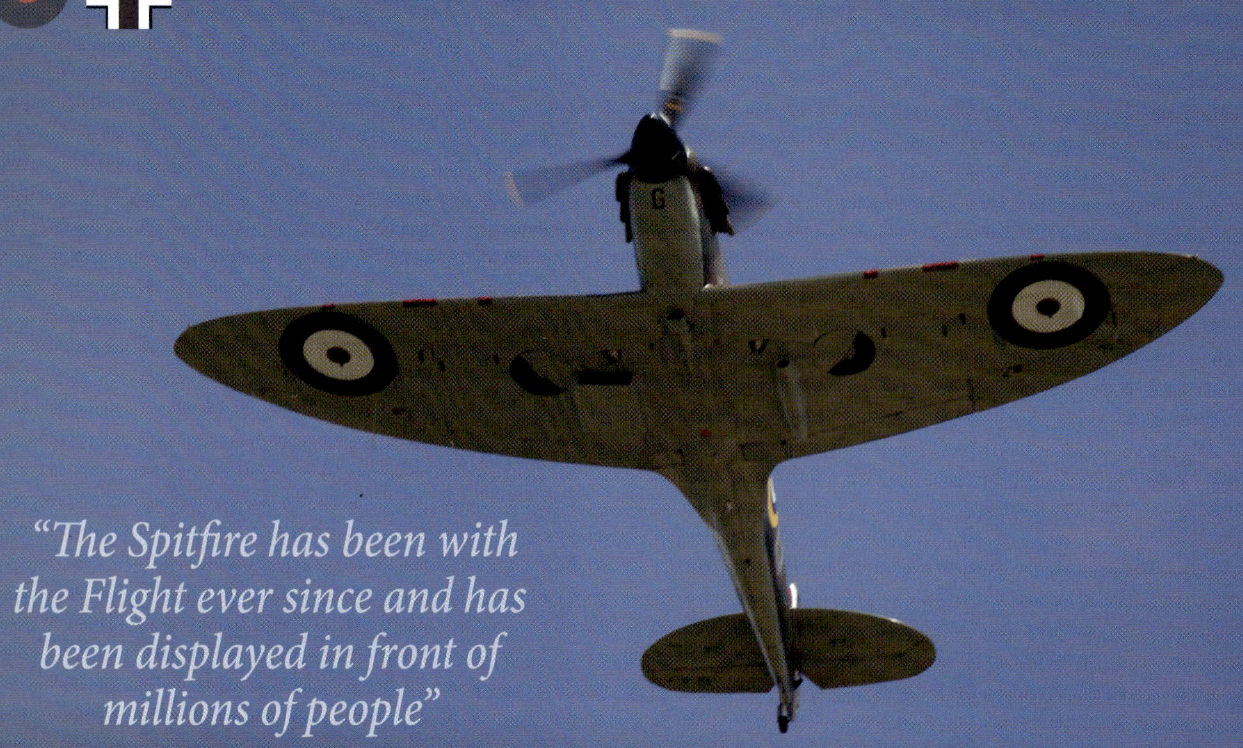

"The Spitfire has been with the Flight ever since and has been displayed in front of millions of people"

TOP: The undersides of P7350 in 2015, when the Spitfire carried the 41 Squadron codes 'EB-G', carried by Pilot Officer Eric Lock's aircraft, N3162, during the Battle of Britain.

17. It crash landed after combat on October 31 and went to 1 Civilian Repair Unit (CRU) at Cowley in Oxfordshire for repairs, the work being completed by November 15, after which it went to 37 MU at Burtonwood, Cheshire, for storage.

Its next operational unit was 616 'County of South Yorkshire' Squadron, joining it briefly from March 18, 1941, until transferring to 64 Squadron on April 10. Scottish Aviation at Prestwick overhauled the Spitfire from early August to January 1942, after which it went back into storage with 37 MU. On April 27, 1942, the fighter was issued to the Central Gunnery School at Sutton Bridge, Lincolnshire, where it remained until it was damaged in an accident on February 4, 1943, requiring the attention of Air Service Training at Hamble, Hampshire. It was issued to 57 OTU at Eshott in Northumberland on March 31, 1943, remaining with the unit until it was taxied into another Spitfire on April 22, 1944, resulting in a return trip to Hamble for repairs. It entered storage with 39 MU at Colerne, Wiltshire, on July 24, 1944, where it remained until declared to be non-effective stock on July 8, 1948, and sold.

The scrap merchants purchasing the Spitfire realised the historical importance of the aircraft and presented it to Colerne for preservation, where it remained until transported to Henlow on March 3, 1967, for restoration to airworthy condition for the film *Battle of Britain*. It was registered G-AWIJ to Spitfire Productions Limited on April 25, 1968, for its appearance in the movie, flying again on May 20. Filming over, in October 1968 it was returned to the RAF for the Battle of Britain Flight based at Coltishall, Norfolk, initially wearing the colours of 266 Squadron as 'ZH-T' until 1971. On January 1, 1969 the unit was renamed the Battle of Britain Memorial Flight and moved to Coningsby in Lincolnshire on March 1, 1976. The Spitfire has remained with the Flight ever since and has been displayed before millions of people.

SPITFIRE Ia P9306

On January 24, 1940, Spitfire Ia P9306 was delivered to 24 MU at Ternhill in Shropshire, having completed its first flight five days earlier. It subsequently passed to the MUs at Ruislip in London and Brize Norton, Oxfordshire. The fighter entered operational service on July 6, joining 74 Squadron based at Hornchurch in Essex, although it was frequently forward deployed to Manston in Kent. Two days later, Pilot Officer Peter C F Stevenson used it in combat with Bf 109s, claiming one destroyed and another damaged, and two Bf 110s during another sortie the same day. On August 11, Sergeant Thomas B Kirk was flying P9306 when he

ABOVE: The Science Museum's Spitfire Ia P9444 was one of a number of Battle of Britain airframes selected for preservation by the RAF.

RIGHT: Spitfire Ia R6915 on display at the Imperial War Museum's premises in South Lambeth in London during July 1997.

shot down a Bf 110 off the coast by Clacton-on-Sea in Essex. The aircraft moved with 74 Squadron to Wittering on August 14 and one week later to Kirton-in-Lindsey, and then Coltishall on September 9. Three days later it was placed into storage with 45 MU at Kinloss on the Moray Firth in Scotland, moving around several similar units until it was issued to 131 Squadron on July 17, 1941. In October that year, it passed to 52 OTU and remained in use with the training unit until going to 61 OTU on May 4, 1943.

From January to August 1944, it was stored at various MUs, before being shipped to Illinois in the United States, arriving in Chicago on August 19. The fighter was installed in the Museum of Science and Industry in that American city during November 1944, becoming the first ever Spitfire to be displayed in a museum. It has remained there ever since.

SPITFIRE Ia P9444

The day after making its first flight at Eastleigh in Hampshire on April 2, 1940, Spitfire Ia P9444 was flown to Farnborough in the same county for use by the Royal Aircraft Establishment (RAE) for unspecified trials. After these were completed, on May 23, 1940 it was passed to 6 MU at Brize Norton, before being issued to 72 Squadron on June 4.

The Spitfire was badly damaged in a crash landing on July 3 while being flown by Pilot Officer Robert Deacon-Elliott, repair work being undertaken by 1 CRU at Cowley. It was not until March 14, 1941, when it went to 45 MU at Kinloss, that it was redelivered to the RAF. On July 4, the Spitfire was handed over to 58 OTU at Grangemouth in Falkirk, Scotland, suffering damage in two incidents that required remedial work while with the unit. It was placed into temporary storage with 8 MU

at Little Rissington, Gloucestershire, on June 18, 1942, before being issued on August 5 to 61 OTU at Rednall in Shropshire. Another accident required work at Air Service Training in Hamble between February 7 and March 29, 1943, the aircraft departing for 12 MU at Kirkbride in Cumbria two days later. It went to 53 OTU at Kirton-in-Lindsey on May 12, 1943, which was destined to be its last flying unit. The Spitfire was withdrawn to 39 MU at Colerne on November 28, 1943, and passed to similar units at Lichfield, Staffordshire, and Cardiff in Wales, arriving at the latter in August 1944 for long-term storage.

The airframe was allocated for display purposes in August 1949, entering the Science Museum's store at Sydenham in December 1954. There it remained until 1963, during which it was placed on display within the museum's South Kensington premises. Spitfire Ia P9444 remains suspended from the ceiling in the aviation galley, wearing the codes 'RN-D' it carried during its time with 72 Squadron.

SPITFIRE Ia R6915

The Spitfire was delivered to 6 MU at Brize Norton on July 11, 1940, having flown for the first time at Eastleigh earlier the same day. Ten days later, it was issued to 609 'West Riding' Squadron, then based at Middle Wallop, as 'PR-U'. The aircraft was operational throughout the Battle of Britain, being flown by 13 different pilots during 57 operational sorties between July 20 and October 7, 1940.

Pilot Officer (P/O) Roger F G Miller damaged a Bf 110 flying R6915 on August 12, while P/O Piotr Ostaszewski-Ostoja damaged a pair of Junkers Ju 87s the next day. On August 25, P/O Noel le Chevalier Agazarian shared in the destruction of a Bf 110, followed by a Heinkel He 111 on September 25. The following day, again flying R6915, he shot down a Bf 109 and damaged two Dornier Do 17s. On October 7, the Spitfire was used to down three Luftwaffe aircraft: Flying Officer John C Dundas shot down a Messerschmitt and P/O Agazarian destroyed a Bf 109 and a He 111.

The Spitfire sustained combat damage several times during the Battle of Britain and from October 14 it required work at 1 CRU at Cowley, after which it was dispatched to 12 MU at Kirkbride where it arrived in mid-December 1940. It was next assigned on January 21, 1941, to 602 'City of Glasgow' Squadron at Prestwick.

In July 1941, the fighter was briefly used by 61 OTU at Heston, Middlesex, before going to 43 Group at Hendon on July 22 for less than a week, as it was with General Aviation at Hanworth in west London by the end of the month, presumably for repairs. After a period of storage, it returned to 61 OTU in June 1942, transferring to 57 OTU at Eshott, one year later. The Spitfire was damaged again in a »

ABOVE: A sonar scan of Dornier Do 17Z-2 1160 on the seabed off Goodwin Sands, Kent.

LEFT: Many of the exhibits of the Battle of Britain Experience at Hendon were removed so the building could be refurbished for the 'RAF First 100 Years' exhibition. Spitfire Ia X4590 was dismantled in May 2016.

flying accident on September 21, 1943. After being repaired and stored, the aircraft was briefly used by the Royal Naval Development Unit in early 1944, before returning to storage with MUs at Colerne, Wiltshire; Lichfield, Staffordshire; and Cardiff in Wales.

On August 28, 1946, the Spitfire was transferred to the Imperial War Museum (IWM), going on display in South Lambeth, where it was to remain for the next 66 years. During December 12 and 13, 2012, it was transported to the IWM facility at Duxford for restoration and storage while the South Lambeth site was itself overhauled. It returned to the museum's London premises on January 15, 2014.

SPITFIRE Ia X4590

Built at Woolston in Southampton, Hampshire, Spitfire Ia X4590's first flying unit was 609 'West Riding' Squadron at Middle Wallop, to which it was issued on October 9, 1940, as 'PR-F'. Twelve days later, it was flown by Pilot Officer Sydney J Hill on a low level chase that ended with a Junkers Ju 88A-5 from 1./KG51 – attempting to get home after attacking Old Sarum airfield in Wiltshire – being shot down. Hill was credited with a half share of the kill, which was the 100th enemy aircraft claimed by 609 Squadron. The Spitfire was transferred to 66 Squadron at Exeter in Devon in late February 1941 and two months later was operated by 57 OTU at Hawarden, Cheshire. It was with 303 Squadron at Speke, Merseyside, from mid-July, where it was damaged on the 24th of the month by Flight Lieutenant Stefan Kolodynski while landing after he completed his first flight in a Spitfire. After repair by Scottish Aviation, the fighter passed in February 1943 to 53 OTU at Llandow in the Vale of Glamorgan, Wales, remaining with the unit when it moved in May 1943 to Kirton-in-Lindsey. Further damage was inflicted on the airframe on

October 4, 1943, ending its flying career. By mid-May 1944, it was with 82 MU at Lichfield where it was identified as worth preserving for future generations, travelling to 52 MU at Pengam Moors outside Cardiff in August for storage.

During Battle of Britain Week in September 1954, the Spitfire was displayed at Horse Guards Parade as part of the Air Historical Branch collection usually stored at Stanmore Park. Around 1958 it moved to Fulbeck in Nottinghamshire, along with several other historic airframes owned by the RAF. The Spitfire was at Bicester, Oxfordshire, by August 1959, where it was used as a travelling exhibit by 71 MU, appearing at many venues during the following decade to promote the RAF.

In early 1972, the fighter was transferred to the RAF Museum store at Henlow, Bedfordshire, then joining the growing collection at Finningley in Yorkshire by September 1974, before moving to the Aerospace Museum at Cosford in Shropshire during 1976. It later moved to Hendon and was displayed within the Battle of Britain

Museum when it opened in November 1978. The aircraft sat within a mock-up of an 'E-Pen' shelter, with the codes 'PR-F', but was moved into the main museum building around 2016.

DORNIER Do 17Z-2 1160

The salvage of a Henschel-built Dornier Do 17Z-2 from the sea near Goodwin Sands off the eastern Kent coast in 2013 not only brought back an 'extinct' type, but also a Luftwaffe bomber that served during the Battle of Britain. All surviving He 111s and Ju 88s did not participate in the campaign.

The Do 17Z-2 was assigned to the 7. Staffel of Kampfgeschwader (KG) 3 as '5K+AR', the unit arriving at Saint-Truiden in Belgium during June 1940. On August 26, the bomber was part of a formation of Do 17s on a daylight raid against the airfields at Debden and Hornchurch, during which it was attacked by Boulton Paul Defiants from 264 Squadron, which damaged both engines and hit the cockpit. Pilot Feldwebel (Sergeant) Willi Effmert force-landed the aircraft into the sea and he was one of the two (from the crew of four) who managed to escape the bomber to become prisoners of war.

A high-resolution side-scan sonar and magnetometer survey of the inverted wreck, some 50ft (15m) below the waves, took place in September 2008, followed by another scan in May 2009 and a diving survey in June 2010. Much of the aircraft remained in situ and, given its historic nature, the decision was taken to raise it for preservation with the RAF Museum. The salvage operations occurred on June 10, 2013, after which it was transported to Cosford where the hulk of the aircraft was placed in a hydration tunnel to neutralise the salt and prevent further corrosion. The Bramo 323P-1 Fafnir engines were raised later. In early 2020, the dismantled airframe

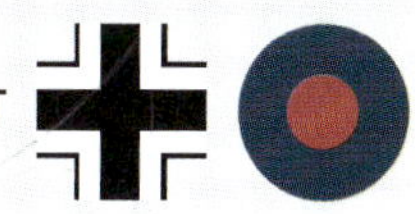

was kept within the Michael Beetham Conservation Centre at Cosford. Considerable work is still required to prepare the bomber for display.

MESSERSCHMITT Bf 109E-3 1190

Rolled out by Erla Maschinenwerk at Leipzig in 1939, Bf 109E-3 1190 is believed to have been flown by the commander of II./JG 26, Hauptmann Karl Ebbighausen during the campaigns in France and the Low Countries. Five of his victories were painted on its fin, achieved on May 13 (two), 18 and 25 and June 14, when the Luftwaffe fighter was shot down by Hurricanes over Beachy Head on September 30, 1940. At the time, the 'Emil' was assigned to 4./JG 26 as 'White 4', based at Marquise-Est. It came down by East Dean in Sussex largely intact, Unteroffizier (equivalent to an RAF corporal) Horst Perez walking into captivity unhurt.

The airframe was inspected by the RAE before being shipped to Canada and the United States as part of a war loans tour. By 1945 it was stored at Arnprior in Ontario with the Canadian Research Establishment, where it remained, becoming increasingly derelict by 1959. After bring rejected by the Canadian War Museum due to its condition, the airframe was sold for scrap, but retrieved from under a pile of wrecked cars by Geoff A Rowe of Stittsville, Ontario, in 1961.

In November 1966, it was shipped to the UK for Peter Foote and Dennis Knight of Bournemouth, Dorset, who slowly restored the aircraft to static condition. On March 17, 1998, the Bf 109E arrived at the Imperial War Museum's Duxford site, where

LEFT:
Messerschmitt Bf 109E-3 1190 on display at the Imperial War Museum at Duxford, Cambridgeshire.
Key-Duncan Cubitt

it was placed on display on its belly with the landing gear raised, guarded by a mannequin masquerading as a British soldier.

MESSERSCHMITT Bf 109E-3 1289

Another Erla-built Bf 109E-3, werke (work's) number (w/n) 1289 was delivered to JG 26 in 1939 and was on the strength of 2./JG 26 as 'Red 2' during the Battle of Britain. While being flown by Unteroffizier Heinz Wolf during a sortie over southern England on November 28, 1940, the fighter crashed on farm land at Udimore, Sussex.

The airframe was shipped to South Africa for a war loans tour in 1942. Two years later, it was presented to the South African National Museum of Military History at Saxonwold in Johannesburg, where it remains on display today, sitting on its belly and still showing evidence of the damage it sustained in 1940.

MESSERSCHMITT Bf 109E-3 1342

Feldwebel Eduard Hemmerling of 6./JG 51 scored his third and final kill over Dover in Kent on July 29, 1940, while flying Bf 109E-3 1342 'Yellow 8'. The Messerschmitt was badly damaged in the fighting and Hemmerling died when it crashed onto a beach at Cap Blanc Nez outside Calais in Normandy, France. His aircraft was written off and eventually disappeared under the shifting sands.

In 1988, the tip of the aircraft's wing became visible and a salvage operation was mounted to recover its remains. They were transported to Colchester in Essex in 1993 for restoration by Charleston Aviation Services, moving to Earls Colne in the same county by December 1997 for final assembly by Hawker Restorations. The project was registered to Sir Tim Wallis' Alpine Deer Group of Wanaka, New Zealand, as G-BYDS on November 24, 1998, ≫

BELOW: Bf 109E-3 1190 in the field at East Dean in Sussex, where it came down on September 30, 1940, after suffering engine failure following combat with Hurricanes.
Key Collection

but instead of travelling south the aircraft was sold to the Flying Heritage Collection at Paine Field in Everett, Washington, USA. It was registered to Vulcan Warbirds Inc as N342FH on November 24, 2004. A certificate of airworthiness was issued on October 15, 2007, and the Bf 109E-3 flew again for the first time since 1940 on March 22, 2008. The aircraft remains airworthy with the retitled Flying Heritage & Combat Armor Museum.

MESSERSCHMITT Bf 109E-7 3579

Originally built by Arado as a Bf 109E-3, w/n 3579 was upgraded as an E-4. While serving with I. Gruppe of Lehrgeschwader 2 as 'White 14', it was hit by bullets fired from a Spitfire over Sheerness in north Kent on September 2, 1940. The unidentified pilot managed to cross the Channel but crash-landed at Calais-Marck in France.

The badly damaged aircraft was rebuilt as a Bf 109E-7 and later served on the Eastern Front, initially with I./JG 77. It was shot down by Soviet Air Force Hurricanes on August 2, 1942, while being operated by 4./JG 51 as 'White 7', coming down at Pya Ozero in the Republic of Karelia in northwest Russia.

The hulk was salvaged from a marsh in 1991, although the fuselage was badly damaged during the recovery operation. It arrived at Jim Pearce's Sussex Spraying Services workshop at Lancing before moving in December 1992 to the workshops of Craig Charleston in Colchester, for restoration on behalf of the Museum of Flying at Santa Monica, California, USA. It was registered as N81562 in August 1998, departing the UK for California during January 1999. The airframe was fitted with a DB601A engine and reflown at Chino in California for the first time on September 29, 1999.

In 2003, the Bf 109E-7 was registered to Ed Russell of Niagara Falls in Ontario, Canada, as CF-EML. It was later sold and registered to the Biggin Hill Heritage Hangar Limited as G-CIPB, arriving at the Kent airport on January 6, 2015. It returned to the British skies in the hands of its new owner on June 17, 2017 although its permit to fly expired in November, 2019.

MESSERSCHMITT Bf 109E-4/B 4101

The RAF Museum's 'Emil' was built as a Bf 109E-4 by Erla during September 1940. It was ferried to Pihen in northern France on September 5, and modified as a Bf 109E-4/B fighter-bomber in the 'field'. Briefly used by 6./JG 51 as 'Yellow 8', it was later transferred to the Jagdgeschwader's 2. Staffel at Wissant near Calais as 'Black 12'. During a sortie over Kent on November 27, it was intercepted by three Spitfires of 66 Squadron and shot down by Flight Lieutenant George P Christie, the pilot Leutnant Wolfgang Teumer making a

wheels-up landing at Manston, Kent. The wreck was moved to the 49 MU dump at Faygate, West Sussex, for scrapping, but the decision was taken to repair it for evaluation. The director general of research and development of the Air Ministry handed the aircraft over to Rolls-Royce at Hucknall, Nottinghamshire, for repair and return to airworthy condition on December 14, 1940, a process that made extensive use of parts from other salvaged Bf 109s. Allocated the serial DG200, it flew again on February 25, 1941.

Rolls-Royce flew the Messerschmitt for 23 hours and 25 minutes during 32 sorties, during which it evaluated the Daimler-Benz DB601A-1 engine. Towards the end of the test programme, the canopy was removed so the aircraft could be flown by Rolls-Royce's test pilot Harvey Hayworth – he was over 6ft (1.8m) tall and could not comfortably fit into the cramped cockpit otherwise! The original canopy was never reinstalled and subsequently lost. In February 1942, de Havilland investigated the variable pitch propeller, after which the aircraft went to the Aeroplane & Armament Experimental Establishment at Boscombe Down in Wiltshire.

On April 28, 1942, the Bf 109E was transported by road to Duxford for the use of 1426 (Enemy Aircraft) Flight, moving with the unit to Collyweston, Lincolnshire, one year later. It was retired to 16 MU at Stafford in Staffordshire during September 1943 and selected for long-term storage, moving to 52 MU at Pengam Moors in Wales 12 months later. By 1947, it was at Stanmore Park, moving on to Wroughton (late 1955); Fulbeck (mid-1958); and Biggin Hill (by 1960); before settling at St Athan in South Wales from September 1969. During its time at St Athan the fighter was refurbished and it was one of the exhibits in the Battle of Britain Hall at Hendon when it opened in May 1978.